Post-Sustainability

Tragedy and Transformation

T0362257

The sustainability discourse and policy paradigm have failed to deliver. In particular, they have failed to avert the dangerously disruptive climate change which is now inevitable. So, if there is still a case for some transformed or revitalised version of sustainability, that case must now surely be made in full acknowledgment of deep-seated paradigm-failure to date. But if we really take ourselves to be living in a post-sustainable world, the issue of 'what next?' must be faced, and the hard questions no longer shirked. What options for political and personal action will remain open on a tragically degraded planet? How will economic and community life, political and social leadership and education be different in such a world? What will the geopolitics (of crisis, migration and conflict) look like? Where does widespread denial come from, how might it be overcome, and are there any grounds for hope that don't rest on it?

The urgent challenge now is to confront such questions honestly. This collection of essays by thinkers from a diversity of fields including politics, philosophy, sociology, education and religion, makes a start.

This book was originally published as a special issue of *Global Discourse*.

John Foster is a freelance writer and philosophy teacher, and an Associate Lecturer in the Department of Politics, Philosophy and Religion at Lancaster University, UK. His relevant publications include *Valuing Nature?* (ed.) (Routledge, 1997), *The Sustainability Mirage* (Earthscan, 2008), and *After Sustainability: Denial, Hope, Retrieval* (Earthscan/Routledge, 2015).

Post-Sustainability

Tragedy and Transformation

Edited by
John Foster

LONDON AND NEW YORK

First published 2018 by Routledge

2 Park Square, Milton Park, Abingdon, Oxfordshire OX14 4RN
52 Vanderbilt Avenue, New York, NY 10017

Routledge is an imprint of the Taylor & Francis Group, an informa business

First issued in paperback 2019

Introduction, Chapters 1–4 and Chapters 6–18 © 2018 Taylor & Francis
Chapter 5 © 2018 Ingolfur Blühdorn. Originally published as Open Access

British Library Cataloguing in Publication Data
A catalogue record for this book is available from the British Library

ISBN 13: 978-1-138-29649-7 (hbk)
ISBN 13: 978-0-367-89128-2 (pbk)

Typeset in Myriad Pro
by RefineCatch Limited, Bungay, Suffolk

Publisher's Note
The publisher accepts responsibility for any inconsistencies that may have
arisen during the conversion of this book from journal articles to book chapters,
namely the possible inclusion of journal terminology.

Disclaimer
Every effort has been made to contact copyright holders for their permission to
reprint material in this book. The publishers would be grateful to hear from any
copyright holder who is not here acknowledged and will undertake to rectify
any errors or omissions in future editions of this book.

Contents

CONTENTS

Citation Information

The chapters in this book were originally published in *Global Discourse*, volume 7, issue 1 (2017). When citing this material, please use the original page numbering for each article, as follows:

Editorial

Hope after sustainability – tragedy and transformation
John Foster
Global Discourse, volume 7, issue 1 (2017), pp. 1–9

Chapter 1

Paris: optimism, pessimism and realism
Brian Heatley
Global Discourse, volume 7, issue 1 (2017), pp. 10–22

Chapter 2

Transformation, adaptation and universalism: reply to Heatley
Nadine Andrews
Global Discourse, volume 7, issue 1 (2017), pp. 23–27

Chapter 3

After development? In defence of sustainability
Mike Hannis
Global Discourse, volume 7, issue 1 (2017), pp. 28–38

Chapter 4

Response to 'After development? In defence of sustainability'
Lawrence Wilde
Global Discourse, volume 7, issue 1 (2017), pp. 39–41

Chapter 5

Post-capitalism, post-growth, post-consumerism? Eco-political hopes beyond sustainability
Ingolfur Blühdorn
Global Discourse, volume 7, issue 1 (2017), pp. 42–61

Chapter 16

Caring for the future? – a response to Rupert Read
John Foster
Global Discourse, volume 7, issue 1 (2017), pp. 168–170

Chapter 17

On letting go
John Foster
Global Discourse, volume 7, issue 1 (2017), pp. 171–187

Chapter 18

The future: compassion, complacency or contempt?: reply to Foster
Rupert Read
Global Discourse, volume 7, issue 1 (2017), pp. 188–191

For any permission-related enquiries please visit:
http://www.tandfonline.com/page/help/permissions

Notes on Contributors

Nadine Andrews is a Visiting Researcher at the Pentland Centre for Sustainability in Business, Lancaster University, UK, and also Science Officer in the Technical Support Unit of the Intergovernmental Panel on Climate Change Working Group II.

Rachel Bathurst is a Postgraduate Researcher in the Lincoln Theological Institute at the University of Manchester, UK

Ingolfur Blühdorn is Professor for Social Sustainability and Head of the Institute for Social Change and Sustainability (IGN) at the University of Economics and Business in Vienna, Austria.

Katie Carr is the Director of Cumbria Development Education Centre, UK.

Ulrike Ehgartner is a doctoral student at the Sustainable Consumption Institute of the University of Manchester, UK.

John Foster is a freelance writer and philosophy teacher, and an Associate Lecturer in the Department of Politics, Philosophy and Religion at Lancaster University, UK.

Steve Gough is Professor of Environment and Society at the University of Bath, UK.

Patrick Gould is a doctoral student at the Sustainable Consumption Institute of the University of Manchester, UK.

Mike Hannis is Senior Lecturer in Environmental Humanities at Bath Spa University, UK.

Daniel Hausknost is an Assistant Professor at the Institute for Social Change and Sustainability (IGN) at the University of Economics and Business in Vienna, Austria.

Brian Heatley is a former senior civil servant, based in the UK.

Marc Hudson is a doctoral student at the Sustainable Consumption Institute of the University of Manchester, UK.

Nina Isabella Moeller is currently Independent Social Research Foundation Fellow at the Oxford Department of International Development, UK.

Rachel Muers is Senior Lecturer in Christian Studies at the University of Leeds, UK.

J. Martin Pedersen is an independent researcher currently working on real food systems and seed commons, Amazonian medicine and microbiology.

Panu Pihkala is a postdoctoral researcher at the University of Helsinki, Faculty of Theology, Finland.

Rupert Read is Reader in Philosophy at the University of East Anglia, UK and Chair of *Green House*.

William Scott is Emeritus Professor of Education at the University of Bath, UK.

Lawrence Wilde is Emeritus Professor of Political Theory at Nottingham Trent University, UK.

Hope after sustainability – tragedy and transformation

Claims to sustainability are everywhere, from the sides of motorway juggernauts to the spin of a UK government arguing for airport expansion in London while notionally signed up to its carbon emissions targets. Scarcely a week passes without the launching of some initiative on sustainable cities, or sustainable agriculture or sustainable something else. In universities, modules and courses referencing sustainability abound. Research money flows generously (well, comparatively so) for projects purporting to increase our understanding of the concept or its applications. Meanwhile, academic and other voices raising awkward questions have been all but inaudible in the approbatory hubbub.

Until just recently, that is – but latterly, there has been a sea-change. It is no longer completely out of court for thinkers and scholars concerned with environmental issues to argue that the 'sustainability' discourse and policy paradigm have failed, and that we are moving into a new and much bleaker era. Take sustainability (for the sake of a working definition) to be the condition of so governing human usage of the planet's natural resources that succeeding human generations can go on into the indefinite future depending on these resources to provide them with levels of well-being at least equivalent to our own. The argument is beginning to gain traction, then, that turning the aspiration towards this condition into a set of policy options represents a strategy which has had a good run for its money since the 1980s, but should now be recognised as well past its use-by date. A recent policy review paper in the journal *Society and Natural Resources* (Benson and Craig 2014) is bluntly entitled 'The End of Sustainability'. Authors as diverse as Clive Hamilton (2010), Tim Mulgan (2011), Kevin Anderson (2011), Dale Jamieson (2014) and myself (Foster 2015) write with the working assumption that climate change on a scale lying unpredictably between the seriously disruptive and the catastrophic, as the Intergovernmental Panel on Climate Change (IPCC) has characterised it (UNFCC 2009, since when the outlook has not improved), is no longer something we must find ways of avoiding, but something we are going to have to live with. And if climate change of that order is indeed coming, then all bets about sustaining other aspects of our natural resource usage are off (hence the recent almost overwhelming focus on this single, dominating issue). Parallel to this recognition is the rise to prominence of the 'anthropocene' trope (e.g. Hamilton et al. 2015) with its defining acceptance that human beings have decisively altered the atmosphere and set in motion a now-inevitable mass extinction as drastic as any produced by Earth system changes over geological time.

Why, on this account, has sustainability failed? It has failed, of course, to be faithful to the motivations of 1960's and 1970's ecological protest which it was supposed to translate into mainstream political terms – but that faith it was never going to keep, as soon as it adopted the anthropocentric language of economics and of the planet as a set of resources. For some, it has failed because it thereby hitched its waggon decisively to liberal consumer capitalism, which, since the global banking crisis, looks to some rather hopeful eyes itself to be (independently) failing. But the real argument is that the trouble goes deeper. The sustainability aspiration has failed on its own terms, it hasn't enabled us to make even a plausible start on governing our natural resource usage by the appropriate criteria, and this is for reasons inherent in the aspiration itself.

Retrospectively, indeed, one can surely see how impotent that aspiration was always going to prove. Constraining immediate needs (or desires) to serve future needs, the identification and measurement of which were all to be carried out under pressure of the immediate needs and desires supposedly to be constrained, could never have offered us anything but a toolkit of lead spanners, capable only of bending helplessly when any serious force was applied. Is it any wonder, then, that we have continued to find the nuts and bolts of unsustainable living so stubbornly unshiftable?

In mainstream political discourse, however, such questions remain resolutely unasked. Here, there reigns an almost complete lack of acknowledgement of the possible paradigm failure of sustainability. In the world of the United Nations and other international and national policy fora, less and less promising environmental and climate prospects are met only by a more and more firmly fixed grin of willed optimism. A recent monitoring report for the EU's Sustainable Development Strategy, for instance (Eurostat Press Office 2015), claims that in respect of sustainable consumption and production, demographic changes and greenhouse gas emissions, changes in headline indicators mark developments that are 'clearly favourable' – although *only* willed optimism could celebrate the last of these without a glance in the direction of China or India. And since then, of course, we have had the Climate Change Conference in Paris, latest in a long line of last-chance saloons, where 'targets' were agreed which are avowedly aspirational, not legally binding, and don't add up to keeping below the crucial 2°C threshold even if they could be delivered: an achievement comparable, as Brian Heatley (2017) points out in the first paper here, to the 1919 Treaty of Versailles which rounded off World War I by laying all the necessary groundwork for World War II. This latter-day Parisian *débâcle* is nevertheless hailed worldwide as a triumph of UN diplomacy – except, of course, by the new US President, whose scepticism however expresses crass ignorance rather than insight.

The nearest the official policy world comes to recognition that we actually won't prevent (above all) unsustainable climate change, is in the increasing volume of talk about mitigation rather than prevention. But for all that, denial is plainly still at work. How do you *mitigate* a set of outcomes which can only honestly be described as tragic? What, for example, could conceivably mitigate the loss of countless millions in sub-Saharan Africa to ultimately-anthropogenic drought, famine and disease? The very question is a kind of obscenity, which we screen out by making ourselves believe that somehow, technological intervention will ensure that things won't after all be anything like so bad. Cognitive dissonance is still powerfully operative here, even as the willed optimism begins to falter.

It is at this critical juncture in thought and practice that we have brought together the explorations and anticipations comprising the present Special Issue of *Global Discourse*. If there is still a case for sustainability – if it still offers us, in some transformed or revitalised version, a graspable policy handle on our collective plight – that case has now surely to be made in full acknowledgment of all the accumulating evidence of deep-seated paradigm-failure to date. But if we really take ourselves to be living in the irreversible aftermath of that failure, the issue of 'what next?' must be honestly faced, and the hard questions no longer shirked. What options for political and personal action will remain open in a tragically degraded world? What are the conditions of habitability of such a world? How will economic and community life, political and social leadership and education be different in such a world? What will the geopolitics (of crisis, migration and conflict) look like? Where does widespread denial come from, how might it be overcome, and are there any grounds for *hope* that don't rest on it?

The following papers divide (roughly equally) between those arguing that the sustainability paradigm can still be redeemed, and those which start to ask questions premised on its being irredeemable. As editor, I have done little more than arrange them to compose a suite of variations on the themes just identified, counterpointed by the brief critical responses from reviewers of each article which it is *Global Discourse*'s excellent habit to include. Papers and responses are drawn from a deliberate diversity of perspectives, including both academic and non-academic contributors as well as some who would probably claim to be both. Some of the contrasts generated between these diverse perspectives are, equally deliberately, fairly stark – as for instance between the interpretive frameworks of environmental social science and of Christian theology, or the assumptions of practical policy-making and those of the philosophy of tragedy. The main intention in setting up both the diversity and the contrasts has been to jolt expectations, perhaps spring new alignments, and in any case provoke debate.

The first movement, as it were, of this suite of variations concerns *policy*. Brian Heatley, a former senior British civil servant and current Green activist, leads it off with an excoriating analysis of the 2015 Paris Climate Change Conference and the resoundingly hollow claims for it which have followed. The consequences of this culminating expression of the sustainability paradigm, he argues, will require us to abandon not only material 'progress' but also the at least notional universalism which has hitherto characterised it. The second claim is one which Nadine Andrews (2017), who works on psychosocial factors in the environmental domain as a Science Officer for the IPCC, challenges in her response while accepting Heatley's general account. Mike Hannis (2017), however, a researcher in environmental ethics and politics and also a sustainability activist, distinguishes between 'sustainability' and 'sustainable development', suggesting that it is only the latter which has failed as a policy framework, the former having never really been tried. Attempting it is still possible, he insists, if an ethic of human flourishing can inform new principles of social organisation. The response by Lawrence Wilde (2017), Emeritus Professor of Political Theory at Nottingham Trent University, accepts the spirit of this approach but seeks to rescue the idea of 'development' for a Sen-Nussbaum style 'capabilities' model.

Then comes a movement unified, if somewhat loosely, under the broad head of *culture and value*. Ingolfur Blühdorn (2017) of the Institute for Social Change and Sustainability in Vienna traces the socio-cultural history of what he identifies as the current deliberate 'sustaining of unsustainability', in which the now non-negotiable values of 'liquid modernity' – essentially, individual consumerist self-realisation – are accommodated to the imminent breaching of recognised ecological limits which they entail. In this 'politics of simulation', which Blühdorn seeks to distinguish from mere denial, we consciously organise ourselves to pursue what we also know we cannot go on having. In his response, Daniel Hausknost (2017) of the Institute of Social Ecology, Alpen-Adria University Klagenfurt, raises some issues with the historical basis of this analysis. Our understanding of the dynamics of simulation, he suggests, needs complementing by attention to the way in which global-systemic issues such as climate change have remained intractable – to address them effectively requiring a challenge to the capitalist state's essential legitimation strategy of ever-increasing material prosperity.

Offering an intriguingly different take on some of the same phenomena, Ulrike Ehgartner and her colleagues Patrick Gould and Marc Hudson from the Sustainable Consumption Institute at the University of Manchester (Ehgartner, Gould, and Hudson 2017) draw on the work of the twentieth-century German philosopher Günther Anders for an account of the human relation to modern technology which lies behind either simulation or (as others might see it) willed denial. The concept of 'apocalyptic blindness' which Anders originally developed for a then-new atomic age is here suggestively applied to the slow-motion holocaust of climate change and ecological degradation. Responding, Nina Moeller of the Oxford Department of International Development and independent researcher John Martin Pedersen (Moeller and Pedersen 2017), both involved in front-line social-ecological work in the Ecuadorian Amazon, offer a perspective on this 'blindness' from a world which, they argue, still remains outside the capitalist 'rule of machines'.

The movement shifts in closing to a different and initially rather distant key with the paper by Rachel Bathurst (2017) of the Lincoln Theological Institute, also at the University of Manchester, which explains sustainability paradigm failure from a frankly Christian perspective, appealing to a theology of the divine intentions for Creation. This alternative, and perhaps now to many people quite remote, mode of thinking has nevertheless the great merit of suggesting powerfully how far from utilitarian naturalism we might actually have to go in order to find a framework which does justice to both the integrity and the sensed preciousness of the whole world, humankind included. Rachel Muers (2017) of the University of Leeds reinforces this intimation with some cogent questions about the role of humility.

A transition less discordant than might perhaps be expected then takes the reader into a third movement concerned with *education*. Panu Pihkala (2017) of the University of Helsinki, who is also a Lutheran pastor, argues that environmental education needs to deal with 'eco-anxiety' in a way that lets 'a certain sense of tragedy' into the frame. Avoiding acknowledgement of the seriousness and intractability of the environmental and climate crisis for fear of seeming negative only encourages disavowal, which drives anxieties underground. The new, quasi-therapeutic roles of an honest environmental-educational approach would involve awakening students from false hope, admitting and confronting anxieties, renewing a sense of present wonder and cultivating energies that can act in uncertainty. This constitutes a very demanding task for educators, who have to go through all this for themselves first, but it is one they can't any longer shirk. Katie Carr (2017) of the Cumbria Development Education Centre, herself a practising environmental educator, responds sympathetically, but notes just how wide is the gap between this aspiration and anything which the formal education system (whether or not it addresses environmental and climate issues) now takes itself to be doing.

By contrast, Stephen Gough's speculative and wide-ranging paper (Gough 2017) considers education from both a Darwinian and an institutionalist perspective. He makes the disturbing, but on reflection compelling point that education, as a formative element in launching the expansion of human economies must always have been inextricably linked to *un*sustainability. If so, then contemporary educational attention to recovering from that condition can perhaps be seen as our evolved species mode of being both resiliently separate from and actively embedded in the natural world. William Scott (2017), responding, picks up on this to emphasise that schools (and by implication, education generally) are always shaped by society faster than society can be shaped by schools, so that maybe the best we can hope for from environmental education is the creation of space for improved choices, whether or not people are then inclined to make them.

The final movement, understandably after all this, is essentially about *hope*. It assumes a quasi-antiphonal form: the paper by Rupert Read, philosopher and Green politician, responded to by myself, is followed by my paper which includes some discussion of Read, to which his response then includes a response to my response to him. This extended dialogue arose in part accidentally, but works in the reading better than it maybe sounds in the description. Read's argument (2017a) is twofold. Firstly, we can legitimately hope that climate disaster, which we must now expect, will bring with it the compensation – he is bold enough to call this a prospective 'great gift' – of enabling new kinds of local community to be born. Secondly, however, this retrieval of a strong local focus is still compatible with caring passionately for the welfare of future generations distant in both space and time. I challenge in my response (Foster 2017a) the way this latter claim is argued, and in my own paper (Foster 2017b) offer reasons for viewing the process of value-transformation which disaster will entail as genuinely tragic rather than in any sense compensatory. While this transposes hope into a different mode, I suggest – hope as value-creativity – it does not eliminate it, but rather strengthens the chance of hope's being what we actually emerge with.

Read (2017b), in then concluding this exchange, makes a surely unanswerable point, on which the whole special issue can fittingly end: if we aren't in control and don't really know what's coming, we also can't *know* that our creativity won't be enough to take us through it.

The upshot of bringing all these papers and responses together is, I trust, a lively ongoing dialogue with (as in all genuine exchange) some fierce disagreement, some unanticipated convergences, multiple loose ends and no clear conclusion in sight. Indeed, probably the only thing on which all the contributors are tacitly united is that maintaining this kind of dialogue about these very difficult issues is, in our present situation, an urgently pressing intellectual responsibility. It is one which we hope that our readers will recognise, embrace and now take forward.

Disclosure statement

No potential conflict of interest was reported by the author.

References

Anderson, K. 2011. "Climate Change Going beyond Dangerous." http://www.whatnext.org/resources/Publications/Volume-III/Single-articles/wnv3_andersson_144.pdf

Andrews, N. 2017. "Transformation, Adaptation and Universalism." *Global Discourse* 7(1): 23–27. doi: 10.1080/23269995.2017.1300403.

Bathurst, R. 2017. "Beyond Sustainability: Hope in a Spiritual Revolution?" *Global Discourse* 7(1): 86–104. doi: 10.1080/23269995.2017.1300410.

Benson, M., and R. Craig. 2014. "The End of Sustainability." *Society & Natural Resources* 27: 777–782. doi:10.1080/08941920.2014.901467.

Blühdorn, I. 2017. "Post-Capitalism, Post-Growth, Post-Consumerism?" *Global Discourse* 7(1): 41–60. doi: 10.1080/23269995.2017.1300415.

Carr, K. 2017. "Response to 'Environmental Education after Sustainability: Hope in the Midst of Tragedy'." *Global Discourse* 7(1): 127–129. doi: 10.1080/23269995.2017.1300413.

Ehgartner, U., P. Gould, and M. Hudson. 2017. "On the Obsolescence of Human Beings in Sustainable Development." *Global Discourse* 7(1): 65–82. doi: 10.1080/23269995.2017.1300417.

Eurostat Press Office. 2015. "Is the European Union Moving Towards Sustainable Development?" *News Release 148/2015*, September 1.

Foster, J. 2015. *After Sustainability*. Abingdon: Earthscan from Routledge.

Foster, J. 2017a. "Caring for the Future?" *Global Discourse* 7(1): 167–169. doi: 10.1080/23269995.2017.1300441.

Foster, J. 2017b. "On Letting Go." *Global Discourse* 7(1): 170–186. doi: 10.1080/23269995.2017.1300442.

Gough, S. 2017. "Education after Sustainability." *Global Discourse* 7(1): 130–144. doi: 10.1080/23269995.2017.1300435.

Hamilton, C. 2010. *Requiem for a Species*. London: Earthscan.

Hamilton, C., et al., eds. 2015. *The Anthropocene and the Global Environmental Crisis*. Abingdon: Routledge.

Hannis, M. 2017. "After Development? in Defence of Sustainability." *Global Discourse* 7(1): 28–38. doi: 10.1080/23269995.2017.1300404.

Hausknost, D. 2017. "There Never was a Categorical Ecological Imperative: A Response to Ingolfur Blühdorn." *Global Discourse* 7(1): 61–64. doi: 10.1080/23269995.2017.1300416.

Heatley, B. 2017. "Paris: Optimism, Pessimism and Realism." *Global Discourse* 7(1): 10–22. doi: 10.1080/23269995.2017.1300402.

Jamieson, D. 2014. *Reason in a Dark Time*. Oxford: Oxford University Press.

Moeller, N., and J. Pedersen. 2017. "Apocalyptically Blinded." *Global Discourse* 7(1): 83–85. doi: 10.1080/23269995.2017.1300418.

Muers, R. 2017. "Response to 'Beyond Sustainability: Hope in a Spiritual Revolution?'." *Global Discourse* 7(1): 105–107. doi: 10.1080/23269995.2017.1300411.

Mulgan, T. 2011. *Ethics for a Broken World*. Durham: Acumen.

Pihkala, P. 2017. "Environmental Education after Sustainability: Hope in the Midst of Tragedy." *Global Discourse* 7(1): 108–126. doi: 10.1080/23269995.2017.1300412.

Read, R. 2017a. "On Preparing for the Great Gift of Community that Climate Disasters Can Give Us." *Global Discourse* 7(1): 148–166. doi: 10.1080/23269995.2017.1300440.

Read, R. 2017b. "The Future: Compassion, Complacency, or Contempt? A Response to John Foster." *Global Discourse* 7(1): 187–190. doi: 10.1080/23269995.2017.1300443.

Scott, W. 2017. "Learning and Education after Sustainability." *Global Discourse* 7(1) : 145-147. doi: 10.1080/23269995.2017.1300439.

UNFCC. 2009. "Future Effects." *Feeling the Heat*. http:/unfccc.int/essential_background/feeling_the_heat/items/2903.php

Wilde, L. 2017. "Response to 'After Development? in Defence of Sustainability'." *Global Discourse* 7(1).

John Foster

Paris: optimism, pessimism and realism

Brian Heatley

ABSTRACT

The climate agreement signed in Paris in December 2015 has been widely hailed as a huge step towards limiting climate change to a safe 2°C. It is not; Paris locks the world into a future where at least a 3–4°C rise by 2100 is virtually inevitable. This will mean a world where there will be massive famine and conflict in much of Africa and the Middle East, serious hunger in South Asia, huge migration pressures but manageable problems in the Americas and more difficult but probably still manageable problems in Europe. Globalisation may collapse, which will be particularly challenging for the UK with its dependence on food imports and international trade. In politics the 200-year hegemony of the idea of progress will be over, while our focus will become more local, putting great pressure on the idea of human universalism.

Introduction

A climate agreement has been signed in Paris (United Nations 2015a). After years of squabbling all the Great Powers, followed rather less enthusiastically by almost the entire international community, have, for the first time come to an agreement. Optimistic up beat press releases claim that this at last is the deal that will put us on the way to limiting dangerous climate change to a manageable and safe 2°C, or even 1.5°C. Obama has his 'turning point for the world' and the world is on the way to being saved! And enthusiasm for this second great Treaty of Paris and French diplomatic triumph ominously matches that for the Treaty signed by the Great Powers almost a century ago at Versailles.

The rich world's environmental movement's public response has largely reflected this optimism: Greenpeace UK concluded that COP21 shows the end of fossil fuels is near (Greenpeace UK 2015). The message from environmentalists up until Paris has been that if the world's politicians act now, drastically cut emissions and invest massively in renewables, then the climate will by and large be OK, and the massive investment required will spark a new sustainable economic boom, dragging us out of the great recession. Otherwise we are all doomed, on a planet that will fry us. We contemplate nothing in between, or at least try very hard not to think about it, and the main point therefore is to prevent climate change, not to be forced to live with it. As for Paris, of course, there is much more to be done, but the agreement is a big step in the right direction.

In reality, despite the hype, Paris punctures this optimism. The world has not been saved any more than it was in 1919. Too little has been agreed far too late. The real meaning of Paris is that dangerous climate change by 2100 is now all but inevitable, and that after 2100 it will get worse. It was probably already too late before Paris. Many poor world environmentalists already knew this, despite their quixotic but successful quest for a reference to a now impossible 1.5°C rise in the agreement. A lot of us in the rich world already really knew it too, but didn't like to come to terms with it, or even talk about it. This is probably because it conflicts with our deep belief in and commitment to progress; the idea that the world, for everyone, and despite setbacks, is getting better and better (see also Foster 2015). And with progress in mind, many have a pervasive faith that technology will somehow clear up the problem. However, even if the world sticks to the path implicitly agreed in Paris, at the very best we are now locked in to global warming of at least 3–4°C by 2100, and more thereafter. At worst it may be much more, and either way we face many uncertainties including catastrophic runaway climate change.

The main argument of this piece is that the Green Movement has to come to terms with this awful fact; we have failed in our mission to prevent damaging climate change. Acceptance of that will have profound consequences for our politics:

- while we must of course continue to act to prevent further climate change, we must also begin to prepare for the world as it will inevitably become;

- that world in 2100 will be profoundly altered, where perhaps a billion people in the poor south will die from famine or disease or migrate, and even places less directly affected like the UK will face huge challenges; and

- two cherished political ideas, currency not just of the green movement but also of all on the liberal left, progress and human universalism, and explained in greater detail towards the end of this piece, face crumbling before an assault by brute events.

We first set out why Paris won't work. Then we speculate on the consequences of a 3–4°C rise by 2100, and more thereafter, for the world system, by first looking at regional climate change and then considering the likely economic and political effects. We turn then to what this means for the UK and its politics and security, ending with a plea for progressives to forget progress, at least for a hundred years, and be realistic about how far human universalism can be preserved.

Why Paris makes at least a 3–4°C rise by 2100 virtually inevitable

The substance of the Paris agreement (the 1.5°C and 2°C targets are no more than pious aspirations; Article 2 of the Agreement makes it clear that these are simply 'aims') essentially amounts to a series of unilateral 'Intended Nationally Determined Contributions' (INDCs) by individual countries, which will after the agreement comes into effect become registered and monitored actual 'Nationally Determined Contributions'. They are no more than what each country has been prepared to contribute. The EU countries, for example, have promised collectively a 40% reduction on domestic greenhouse gas emissions by 2030. China says that its emissions will peak in 2030 at the latest, and that it will lower the carbon intensity of GDP by 60–65% below 2005 levels by 2030. And there is a bit more on renewables and forests. The US has undertaken to reduce net greenhouse gas emissions by 26–28% below 2005 levels in

2025, and so on. In total, 185 countries covering around 94% of world emissions made such promises (Climate Action Tracker 2015). Half of the remaining 6% is international aviation and shipping not covered by the agreement. There is also an agreement to try to do better in the future: National Contributions will be revised every 5 years, and must always improve on previous aspirations, but they are not legally binding. And the rich countries have promised $100 billion in extra aid to help the poorer countries develop renewables and adapt to climate change – but are not legally bound to provide it.

So what's wrong with that? Progress moving towards the 2°C target combined with commitments from the biggest emitters seems great. The problem is that *quantitatively* this simply doesn't remotely add up to sufficient reductions to contain human-induced climate change within a 2°C rise within the current century. At best it means that the temperature will rise by about 3–4°C by 2100. While this prediction is the result of a detailed calculation to which we will return, the big picture that we will breach 2°C is very simple to understand. To keep within the 2°C limit the Intergovernmental Panel on Climate Change (IPCC) estimated that the whole world could not add after 2010 more than a total of about 1000 further gigatonnes of greenhouse gases to the stock already in the atmosphere (IPCC 2015, 10). We now add to that stock at a rate of about 50 gigatonnes a year. Even with the Paris pledges we will go on emitting over 50 giga-tonnes a year for the next 20 years, or a total of 50 times 20 which equals 1000 gigatonnes. It defies everything we know about the longevity of energy infrastructure investments and how the economy works to suppose that emissions will just stop altogether in the 2040s, especially in growing economies. So 2°C must inevitably be substantially breached.

An alternative approach to seeing that remaining within 2°C is impossible follow-ing Paris is to look at the UN's own graph (United Nations 2015b, Figure 2, p. 11) produced this October on the effects of the intended national contributions as compared to what is needed to have a two-thirds chance of staying within 2°C. However, while the UN has simply concentrated on the years around Paris, we gain a different perspective by embedding a simplified version of their graph within the whole time period 1950–2100 (Figure 1).

The heavy solid line on the left shows what has happened from 1950 until 2010. The steeply rising dotted line from 2010 to 2030 and then on to 2100 shows what is expected to happen without Paris, so-called Business as Usual (BAU). The still rising dashed line from 2010 to 2030 shows what is expected if Paris were fully implemented. No, it's not very different from the dotted line. If at Paris it had really been agreed to stay within 2°C, and this started in earnest in 2020 then the reduction would have to follow the steeply descending dashed and dotted line on the graph, with emissions reaching zero by 2040. This is simply not going to happen; such a reduction would imply a commitment in the rich countries to a radical degrowth strategy, which does not exist.

UN Press reports have suggested however that Paris will result in a 2.7°C rise, which looks comfortably close to 2°C. Christiana Figueres, the Executive Secretary of the UN Framework Convention on Climate Change said on 30 October 2015 *'The INDCs have the capability of limiting the forecast temperature rise to around 2.7 degrees Celsius by 2100, by no means enough but a lot lower than the estimated four, five, or more degrees of warming projected by many prior to the INDCs'* (UNFCCC 2015). The 2.7°C rise prediction comes from one of a number of scenarios explored by Carbon Action Tracker (Climate Action Tracker 2015). It optimistically

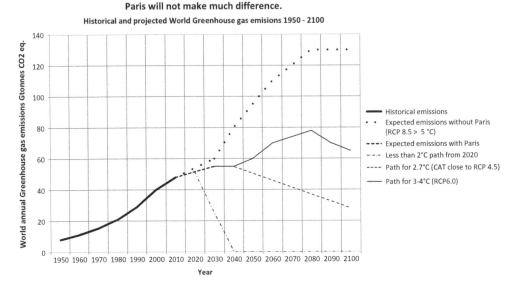

Paris will not make much difference.

Historical and projected World Greenhouse gas emisions 1950 - 2100

Figure 1. Historical and projected world greenhouse gas emissions 1950–2100.

assumes countries will continue to accelerate the rate of reduction in greenhouse gases as they have done for Paris, so emissions peak in 2030 and then decline gradually to about 1990 levels by 2100. It is represented by the light dashed line on our graph. This path bears some resemblance to the IPCC's RCP 4.5, (IPCC 2015) and the assignation of the average temperature rise of 2.7°C to such a path is reasonable, if much too precise.

However, surely the most optimistic assumption we are entitled to make based on current political agreements and actions across the world is that emissions will continue to rise after 2030, perhaps levelling off later in the century. This is broadly represented by the light solid line on the graph, which is associated with a 3–4°C rise, and follows the IPCC's RCP 6.0. We might instead expect the future simply to reflect the past, and follow the top light blue line, which is the IPCC's 'BAU' case, where the temperature rise is in the range 4–5°C.

The notion that emissions really are after all going to go down after about 2040 is altogether too reminiscent of St Augustine's *'Oh Lord make me pure, but not yet'*, or the business plan that predicts recovery, but always starting the year after next, never now. The danger is that 'BAU' might yet prevail.

OK, Paris said that everyone was going to try harder next time. But equally there is no international legal machinery to enforce the Paris commitments, and there must be severe doubts whether some countries will actually keep to their commitments; the US Senate, for example, may simply not ratify the US commitment, or the next US President may not even ask Congress. The great powers and their energy companies are simply not suddenly going to turn round and leave pretty much all the remaining fossil fuels in the ground. If the people with money and power in the world believed that really was going to happen, share prices of the major fossil fuel companies would have collapsed by now. They have not.

So the most probable and prudent assumption – still perhaps a bit optimistic – must be that the level of global temperature rise associated with carrying on as we are with emissions limited to broadly current levels – at least 3–4°C rise by 2100 – will now happen. This view is shared by one of the UK's foremost climate scientists, Professor Kevin Anderson, former Director of the Tyndale Centre. With his colleague Alice Bows-Larkin, Anderson's work on carbon budgets has revealed the gulf between political rhetoric on climate change and the reality of rapidly escalating emissions. His work makes clear that 'there is now little chance of maintaining the rise in global temperature at below 2°C, despite repeated high-level statements to the contrary. Moreover, his research demonstrates how avoiding even a 4°C rise demands a radical reframing of both the climate change agenda and the economic characterisation of contemporary society' (Anderson 2015).

The UNFCCC technical documents simply do not address what will happen to temperatures in the longer term after 2100. They say 'the use of climate models to estimate end-of-century temperatures resulting from specific post-2030 assumptions (like constant or linear extensions of emissions or assumed constant climate policies) is considered to be out of its (i.e. the report's) scope' (United Nations 2015b, para 208). Moreover, a 3–4°C rise by 2100 is the lower bound; there is huge uncertainty about the potential for various types of positive feedback, where warming initiates further warming mechanisms, such as die back of tropical forests, methane emissions from the tundra and methyl hydrate emissions from the deep ocean, all of which could result in runaway climate change leading to a 6°C rise or more in the longer term. And apart from feedback effects, there are major uncertainties about other possible effects, such as how quickly the Greenland and parts of the Antarctic ice caps will melt, radically changing sea levels and altering how far heat is reflected back or absorbed (the albedo effect), or whether northern Europe will continue to be warmed by ocean currents. These are just the 'known unknowns'; there will surely be other effects no one has even thought of. Because of these effects, there is a case for arguing that a 3–4°C rise simply implies a rise of at least 6°C, albeit slightly later.

Moreover, global average temperatures are expected to continue to rise after 2100 even without feedback effects and assuming optimistically that there are no further emissions after that date. Even a further 1°C or 2°C rise will massively increase the effects of climate change set out in the next section.

So we must now face our future on the assumption of very substantial climate change. This is not to give up on the struggle for mitigation, but it is to recognise that major damage is already virtually inevitable. The focus of mitigation must be to prevent even worse damage. Indeed, focussing on the damage we have already done will increase the case for mitigation.

It's not just dangerous climate change. Climate change is simply where the environmental shoe is pinching first. But it is combined with a still increasing world population, depletion of non-renewable resources, exhaustion of some renewable resources, other pollution such as plastics in the oceans and synthetic chemical in the Arctic, and the destruction and degradation of ecosystems and the services they provide us, including clean water, flood prevention and clean air.

The effects of 3–4°C of warming by 2100

What are the consequences of a 3–4°C rise by 2100? The IPCC has produced in its Fifth Assessment Report a detailed account of the likely risks for the main regions of the world (see IPCC 2014). It is insufficiently appreciated that damaging climate change will affect different parts of the world unequally. Broadly the tropics will suffer far more than the higher latitudes. It will also do so deeply unfairly; the countries and regions least to blame historically for climate change will generally fare worse than the very countries responsible for causing it. Some blameless small island states will literally disappear.

Specifically, and paying particular attention to the 'great powers' for it is they who will continue to dominate the world system into the twenty-second century, and taking some account of other already existing resource and ecological issues, but largely ignoring changes to wildlife that do not directly affect people, this what we might expect (see IPCC 2014):

- the US and wider North America will suffer primarily from increased wildfires, heat induced deaths and flooding, compounded by existing problems of water stress in some areas. But the US is a wealthy country, with an effective government and has relatively recent history in the last two centuries of internal migration. The US will cope, even if it resorts to ever more draconian measures to protect its southern border from migration;

- Despite facing huge ecological changes, especially in the forests of the Amazon basin, the prospects for Central and South America are highly variable, and include decreased food production and an increase in diseases. But population pressures are relatively low, and severe problems on a huge scale are unlikely. In particular the numbers seeking to migrate will be large, but not on the same scale as in Africa or Asia;

- Europe faces considerable challenges, only partly mitigated by its relative wealth. Perhaps the main problem will be increasing aridity in southern Europe, devastating agriculture and creating pressures for northward migration. Flooding and occasional extreme heat will also be hazards. It is not clear that the European Union can survive these pressures; the recent refugee crisis has shown that its solidarity is fragile. Without the EU the weight of the individual European powers in world affairs will be much diminished, and their economic, diplomatic and military ability to secure a disproportionate share of world resources may be compromised, leading to a decline in living standards but starting from a high base;

- Asia's great powers Russia, India and China face contrasting futures. Russia is a vast country and the effects of climate change will vary greatly, but on balance it might face greater opportunities than threats. The ability to expand its agriculture northwards, despite the disruption to its infrastructure caused by melting permafrost, and opportunities in the warming arctic might well outweigh problems in its drying south. The main question is how far it has the political and economic ability to respond to these changes. India and Pakistan on the other hand face huge problems. Lower rice yields on the whole are expected with rising temperatures. Heat stress will severely damage wheat growing and create severe food insecurity in the Indus and Ganges valleys. Flooding will displace millions of people in Bangladesh. The Indian sub-continent faces famine in many areas and forced migration for huge numbers of people. China looks less vulnerable, although climate change will compound its already existing severe environmental problems. Increased rain should compensate for reduced meltwater in its great river valleys, posing problems of water management but in a country with a two millennium history of controlling its water supplies on a sub-continental scale. Although major overall food insecurity is unlikely, local problems will arise and probably cause famines as in the 1970s. The prospects for the countries of central Asia are mixed, with increased aridity being the major problem, perhaps putting migratory pressure on both Russia and China.

- The poorest continent containing a billion of the world's poorest people, Africa, together with the already troubled Middle East, will be the hardest hit by climate change. The relentless expansion north, south and east of the Sahara desert, will displace hundreds of millions of people by making food security impossible. In tropical Africa diseases will increase their range and incidence. Already fragile states in both Africa and the Middle East inhabited by already very poor people will probably collapse, bringing war and forced migration on an unprecedented scale;

- while damage to unique ecosystems, such as coral reefs will be terminal in Australasia, and already arid but thinly populated regions may get drier, the main effects in Australia and New Zealand will be increased floods and coastal erosion, to which these comparatively rich countries should be able to adapt;

- some particular but relatively quite small groups, such as those living in the Arctic or on low lying islands will face total changes to their way of life as the traditional ecosystems on which they depend are destroyed or their land is simply flooded; and

- the oceans will warm and become more acid, causing decline in tropical fisheries in particular, affecting the ability of a large number of people in coastal communities mainly in the poorest parts of the world to obtain protein from the sea.

Overall, a vast genocide is likely to take place, greater than any in the twentieth century, with the perpetrators in the rich North retaining their power while the victims in the poor South may batter at the doors of the North but will probably not be able to gain entry. The US will be strong enough to retain its overall global hegemony over a diminished world if it chooses to do so, with Russia gaining strength in Eurasia. China's march to prosperity and power will be stunted as it grapples with colossal environmental problems, while the Indian subcontinent, and especially Africa and the Middle East will slip into war, famine and massive population loss.

What will happen to the British Isles?

The likely direct effects of 3–4°C of global warming on the British Isles look quite mild compared to this global holocaust. We can expect milder wetter winters, and drier hotter summers (especially in our most densely populated and most prosperous region, the South East), combined everywhere with more extreme and unpredictable weather. Flooding and coastal erosion will become more frequent and more destructive. Our wildlife will suffer much more than we do, with many species, as elsewhere in the world, being unable to adapt or move quickly enough.

Much more will need to be done on a fairly familiar list of additional investment, which while not depressing the economy as a whole will reduce consumption and divert resources to investment:

- flood defences;

- water conservation infrastructure, especially in the South East;

- changes to agricultural practices and crops; and

- loss of some land altogether to coastal erosion and sea level rises, and in particular increased flooding risk to London.

While it might not seem like it to those currently affected by flooding (I am writing at New Year 2016), coping with this is well within the capabilities of the British economy and state if it puts its mind to it; the warmer climate will be welcomed by many and will reduce heating costs.

But these direct effects on the UK are only the tip of the iceberg, and the only parts to have engaged our domestic political consciousness. Far more important is preparing for the breakdown of the current international system of trade and security. We are an economy far more engaged in the wider world than most, and crucially depend on the rest of the world biologically in the form of massive food imports. We cannot easily and quickly feed ourselves, and not at all in the meat intensive ways that we do now. The UK has a specialist economy heavily dependent on international trade; just like a specialist organism in any ecosystem we rely on the survival of that ecosystem. So we must think about what the economics and politics of the international ecosystem in 2100 might look like.

Perhaps the biggest single question is how far the present system of international free trade and easy movement of people known as globalisation will endure. There are at least two major ways in which it might collapse. The first is a serious and at least partially global war, which might act in the same way as World War I did to end the first period of globalisation. The fragile and fractious world described in the previous section would seem to provide plenty of opportunities for such a calamity, which of course could itself have huge implications for our security.

The second is the attitude of the US. Since World War II, the US has both engaged, often militarily, with the whole world and promoted and hugely benefited from international free trade, the sea lanes policed by the huge and dominant US navy. It is US corporations who are at the forefront of promoting the World Trade Organisation, and it is the US that dominates world economic organisations like the International Monetary Fund and the World Bank. The US is the state embodiment of international capitalism, and it seems unimaginable that it should withdraw from that position.

Yet, it has not always been that way. Between 1812 and 1914, and again between 1920 and 1941 the US foreign and trade policy was essentially isolationist. After World War II, it looked entirely possible that the US would withdraw again; keeping the US engaged in Europe was regarded as Ernest Bevin's great post-war foreign policy triumph. Isolationist voices have never been absent in US politics, and it is entirely possible that faced with a collapsing, unstable, war-ridden Eastern hemisphere the US may simply retreat to its self-sufficient Western hemisphere fastness, protected in particular from the vast potential migrations in the Eastern hemisphere by the Atlantic and Pacific oceans.

The future of globalisation, whether destroyed by general war, or by US isolationism, or both, has a potentially profound impact on the UK. While UK Governments will no doubt pursue their long traditional policy of trying hard to use their influence to maintain a world with free and plentiful international trade, it is unlikely they can be decisive; the decision will be made in Washington. That has the consequence that the UK must at least prepare for a world with much reduced international trade, and cease regarding an alliance with the US as being the cornerstone of its security policy. Other consequences are that:

- a breakdown in world trade would threaten our very biological survival through a reduction in food and animal feed imports, rather as occurred in the World Wars of the last century. Food security policy, based on much greater self sufficiency, though possibly within northern Europe, must be a priority. This will need at least more labour intensive and land efficient husbandry, fewer animals and less meat. The most glamorous, exciting job in the cabinet by 2080 will be Minister of Agriculture;

- we may face possible worldwide epidemics of existing or new diseases, and need to develop the epidemic management policies to deal with them;

- quite apart from mitigating climate change, maintaining our energy security will mean that we need to shift anyway from our current increasing (fossil fuel) energy imports to being self-sufficient in energy supplies in the UK;

- massive security challenges. In future we must expect more fragile states and more local or even global wars – which may directly affect the British Isles. Our concerns will become more local simply because of our inability to influence events in the wider world. A priority will be to keep the peace near us in Europe, and at least maintain a reasonable level of trade with Europe, especially in food. This means a security policy based on the actual threats we might face, concentrating more on defence of our home territory and less on expeditionary capacity;

- huge levels of forced and often unavoidable migration, perhaps akin to the fifth century, and possible forcible attempts to take over the remaining habitable parts of the world, including the UK, by people displaced from elsewhere. It is hard to imagine the UK maintaining an open borders policy in these circumstances.

It may be objected to all the forgoing that it is conjecture piled upon speculation, situated in a sea of uncertainty. We have to assume what the likely emissions following Paris will be; we have to believe the climate models that predict 3–4°C rise; we have to accept the consequences of this average rise for different parts of the world; we have to engage in a kind of futurology concerning the evolution of the world political system; and finally make an assessment of the effects of all this on the UK. Surely it's just all too uncertain to act on such a wobbly pile of propositions.

But what is the alternative? Food, health, foreign, aid, and security policy planning in particular need to take account of the long term, and must therefore proceed on some assumption about what we might think the future might look like. The main alternative hypothesis, which is that the world will continue to look much as it has before, is plainly not adequate. OK, we face colossal uncertainties, but that doesn't mean that the best thing to do is to be like the rabbit and stare at the headlights bearing down on us. Others more expert could no doubt come up with a more informed account of our future; the main point of this report is to argue that climate change will happen and that this assessment must be done.

The UK, together with the other rich countries, will also face a huge moral and political choice. How much of their effort should go into helping poorer countries adapt to climate change so far as that is possible, and how much into defending our own population and territory from the potential collapse in the international order, and in particular the pressures of mass migration? Of course some part of any help to poorer countries will help reduce the pressures on our own countries, and so is self-serving. But humanitarian concerns and our responsibility for the bulk of the historical emissions that have caused the problem suggest we should do much more than that. It is doubtful however whether even if the rich world gave as much support as it possibly could, even setting aside domestic political constraints, to the poor world's adaptation effort, it could ever be enough to prevent all the perils to international order and the UK security listed above. But where will the balance be drawn?

Universalism and progress – implications for political principles

With this end of innocence two great political principles dear to the hearts of all on the left, not just the green left, will also perish. First to die must be the idea of progress. And with that we will also have to come to terms with the impossibility of the aspiration of human universalism. Let me explain.

Modern politics is almost universally optimistic. Above all politicians promise a better future, generally predicated on economic growth. Green and other progressive politicians in particular exemplify this; the green, sharing, caring future will not only save the planet, but will also be better than the past. This applies both to those who believe that green growth and sustainable development is possible and those, like Green House, who see material growth in the economy as ending and envisage a smaller economy, but which will still nevertheless offer a better life. With Corbyn's election as Labour leader, the project to build a new alliance on the left of politics is above all seen as a 'progressive' project; let the progressives unite.

Yet, the bleak world presented above does not represent progress; the twenty-first century for most people in the world is going to be worse than the second half of the twentieth century, not better, however you dress it up. It will be worse not only materially (and many of us unhappy with rampant consumerism in the rich north may worry little about that, but poor people in both the rich north and the poor south will be genuinely less well off) but also morally and politically. As John Gray has argued (Gray 2013), while progress in science and human knowledge is cumulative, moral and political progress is always at risk, and it cannot be taken for granted that a success in one generation, such as the abolition of slavery, will hold forever from then on.

Failure to come to terms with the end of progress is part of the reason we find it so very hard to think about the world we face. Thinking about it confronts our most basic belief, cemented by ten generations of economic growth that the world is getting better. We will need to get closer to one aspect of the mind-set of the last genuinely sceptical Prime Minister, Lord Salisbury, in the 1890s, who aimed to do no more than prevent the world from getting worse. (Of course, he was worried about different things, like Britain's relative decline as a power, and the decline of the aristocratic landed interest in an era of advancing democracy, but the point is he was not, unlike his great opponent Gladstone, 'progressive'; rather unfashionably even then, he did not expect the world to get 'better'.)

But it's not just progress that is threatened. One central point of this report is to suggest that green-minded politicians and the environmental movement need to be honest with the public. It is no longer a matter of saving the world, the world is already at least half doomed. It is more a matter of coming to terms with what we have done, and preparing to meet that world. In the jargon, we need increasingly to emphasise adaptation to climate change, not forgetting we still need mitigation, that is reducing and soon eliminating, our greenhouse gas emissions.

Those of us who call themselves 'progressives' have always been more comfortable with preventing climate change, mitigation, rather than adapting to it. Partly that is just a commitment to the long term, the conviction that we should not leave these problems to our grandchildren. As responsible people, we should deal with the causes, not the effects of problems, prevent the problem arising, not cure it after the event. And the forces ostensibly behind climate change, the oligopoly of big fossil fuel companies, power companies, and the motoring lobby make attractive political targets for those on the left.

But there is a deeper reason for prioritising mitigation. When I cut my personal emissions, the benefit will be felt, in an infinitesimal way, by everyone on the planet and by future generations. Personally I get no meaningful benefit. If the UK cuts its emissions, the UK actually benefits just a little, but all other countries and their inhabitants benefit a little bit too. The point is that mitigation is necessarily a *universalist* project; an altruistic act that benefits everybody on the planet. Progressives are comfortable with universalism. It is after all what motivates our interest in alleviating poverty everywhere, or seeking universal peace and disarmament, or being sympathetic to the needs and aspirations of migrants. Un-selfishness, altruism, expanding the moral universe beyond myself, my family, my generation, my race, my gender, our country and even our species is what 'progressives' are all about.

It is in particular the opposite of far right nationalist or fascist ideas, which confine moral sympathy to one's own nation or race, and regard ourselves as locked in a struggle to the death with other races and nations for lebensraum, for an ecological niche. It is easy to forget that whole nations accepted these ideas only 70 or 80 years ago, and under far less provocation by events. The challenge for our politics will be to preserve some of our universalism in the face of events that will make its practical application impossible, and which will fan much more extremist and right-wing alternatives.

Increasing our focus on adaptation changes the political and moral emphasis. Adaptation is a local project. How do we protect our locality, our country, our way of life, from the effects of the climate change? While governments in the rich world may be persuaded to give help to poorer countries' adaptation needs, this is ultimately voluntary, and rich country electorates will come down to demanding priority for the preservation of their countries' security and basic living standards. Conservative politicians and thinkers have this local focus naturally, given their commitment to nation, kith and kin, and perhaps that is why they have always been lukewarm about mitigation. It is an approach implicit for example in Roger Scruton's *Green Philosophy* (Scruton 2012) or Nigel Lawson's *An Appeal to Reason* (Lawson 2008). And perhaps too conservatives are less attracted to progress, despite their politicians' rhetoric, and more concerned, as was traditional for them, with defending what we have. The electorate sense this, and this may be at the root of conservative electoral success that many progressives find hard to understand. But we should not forget that what we have includes political ideas like tolerance, respect for others, freedom of expression, and politics will become more a matter of preserving these than expecting their expansion.

However uncomfortable politically and morally, 'progressives' must nevertheless now face up to the need for adaptation. There is no longer a choice between mitigation and adaptation. It is too late, damaging climate change will happen, and no responsible politicians can ignore it. That is not to say we should not continue pressing for mitigation, we must, but an emphasis on mitigation alone is no longer tenable. Indeed, facing up to adaptation and seeing how difficult it is will strengthen the case for preventing worse damage, that is, for mitigation.

Conclusion

So, in short, Paris means that it is now too late to avoid profoundly damaging climate change. We must both not let our belief in progress prevent us from facing that, and accept that, as in the European Early Middle Ages, we are entering a new Dark Age; for a century or so progress is over.

Nor must we let the relatively small direct climate challenges to the UK blind us to the fact that the effect on the current world system will be profound, and that a nation extremely integrated with that system must prepare for huge uncertainties. For many of us on the left this concentration on UK security will be extremely challenging, under-mining our commitment to a human universalism which while still morally right will become a project impossible to achieve or even contribute much to through participa-tion in UK politics, though it is imperative that the idea is kept alive.

I said earlier in this piece that the last pessimistic Prime Minister was Salisbury. Actually that's not quite right. Before he was Prime Minister, Churchill was universally pessimistic in the later 1930s, holding up correctly the prospect of another awful war with Germany. He paid for it by being in the political wilderness. And he swiftly returned to total, if improbable, optimism during the war itself. But it was a grim optimism based on an appreciation of realities, and that's what I think we need here. Yes, the prospects are awful, but we can make them less awful if we prepare for them, and then we would have a chance that we might preserve much that is good about our democratic structures, and a commitment to universalism and the wider and poorer world tempered by realism. We cannot pretend we can avoid it altogether, or, alternatively, simply decide, as many have, that we are now doomed whatever we do, avert our eyes and retreat into a merry but short private life. It's much more complicated than that lazy dichotomy, and my 3-year-old granddaughter doesn't have the second option.

Acknowledgements

I started writing this piece before I was aware of and read John Foster's book, *After Sustainability* (Foster 2015). This paper is complementary I hope to Foster's work, trying to address some of the political and economic implications of climate change, but I took much inspiration from his book, and from subsequent exchanges with him.

I am as ever grateful to my Green House colleagues for their comments on earlier drafts of this paper, and in particular to Ray Cunningham for first suggesting this topic, and to Rupert Read, Jonathan Essex and Victor Anderson (who wasn't at all happy about it).

Disclosure statement

No potential conflict of interest was reported by the author.

References

Anderson, K. 2015. Kevin Anderson's University of Manchester Page. Accessed October 26 2015. http://www.manchester.ac.uk/research/kevin.anderson/.
Climate Action Tracker 2015. Accessed December 13 2015. http://climateactiontracker.org/indcs. html
Foster, J. 2015. *After Sustainability: Denial, Hope, Retrieval*. Abingdon: Routledge.
Gray, J. 2013. *The Silence of Animals: On Progress and Other Modern Myths*. London: Allen Lane.

Greenpeace UK. 2015. accessed December 14 2015. http://www.greenpeace.org/international/en/news/Blogs/makingwaves/cop21-climate-talks-paris-negotiations-conclusion/blog/55092/

IPCC. 2014. "Climate Change 2014, Impacts, Adaptation, and Vulnerability; Part B: Regional Aspects." In *Intergovernmental Panel on Climate Change*. New York: Cambridge University Press.

IPCC. Intergovernmental Panel on Climate Change. 2015. *Fifth Assessment Report, Summary for Policymakers*. Geneva: IPCC.

Lawson, N. 2008. *An Appeal to Reason: A Cool Look at Global Warming'*. London: Duckworth Overlook.

Scruton, R. 2012. *Green Philosophy: How to Think Seriously about the Planet*. London: Atlantic Books.

UNFCCC 2015, Press release at http://newsroom.unfccc.int/unfccc-newsroom/indc-synthesis-report-press-release/.

United Nations. 2015a. *Framework Convention on Climate Change; Adoption of the Paris Agreement, FCCC/CP/2015/L.9*. Paris: UN.

United Nations. 2015b. Synthesis Report on the Aggregate Effect of the Intended Nationally Determined Contributions. *FCCC/CP/2015/7*. Paris, UN.

REPLY

Transformation, adaptation and universalism

Nadine Andrews

A reply to:

Heatley, Brian. 2017. "Paris: optimism, pessimism and realism." *Global Discourse*. 7 (1): 10–22.
http://dx.doi.org/10.1080/23269995.2017.1300402

May 2016 was the 13th month in a row to break global temperature records, with 2016 set to become the hottest year ever recorded, completing a run of three record years in a row (Carrington 2016). Temperatures have risen by 1°C since pre-industrial times, and the symbolic milestone of 400 ppm of CO_2 in the atmosphere has now been passed. As Heatley (2017) argues, optimism about preventing dangerous climate change is unrealistic. And it is diverting attention away from where it needs to be focussed: planning our adaptation to the 3–4°C increase that seems more likely, and acting to prevent even higher temperature increases.

I will discuss optimism later but first I respond to the issue of adaptation.

Adaptation begins with accepting the reality of the situation we are in. Acceptance enables us to make the psychological adjustments necessary for responding in ways appropriate to the new reality (Crompton & Kasser 2009). But according to the Intergovernmental Panel on Climate Change's (IPCC's) most recent Assessment Report (AR5), maladaptation is a growing concern. There are many factors thought to be contributing to maladaptation, including different perceptions of risks, competing values, as well as assumptions that adaptation will be a rational-linear problem-free process (IPCC 2014, 187, 199), thereby underestimating the complexity of adaptation decision-making.

AR5 describes two types of adaptation: incremental and transformational. Incremental adaptation is often referred to as 'business-as-usual' because unlike transformational adaptation, it does not challenge or disrupt existing systems and structures. Given these are the systems that are contributing to climate change in the first place, how effective incremental adaptation can really be is doubtful. AR5 states that for avoiding intolerable risks 'transformational adaptation may be required if incremental adaptation proves insufficient' (189). Based on the success of our mitigation track record to date, it's not a wild guess that incremental adaptation will indeed prove to be insufficient and that transformational adaptation will be needed. AR5 explains that transformational adaptation may be reactive, forced, induced by random factors or deliberately created through social and political processes (1105). But however it happens, it is not a neutral process (1121) and there are concerns about the equity and ethical dimensions (1105). Planning for transformational change will not be easy: there are many social, political and cultural and psychological barriers and resistances to changing the fundamental attributes of existing systems and structures, not least that it may pose a threat to vested interests (1121). Even if we could reach agreement about what constitutes 'proof' of incremental adaptation insufficiency (which is a big 'if'), by the time this point of incontrovertible proof is reached, it will be too late to do much in the way of advance planning especially for transformations that are equitable and ethical.

Transformational adaptation is also likely to involve changes in values, although AR5 does not specify which ones. However, Heatley does in referring to universalism, which I discuss now.

Universalism values are to do with understanding, appreciation, tolerance and protection for the welfare of all people and for nature (Schwartz 1992). Universalism and benevolence, which is concerned with caring for in-group members, form a self-transcendence set of values beyond individual self-interest. In Schwartz's model (1992; Schwartz et al. 2012), self-transcendence values are structured in the mind in an oppositional relationship with self-enhancement values. Self-enhancement values are to do with power over others, social status and prestige, and material and financial wealth. The oppositional nature means that when one set of values is activated in the mind, the other set is suppressed: it is difficult to think about and act from both sets of values at the same time. The more a value is activated, the stronger it becomes, and the easier it is to subsequently activate. This matters because universalism values are associated with ecologically responsible behaviour, whereas self-enhancement values are associated with lack of concern for the natural world (Schultz et al. 2005; Bardi and Schwartz 2003; Sheldon and Kasser 2011). Self-enhancement values are anxiety-based: they are self-protective values pursued to cope with anxiety in situations of uncertainty (Schwartz et al. 2012).

Looking ahead to 2100, Heatley anticipates that universalism values will come under threat from the impacts of 3–4°C warming. In the UK these impacts are likely to include the breakdown of systems and structures of globalisation upon which the UK depends, as a result of war and other security threats, mass migration, and the isolationist policies of other nations undermining collaborative universalism approaches. The fragile solidarity of the European Union (EU) may not survive the pressures, he warns. But we do not have to wait till 2100 for the breakdown of solidarity and disruption of international systems of trade and security. As we enter a post-Brexit world, it is already within sight. The self-protection values and isolationist tendencies that have been developing in the UK for some time have erupted to the surface, creating political chaos. The fear now is that this referendum result will spur on those in other EU countries with similar concerns, 'making the disintegration of the EU practically irreversible' (Soros 2016).

Universalism values are already under threat. So why is it that self-protection values are becoming stronger in society? Climate change is a situation of huge uncertainty and poses profound existential threat. It threatens sense of safety, and stability and integrity of self-identity by threatening life plans and subverting internalised expectations of the future (Crompton and Kasser 2009; Hamilton and Kasser 2009; Weintrobe 2013; American Psychological Association 2009; Norgaard 2006; Lertzman 2015; Hoggett

2011). The human tendency is to alleviate the stress and anxiety caused by psychological threat through defence mechanisms and coping strategies (Cramer 1998).

One defence is to retreat into self-protection. But such a retreat is not a purely individual, personal response: defences are culturally sanctioned and maintained by social norms and structures (Randall 2013). As a society, explains Macy (1993), 'we are caught between a sense of impending apocalypse and an inability to acknowledge it' (15). This allows individuals and institutions to simultaneously *acknowledge* climate change and its risks (e.g. COP21 pledges) and *deny* it (e.g. the pledges are below the level needed to restrain warming to within 2°C) in a process known as disavowal. Interestingly, a recent survey found that Brexit voters were more likely to deny that climate change is human-caused (Vaughan 2016).

Another defence is unrealistic optimism. Optimism is often pursued because of a fear that to do otherwise would be to fall into despair and dysfunction (Andrews, Fahy & Walker 2016). Despair, Macy (1993, 18) reminds us, 'is tenaciously resisted because it represents a loss of control, an admission of powerlessness'. This takes us to the issue of progress: climate change renders the dominant cultural worldview of progressivism untenable and this is profoundly threatening because progressivism is about being in control. Progressivism is the belief that is through advancement of technoscience, industrialisation and economic development that the human condition can be improved (Foster 2015). The supposition is that humans are separate from, and superior to, nature. That we can transcend nature's limits, harness its forces and exploit its resources for our own ends (Plumwood 1993; Merchant 1983; Midgley 2003). It is exactly this cultural worldview that has led us to this situation of ecological crisis (e.g. White 1967; Bateson 1982; Plumwood 1993), and which is also hindering us from responding adaptively. We would do better to let go of such hubris and embrace humility, for we cannot technofix and economically develop our way out of this mess. That, as Wright (2004, 61) argues, is an 'ideological pathology'. We have to forget the project of progress as it is currently conceptualised, not just for a hundred years as Heatley pleads, but altogether, and promote an alternative idea of human flourishing that is infused with different values.

Adaptation should not become a purely local project motivated by narrow self-protection values: that is unlikely to end well for us or for the other living beings with whom we share the planet. But it is not clear who can champion an alternative vision of 'adaptation as universalism'. Who are the custodians of universalism values with sufficient socio-cultural influence to keep these values activated in public, media and political minds? Will spiritual leaders be able to step up and perform this role? The 2015 Papal Encyclical suggests this is Pope Francis' intention, with its fierce critique of capitalism and emphasis on the interconnectedness of humans with the rest of nature. In calling for a subject–subject relationship of mutuality rather than a subject–object relationship of domination and exploitation, Pope Francis echoes indigenous belief systems as expressed by, for example, the Indigenous Environmental Network[1] who campaigned and protested at COP 21 in Paris. AR5 acknowledges that indigenous peoples' holistic view of community and environment is a major resource for adapting to climate change but notes that such non-scientific sources of knowledge have not yet been used consistently in existing adaptation efforts (26, 181). How and why is not explored but a clue is in the term 'non-scientific'. Letting go of ideologies of scientism and progressivism is surely part of the transformational change in existing structures and systems needed for living in more harmonious relationship with the natural world.

Note

1. see http://indigenousrising.org

Disclosure statement

No potential conflict of interest was reported by the author.

References

American Psychological Association. 2009. *Psychology & Global Climate Change: Addressing a Multifaceted Phenomenon and Set of Challenges*. Washington, DC: American Psychological Association.

Andrews, N., S. Walker, and K. Fahy. 2016. "Between Intention and Action: Psychosocial Factors Influencing Action on Climate Change in Organisations." In *Innovation in Climate Change Adaptation*, edited by W. L. Filho 275-287. Cham: Springer International Publishing. doi:10.1007/978-3-319-25814-0_19

Bardi, A., and S. H. Schwartz. 2003. "Values and Behaviour: Strength and Structure of Relations." *Personality and Social Psychology Bulletin* 29: 1207–1220. doi:10.1177/0146167203254602.

Bateson, G. 1982. *Steps to an Ecology of Mind*. Reprint 1987. Northvale, New Jersey: Jason Aronson.

Carrington, D. 2016. "Shattered Records Show Climate Change Is an Emergency Today, Scientists Warn." *Theguardian.com*. Accessed 18 June 2016. https://www.theguardian.com/environment/2016/jun/17/shattered-records-climate-change-emergency-today-scientists-warn

Cramer, P. 1998. "Coping and Defense Mechanisms: What's the Difference?" *Journal of Personality* 66 (6): 919–946. doi:10.1111/1467-6494.00037.

Crompton, T., and T. Kasser. 2009. *Meeting Environmental Challenges: The Role of Human Identity*. Godalming, UK: WWF-UK.

Foster, J. 2015. *After Sustainability*. London: Routledge.

Hamilton, C., and T. Kasser. 2009. "Psychological Adaptation to the Threats and Stresses of a Four Degree World." [conference paper] Four Degrees and beyond Conference, Oxford University, Oxford, UK, September 28–30.

Heatley, B. 2017. "Paris – Optimism, Pessimism and Realism." *Global Discourse* 7 (1).

Hoggett, P. 2011. "Climate Change and the Apocalyptic Imagination." *Psychoanalysis, Culture & Society* 16 (3): 261–275. doi:10.1057/pcs.2011.1.

IPCC. 2014. "Climate Change 2014 Impacts, Adaptation, and Vulnerability Part A: Global and Sectoral Aspects." Working Group II Contribution to the Fifth Assessment Report of the Intergovernmental Panel on Climate Change. New York, NY: Cambridge University Press.

Lertzman, R. 2015. *Environmental Melancholia: Psychoanalytic Dimensions of Engagement*. East Sussex: Routledge.

Macy, J. 1993. *World as Lover, World as Self*. Berkeley: Parallax Press.

Merchant, C. 1983. *The Death of Nature*. San Francisco: Harper & Row.

Midgley, M. 2003. *Myths We Live By*. London: Routledge.

Norgaard, K. M. 2006. "'People Want to Protect Themselves a Little Bit': Emotions, Denial, and Social Movement Non-Participation." *Sociological Inquiry* 76 (3): 372–396. doi:10.1111/soin.2006.76.issue-3.

Plumwood, V. 1993. *Feminism and the Mastery of Nature*. London: Routledge.

Randall, R. 2013. "Great Expectations: The Psychodynamics of Ecological Debt." In *Engaging with Climate Change: Psychoanalytic and Interdisciplinary Perspectives*, edited by S. Weintrobe, 87–102. Hove, UK: Routledge.

Schultz, P. W., V. V. Gouveia, L. D. Cameron, G. Tankha, P. Schmuck, and M. Franek. 2005. "Values and Their Relationship to Environmental Concern and Conservation Behavior." *Journal of Cross-Cultural Psychology* 36 (4): 457–475. doi:10.1177/0022022105275962.

Schwartz, S. H. 1992. "Universals in the Content and Structure of Values: Theoretical Advances and Empirical Tests in 20 Countries." *Advances in Experimental Social Psychology* 25: 1–65.

Schwartz, S. H., J. Cieciuch, M. Vecchione, E. Davidov, R. Fischer, C. Beierlein, A. Ramos, et al. 2012. "Refining the Theory of Basic Individual Values." *Journal of Personality and Social Psychology* 103 (4): 663–688. doi:10.1037/a0029393.

Sheldon, K. M., and T. Kasser. 2011. "Americans Recommend Smaller Ecological Footprints When Reminded of Intrinsic American Values of Self-Expression, Family, and Generosity." *Ecopsychology* 3 (2): 97–104. doi:10.1089/eco.2010.0078.

Soros, G. 2016. "Brexit and the Future of Europe." Project-Syndicate.Org. Accessed 26 June 2016. https://www.project-syndicate.org/commentary/brexit-eu-disintegration-inevitable-by-george-soros-2016-06

Vaughan, A. 2016. "Brexit Voters Almost Twice as Likely to Disbelieve in Manmade Climate Change." *Theguardian.com*. Accessed 17 June 2016. https://www.theguardian.com/environment/2016/jun/16/brexit-voters-almost-twice-as-likely-to-disbelieve-in-manmade-climate-change

Weintrobe, S., ed. 2013. *Engaging with Climate Change: Psychoanalytic and Interdisciplinary Perspectives*. Hove, UK: Routledge.

White, L. 1967. "The Historical Roots of Our Ecological Crisis." *Science* 155 (3767): 1203–1207. doi:10.1126/science.155.3767.1203.

Wright, R. 2004. *A Short History of Progress*. Edinburgh: Canongate Books.

After development? In defence of sustainability

Mike Hannis

ABSTRACT

The Paris Agreement was a success only for the carbon traders, sequestrators and geoengineers who are now expected to 'balance emissions with removals' by 2050, against a background of continued economic growth. If this is sustainable development, it is indeed discredited. But the problem is with the 'sustainable development' paradigm, not with the idea of sustainability. The UN's Sustainable Development Goals explicitly call for intensified economic growth and are clearly incompatible with the allegedly overarching goal of ecological sustainability. To aim at *this* very different goal is simply to aim at living in a way that does not contain the seeds of its own destruction. Far from invalidating this objective, diagnoses of crisis make its pursuit more urgent than ever. 'Why aim at sustainability?' is an odd question to pose, but one that may nonetheless produce illuminating answers. One answer derives from intergenerational obligations, but this may not even be the most important. An orientation towards sustainability is also beneficial in its own right, since it is a key part of aiming at the good life.

Sustainability stands charged with having failed (Benson and Craig 2014; Foster 2015): but it remains a useful and important guiding principle, albeit one that is more ethical than technical. By contrast, sustainable development (SD) could clearly be said to have failed, if its task had been to bring about ecologically sustainable human societies. Documents emerging from two recent sets of protracted UN negotiations confirm however that in reality SD continues to succeed spectacularly in its true objective of sustaining the 'development' paradigm, transforming evidence of ecological crises into arguments for further economic growth.

COP21 – endings, beginnings and contradictions

In the north of England, 2015 ended with the flooding of several major cities. The rain arrived at the margins of an Atlantic storm system so powerful that it raised midwinter temperatures at the North Pole above freezing, for only the second time ever recorded (Griffin 2015). This graphic illustration of climatic disruption came as a swift and sobering corrective to the choreographed euphoria which had just greeted the Paris Agreement on Climate Change.

The primary achievement of the 21st Conference of the Parties to the UN Framework Convention on Climate Change was to get 195 countries to formally agree firstly that anthropogenic climate change is real, and secondly to set targets ('intended nationally determined contributions' or INDCs) for reduction of their own net greenhouse gas emissions. There is no requirement to set INDCs at any particular level, nor any penalties for not meeting them – but all nations have agreed to set them and publicly account for progress towards them, and they are intended to be ratcheted up with each 5-yearly review (UNFCCC 2015).

This apparent consensus masked a significant backward step from the previous Kyoto agreement which, for all its many flaws, had acknowledged 'differential responsibility'. Countries whose current wealth and power derive from early industrialisation and disproportionate past use of fossil fuels were seen as bearing particular responsibility for current greenhouse gas levels and expected to lead the way in reducing emissions. Following 20 years of pressure, primarily though not exclusively from the United States, this acknowledgement has now been abandoned. 'We' are now officially all in it together, and a veil has been determinedly drawn over the fact that some did more than others to get 'us' here. Despite ample historical evidence to the contrary, the politically convenient narrative of the unforeseen Anthropocene has been institutionalised (Bonneuil and Fressoz 2016). 'Loss and damage' provisions on adaptation finance may sweeten this pill, but commitments here are vague.

The other headline from Paris was the unexpected adoption, alongside the widely trailed explicit target of keeping global temperature rise within 2°C, of a more challenging aspiration to limit warming to 1.5°C. This was particularly welcomed by the Alliance of Small Island States, some of whose low-lying territories are predicted to disappear under the sea level rise expected at two degrees. The adoption of a 1.5°C target was a public relations masterstroke, but given that temperatures have already risen by 1°C, and that there is a delay of decades between emissions and the resulting warming, it is almost certainly unachievable even if all available stops were pulled out now. Existing targets, if met, will result in warming of closer to 3°C. To have even a 50% chance of achieving 1.5°C, current emissions levels would need to be cut by 60% within 10 years.

There is of course a large gap here between aspiration and action. The Paris Agreement was presented by excited environmental journalists as signalling 'the end of the fossil fuel era' (e.g. Goldenberg et al. 2015) but it makes no mention of reducing the extraction or use of fossil fuels. Nor does it endorse direct taxation of fossil fuel production. It does not call for any reductions in consumption levels, and it reaffirms (at article 10.5) the importance of 'promoting economic growth'. These multiple contradictions are reconciled by two innocuous words that do a great deal of work in the text: 'net' and 'balance'. The key aim agreed is

> to achieve a balance between anthropogenic emissions by sources and removals by sinks of greenhouse gases in the second half of this century. (article 2.1)

The envisaged reduction is in *net* emissions, rather than in what might be – but never are – called *gross* emissions. By sometime after 2050, the amount of carbon emitted should be matched by the amount being removed. Given the inevitable increased emissions associated with continued economic growth, this balance will presumably be primarily achieved by action on the sink side of the equation, using 'negative emissions' technologies to take carbon back out of the atmosphere. Some such measures, such as increasing carbon sequestration in topsoil, may be beneficial if done sensitively but seem unlikely to be sufficiently scaleable. Others, such as seeding algal blooms in the oceans or pumping carbon dioxide into saline aquifers, could well be disastrous. All are highly speculative.

Whatever the mechanism, the clear intention is that carbon capture and trading will be used to offset continued growth in emissions. The agreement (at article 6) promises new trading mechanisms and standardised accounting rules to help integrate national and regional carbon markets, making this offsetting both easier and more profitable. With remarkable circularity, the resulting Green Economy is itself envisaged as a key driver of the broader economic growth allegedly required to produce the additional financial flows needed for climate change adaptation. Financial engineering is just as much part of this picture as geoengineering – and is arguably just as dangerous (see e.g. Lohmann 2011; Sullivan 2014).

All this represents a massive opportunity for the carbon traders, sequestrators and geoengineers whose 'godlike' redemptive powers are now expected to 'balance emissions with removals' indefinitely, while economic growth continues (Lynas 2012; discussion in Hannis 2012). Aggressively pushing back against the supposed Luddism of steady-state left-green environmentalism, 'ecomodernists' proclaim without any apparent irony that once humanity accepts its true destiny, our creative ingenuity will usher us into a 'good Anthropocene' (Asafuyu-Adjaye et al. 2015; see also Caradonna et al. 2015; Hamilton 2013, 199–205). If this is sustainable development, it is indeed discredited. However the problem is, as it has been all along, with the paradigm of sustainable development, rather than with the co-opted concept of sustainability.

Sustainable development goals?

The salience of the idea of sustainability increased dramatically from 1987, in the wake of the Brundtland report's historic call for sustainable development (WCED 1987). The word 'development' defines what is to be sustained in this paradigm: it is not a neutral term denoting social organisation or human activity in any generic sense but has a very specific (and question-begging) meaning. This usage can be traced back to the inaugural speech of post-war US president Harry Truman, which famously called for

> a bold new program for making the benefits of our scientific advances and industrial progress available for the improvement and growth of underdeveloped areas. (Truman 1949, quoted in Esteva 1992)

The assumed end point of human social and economic 'development' was henceforth defined as industrialised, market-economy societies on the US model. The majority of the world, with its prodigious variety of other social and economic traditions, was redefined at a stroke as 'underdeveloped', and needing to be brought into the fold.

Early attempts by independent-minded countries in the global South to achieve such development autonomously through import substitution were later suppressed. US-dominated global financial institutions insisted on structural adjustment programmes which 'liberalised' such economies, opening their domestic markets to Northern exports and ownership of their assets and industries to Northern capital, while enforcing export-orientated economic policies locking in the historic colonial emphasis on provision of raw materials and cheap labour. Development thus came to inescapably imply participation in globalised markets, usually on highly unequal terms. The powerful organic metaphor of development lent an air of respectability and irresistible teleology to this highly constructed and ideologically driven project, as it still does today.[1]

Brundtland's masterful reinvention of this neocolonial project as *sustainable* development not only pacified the environmentalist objectors of the late 1980s but recruited many of them to the cause. The year 2015 arguably saw an attempt to achieve the same thing with social justice campaigners, as sustainable development was authoritatively updated and redefined through the adoption of the UN's 2030 Agenda for Sustainable Development (United Nations 2015). Once again the document seeks to be all things to all people. This time however the rhetorical technique employed is not to gather allcomers around the campfire of a vague general principle, but to bundle (almost) everyone's demands in together, glossing over any incompatibilities.

Like Brundtland, and indeed Paris, the 2030 Agenda represents the outcome of a tortuous process of consensus-building between several axes of diametrically opposed constituencies. Its 17 sustainable development goals (SDGs) and 169 targets have been roundly criticised from the right as utopian, impossibly expensive and a misguided attempt to shoehorn all available concerns into one document (e.g. Economist 2015). From the left, the accusation is that laudable headline aspirations on issues such as poverty, food security and inequality (goals 1, 2 and 10) are entirely undermined by the failure of the related targets to endorse any policies that might threaten existing power structures, strengthen regulation of corporate bodies or propose significant redistribution of existing wealth (e.g. Hickel 2015).

Both critiques have some merit. The latter though is particularly pertinent to the environmental goals. For instance, the targets underlying goal 7 on energy, while endorsing renewable energy and energy efficiency measures, do not support any reduction in fossil fuel use but in fact call for 'advanced and cleaner fossil-fuel technology'. Most paradoxically of all, while endorsing 'sustainable consumption and production patterns' (goal 12) and 'urgent action to combat climate change' (goal 13), the SDGs are also repeatedly premised on intensified growth in GDP. While artfully broadening the appeal with references to inclusivity and full employment, Goal 8 calls explicitly for 'sustained economic growth'. The key supporting target here is more detailed than most:

> sustain per capita economic growth in accordance with national circumstances and, in particular, at least 7 per cent gross domestic product growth per annum in the least developed countries. (goal 8.1)

This is not the place for detailed argument in support of the contested claim that economic growth is a key driver of ecological crisis, not a solution to it. Suffice it to say that (*pace* ecomodernism) 'weightless' growth decoupled from extractive industries and waste generation remains a myth, and the Jevons effect continues to undermine efforts to square this circle through efficiency gains and technological ingenuity (Jackson 2009; Polimeni et al. 2009). The point here is simply that the SDGs exemplify and clarify the SD paradigm, illustrating its fundamental incompatibility with the supposedly underlying objective of ecological sustainability. The two have definitively come apart, if they were ever together. Sustainability has not failed – it has never been attempted.

Needs and futures

Stepping outside the SD mindset means reopening the question of what is to be sustained. Brundtland brokered an unequal compromise between sustainability and development, and sustainability has been fading into the background ever since (Dresner 2008). Let us then return briefly to that pivotal moment, and to Brundtland's protean definition of SD: 'development which meets the needs of the present without compromising the ability of future generations to meet their own needs' (WCED 1987). In striking contrast to the voluminous SDGs, this apparently unobjectionable formulation is entirely (and notoriously) free of empirical content. In particular, it says nothing explicitly about environmental issues. It simply proposes that a very general ethical principle should govern the activity of 'development'. To spell it out, this principle, once shorn of the word 'development', yields a similarly protean definition of 'sustainable': X is sustainable if it 'meets the needs of the present without compromising the ability of future generations to meet their own needs'.

As noted above, 'development' is a highly disingenuous term which, while masquerading as neutral, smuggles in far more than is apparent. It is essentially *impossible* for the project of 'development' to be conducted in a way that 'meets the needs of the present without compromising the ability of future generations to meet their own needs' – not because the basic principle is at fault, but because it is simply not compatible with what 'development' is. The disconnect is not only ecological but also social, historical and conceptual. As one Indian scholar memorably observed,

> Sustainability and development belong to different, almost incommensurable worlds. … Sustainability is about the ethics of care and concern. It exudes the warmth of locality, of the Earth as a home. Development is a genocidal act of control. … Development is a contract between modern nation-state and modern Western science to reduce all forms of difference – all ethnic forms, all ethnic knowledges – to create a flatland called modernity.
> (Visvanathan 1991, 378–379)

What then if X were something else? What would it be to have a *politics*, a *society* or an *environmentalism* which met the needs of the present without compromising the ability of future generations to meet theirs? Compared to current mainstream discourse, it is hard to imagine what genuinely open-ended conversations about such matters, freed of the unspoken obligation to reach answers compatible with economic growth and 'development', would even look like. But these are conversations which urgently need to take place.

Brundtland thus remains a surprisingly good place to start thinking about sustainability, not just because of its historical significance, but because its basic ethical injunction is so hard to resist. As a principle of social organisation, it seems clear almost to the point of banality that present people should be able to meet their needs, but not at the expense of future people's ability to meet theirs. Of course, the ethical force derives in large part from the fact that the definition talks not about wants, desires or preferences but about needs. It appeals to fundamental notions of respect for the dignity and autonomy of persons, to support a strong ethical claim that genuine human needs should not go unmet. As John O'Neill (2011) points out, such claims are far more compelling when they refer to needs, rather than preferences. Indeed, it could be argued that the one word 'needs' provides *all* the ethical ballast here.

What will future people's needs be? How could anyone in the present possibly know the answer to such a question? One possible response is to say that the ethical imperative that needs be met applies in fact only to 'basic' needs. These are still notoriously difficult to define, but it is nonetheless tempting to think that this reduced task should not be impossible, even in respect of future people. But both reason and compassion militate against seeing present obligations to future generations as limited to safeguarding the provision of their basic needs. The bare minimum is certainly a good starting point for identifying what to pass on, but a starting point is all it is. Present actions should aim at maximising the chances that future people not only survive but also flourish. This remains true however difficult it may seem, or however gloomy we may be now about likely future conditions.

Clearly then, taking the idea of sustainability seriously implies an ethical obligation to reflect now on what future people will need in order to flourish, and then to ensure, as far as possible, that these needs will be able to be met. This does not mean that the needs of the future trump those of the present. It means rather that needs both present and future should be understood in terms not of how markets can satisfy preferences, but of how societies can best satisfy genuine requirements for human flourishing. This opens up many further questions, some new and some ancient, such as what constitutes a flourishing life, and what the relationships might be between human and non-human flourishing. Answers to such questions may be judged by the extent to which they are applicable to past, present and future generations of human beings, and across cultures (Sullivan and Hannis 2016). While this kind of fundamental reflection might seem distant from the urgent practicalities of the Anthropocene, it may well be the only way to understand and (hopefully) escape the drivers of what John Barry (2012) calls 'actually existing unsustainability' (Hannis 2015a).

Temptations of agnosticism

Perhaps though, given the inevitable uncertainty under which such reflection takes place, we present-day humans should not impose our present-day expectations on future people but simply aim to maximise the range of options that will be available in the future, enabling them to fulfil their autonomously defined needs in the widest possible range of ways.

This would be to apply a broader political principle of neutrality about conceptions of the good life to environmental matters. It has been argued that this principle can legitimise or even require robustly precautionary environmental policy (Wissenburg 2006; Dobson 2003; Sagoff 2008). The idea is that if both environmentalists and eco-sceptics are to be able to live the lives they choose, then the future demands of both will need to be met, and making this possible will in practice require the implementation of strong environmental policies. There are significant ethical and political problems with this view, many of which boil down to the fact that the two sets of demands may very well turn out to be not just different but mutually exclusive, and hence to require diametrically opposed sets of policies. To adjudicate between them in any meaningful or effective way will eventually require abandoning neutrality, and replacing it with an overt commitment to some substantive idea of what a flourishing life requires.[2]

Such agnosticism about what will be valued by future people is neither ethically tenable nor politically defensible (Hannis 2005). But there are also formidable practical difficulties in maintaining an agnostic position on future needs. It is not possible to pass on both the option to live in a world free of radioactive waste, and the option to live in a world equipped with nuclear power plants. The option of living in a world containing Yangtze River dolphins, and the option to live in a world in which that river serves as a major freight shipping route, are incompatible. In both of these cases, the choice has already been made, and only one of each pair of options will be passed on. Whether the choice was conscious or deliberate is now largely immaterial. The nuclear waste is here, and the dolphins are extinct. Humanity's current trajectory is closing off options at an accelerating rate, multiplying the choices we in the present are required to make about what is bequeathed to future generations. Rainforests, or biofuel plantations? A briefly increased supply of oil, or intact arctic ecosystems? Expanding economies, or a habitable climate?

Sustainable development, as conceived in both the 2030 Agenda and the Paris Agreement, seeks 'win-win solutions' to such dilemmas which circumvent the need for attitudinal or political change. These frequently rely not only on heroic optimism about technology but often also on deceptive aggregation techniques which assume and enforce unjustifiable commensurabilities of value. For instance, proposals for the 'off-setting' of biodiversity impacts, in their calculative utilitarianism, recognise no ethical, ecological or ontological problems with the idea that ecological degradation arising from overexploitation, overproduction or overconsumption can be cancelled out by additional conservation efforts elsewhere, leaving 'no net loss' (Hannis and Sullivan 2012; Sullivan and Hannis 2015). This is ideology, not ecology. Creative solutions to particular problems may sometimes be able to reconcile ecological sustainability with other conflicting objectives, perhaps even in some contexts with economic growth. But the possibility of such reconciliation cannot be assumed and certainly cannot avoid the need for choices, or for the critical evaluation of options.

It might be the case in a given instance that options opened up by changing parts of the non-human world irreversibly were so valuable as to outweigh the other options thereby closed off. But even for agnostics (or ecomodernists), this would somehow need to have been calculated and demonstrated in advance, if they were to meet their obligations to future people – and such calculations are by definition made in conditions of radical uncertainty. The impact of this year's catch on North Sea cod stocks a decade from now is impossible to calculate without knowing whether quotas in the intervening years will be set to allow recovery or to maximise yield. The ecological impact of cutting down a square mile of forest depends not only on how large the whole forest is now, and on how much intact forest is needed for it to remain a viable ecosystem, but also on how likely the remaining forest is to be left intact in the future. Great uncertainty arises regarding such counterfactuals, both when assessing degradation and when planning conservation interventions (see e.g. Maron, Rhodes, and Gibbons 2013). In evaluating a proposed forest clearance, for instance, it matters not only what species are present now but also what species might have been present in the future had the current trajectory continued. Impacts on livelihoods and climate are of course similarly uncertain, often rendering calculations of what future options are closed off by a given present action close to meaningless.

Flourishing beyond progress

The unsurprising ethical upshot is that we in the present *should* think seriously now about what future people will need in order to flourish, with the equally serious intent of not making it impossible for them to have it. Two qualifications immediately arise. The formidable levels of uncertainty involved suggest firstly that a strongly precautionary attitude is appropriate, and secondly that such reflection should focus on aspects of human experience which *can* be reasonably expected to persist into the future. Both of these point away from any rash assumption that the satisfaction of future needs will require the continuation of present (and historically anomalous) high-consumption life-styles, or their associated economic and political structures.

I have argued elsewhere that making an ethical argument for sustainability requires not consequentialism or deontology, but a eudaimonist virtue approach building on, and contributing to, an ecologically literate conception of human flourishing (Hannis 2015a, 2015b). However in his challenging attack on the very idea of sustainability, John Foster (2015) questions the efficacy of such arguments, on the basis that other visions of human flourishing are possible, and indeed apparently widely shared. Utilitarian arguments urging the avoidance of present-day profligacy in order to avoid a painful future can be undermined by techno-optimistic claims that future problems can and will be fixed. Foster argues that virtue arguments urging the avoidance of present-day profligacy because of their likely effects on future human flourishing are similarly vulnerable to consumerist (or indeed ecomodernist) revisionings of flourishing, in which little or no value is placed on 'wildness' or non-controlling relationships with the nonhuman world.[3]

But Foster glosses over the fact that from a political perspective, virtue ethics tends to be associated with a broadly perfectionist view of the role of government. While such matters should indeed be open to debate, as briefly discussed above it is not the case that action on environmental matters requires neutrality between those who want it and those who don't. Yes, the argument that a fully flourishing human life requires some kind of ecological virtues would need to be cogently put, and competently defended – and yes, if this argument were squarely lost, then perhaps humanity really would find itself in the position Foster evocatively terms 'environmental tragedy'. But we're not quite there yet. Given the tsunami of propaganda required to keep consumerism on track, and the coercive force required to maintain current levels of inequity, Foster's apparent conviction that post-Enlightenment humanity is hopelessly lost in unreflective individualism seems overstated. Gramsci's 'pessimism of the intellect, optimism of the will' seems more appropriate here.

Only a very strange version of human flourishing could deny not only the value of meaningful human relationships with non-human nature, but also the value of caring about the future. Care for the future is not premised only on consequences. *Aiming* at sustainability is something that contributes to human flourishing in the present. Most obviously, it ameliorates present as well as future predicaments. Given sustainability's intricate connection with egalitarianism, honestly adopting it as a genuine goal can also bolster community and help address corrosive inequality. There is a virtuous circle here, since *in*equality drives *un*sustainability (Barry 2012; Wilkinson and Pickett 2009). Lastly, an orientation towards sustainability involves, not just peripherally but centrally, thoughtful reflection on just what it is that constitutes a good human life: and such reflection is itself a key part of a good life.

Foster's is a more nuanced argument against the idea of sustainability than those premised on neutrality or ecomodernism. He yokes it together though with a further argument that sustainability is inevitably associated with progressivism. This I think is mistaken. Unlike sustainable development, sustainability is not about maintaining a trajectory of 'progress'. Caring about – and planning for – the future does not imply this kind of linear narrative. Indeed, it might be argued that the opposite is true. If I believe the future will by some mysterious mechanism be necessarily 'better' than the present whatever I get up to, why would I bother doing anything other than live it up? Conversely, if I believe the future may be harsher than the present, I may feel an intensified obligation to do what I can now to help. Foster is right that it is time to build the post-SD world, and right that this may require accepting that 'catastrophe' is coming – but this does not mean that sustainability is no longer relevant or useful as a guiding concept.

Conclusion – sustainability for the Anthropocene?

To aim at ecological sustainability is simply to aim at living in a way that does not contain the seeds of its own destruction. Far from invalidating this objective, diagnoses of crisis, whether 'entering the Anthropocene' or 'facing catastrophic climate change' make its pursuit more urgent than ever, for both practical and ethical reasons. Getting from here to anything like ecological sustainability will probably require not just conquering the institutionalised addiction to economic growth, but dismantling many existing power structures, and evolving radically different principles of social organisation. The worse things get, the more urgent this becomes. Whether it currently looks politically achievable ultimately has no bearing on whether it is a worthwhile ethical objective. Despite its widespread appropriation by technocrats and market enthusiasts, sustainability is not an apolitical idea, but a rich and powerfully normative concept which may yet prove invaluable.

Notes

1. On the history and genealogy of development discourse, including the emergence of the 'sustainable development' paradigm, see contributions to Crush's (1995) anthology, particularly Porter (1995). Porter discusses the background assumptions of Truman's speech, relating it to Arndt's important (1981) distinction between intransitive (Marxist) and transitive (colonialist, as in the British 1929 Colonial Development Act) usages of the verb 'develop'. See also Deb (2009) on 'developmentality', and discussion in Hannis (2011).
2. Also relevant here is the well-established broader communitarian critique of liberalism, which argues that any attempt at government based on liberal neutrality will in fact inevitably result in the imposition of unexamined liberal conceptions of the good, not least those embedded in the very idea that neutrality is desirable. The related concern that Rawlsian liberal neutrality relies on an untenable conception of persons as 'radically disembodied subjects' (Sandel 1998) is particularly pertinent in the context of environmental policy.
3. 'Wildness' is of course a complex and slippery concept which can be deployed to support many different perspectives. See for example discussion in Sullivan (2015).

Disclosure statement

No potential conflict of interest was reported by the author.

Funding

Completion of this paper has been generously facilitated by funding from the Arts and Humanities Research Council (grant AH/K005871/2).

References

Arndt, H. W. 1981. "Economic Development: A Semantic History." *Economic Development and Cultural Change* 29 (3): 457–466. doi:10.1086/451266.

Asafuyu-Adjaye J., L. Blomqvist, S. Brand, B. Brook, R. DeFries, E. Ellis, C. Foreman, et al. 2015. *An Ecomodernist Manifesto*. Accessed 7 May 2015. http://www.ecomodernism.org

Barry, J. 2012. *The Politics of Actually Existing Unsustainability: Human Flourishing in a Climate-Changed, Carbon Constrained World*. Oxford: Oxford University Press.

Benson, M., and R. Craig. 2014. "The End of Sustainability." *Society and Natural Resources* 27: 777–782. doi:10.1080/08941920.2014.901467.

Bonneuil, C., and J.-B. Fressoz. 2016. *The Shock of the Anthropocene*. London: Verso.

Caradonna, J., I. Borowy, T. Green, P. A. Victor, M. Cohen, A. Gow, A. Ignatyeva, M. Schmelzer, et al. 2015. *A Call to Look Past 'An Ecomodernist Manifesto': A Degrowth Critique*. Accessed 7 May 2016. http://www.resilience.org/articles/General/2015/05_May/A-Degrowth-Response-to-An-Ecomodernist-Manifesto.pdf

Crush, J. S., ed. 1995. *Power of Development*. London: Routledge.

Deb, D. 2009. *Beyond Developmentality: Constructing Inclusive Freedom and Sustainability*. London: Earthscan.

Dobson, A. 2003. *Citizenship and the Environment*. Oxford: Oxford University Press.

Dresner, S. 2008. *The Principles of Sustainability*. 2nd ed. London: Earthscan.

Esteva, G. 1992. "Development." In *The Development Dictionary*, edited by W. Sachs. London: Zed Books.

Foster, J. 2015. *After Sustainability: Denial, Hope, Retrieval*. Abingdon: Earthscan.

Goldenberg, S., J. Vidal, L. Taylor, A. Vaughan, and F. Harvey. 2015. "Paris Climate Deal: Nearly 200 Nations Sign in End of Fossil Fuel Era" *The Guardian*, December 12. Accessed 7 May 2015. http://www.theguardian.com/environment/2015/dec/12/paris-climate-deal-200-nations-sign-finish-fossil-fuel-era

Griffin, A. 2015. "Storm Frank: Freak Weather Pushes North Pole above Freezing." *The Independent*, December 31. Accessed 7 May 2016. http://www.independent.co.uk/news/science/storm-frank-freak-weather-pushes-north-pole-above-freezing-a6792141.html

Hamilton, C. 2013. *Earthmasters: The Dawn of the Age of Climate Engineering*. New Haven: Yale University Press.

Hannis, M. 2005. "Public Provision of Environmental Goods: Neutrality or Sustainability? A Reply to David Miller." *Environmental Politics* 14 (5): 577–595. doi:10.1080/09644010500257862.

Hannis, M. 2011. "Land-Use Planning, Permaculture and the Transitivity of 'Development." *International Journal of Green Economics* 5 (3): 269–284. doi:10.1504/IJGE.2011.044238.

Hannis, M. 2012. "Another God Delusion?" *The Land* 11: 10. Accessed 7 May 2016. http://www.thelandmagazine.org.uk/articles/another-god-delusion.

Hannis, M. 2015a. *Freedom and Environment: Autonomy, Human Flourishing, and the Political Philosophy of Sustainability*. London: Routledge.

Hannis, M. 2015b. "The Virtues of Acknowledged Ecological Dependence." *Environmental Values* 24 (2): 145–164. doi:10.3197/096327114X13947900181437.

Hannis, M., and S. Sullivan. 2012. *Offsetting Nature? Habitat Banking and Biodiversityoffsets in the English Land Use Planning System*. Weymouth: Green House. Accessed 7 May 2016. http://www.greenhousethinktank.org/files/greenhouse/home/offsetting_nature_inner_final.pdf.

Hickel, J. 2015. "The Problem with Saving the World." *Jacobin*, August 8. Accessed 7 May 2016. http://www.jacobinmag.com/2015/08/global-poverty-climate-change-sdgs/

Jackson, T. 2009. *Prosperity without Growth: Economics for a Finite Planet*. London: Earthscan.

Lohmann, L. 2011. "The Endless Algebra of Carbon Markets." *Capitalism, Nature, Socialism* 22 (4): 93–116. doi:10.1080/10455752.2011.617507.

Lynas, M. 2012. *The God Species: How Humans Really Can Save The Planet.* London: Fourth Estate.

Maron, M., J. Rhodes, and P. Gibbons. 2013. "Calculating the Benefit of Conservation Actions." *Conservation Letters* 6 (5): 359–367.

O'Neill, J. 2011. "The Overshadowing of Needs." In *Sustainable Development: Capabilities, Needs and Well-Being*, edited by F. Rauschmeyer, I. Omann, and J. Fruhmann. London: Routledge.

Polimeni, J., K. Mayumi, M. Giampetro, and B. Alcott. 2009. *The Myth of Resource Efficiency: The Jevons Paradox.* London: Earthscan.

Porter, D. 1995. "Scenes from Childhood: The Homesickness of Development Discourses." In *Power of Development*, edited by J. S. Crush. London: Routledge.

Sachs, W., ed. 1992. *The Development Dictionary.* London: Zed Books.

Sagoff, M. 2008. *The Economy of the Earth.* 2nd ed. Cambridge: Cambridge University Press.

Sandel, M. 1998. *Liberalism and the Limits of Justice.* Cambridge: Cambridge University Press.

Sullivan, S. 2014. *The Natural Capital Myth; or Will Accounting Save the World? Preliminary Thoughts on Nature, Finance and Values* Working Paper 3, Leverhulme Centre for the Study of Value. Accessed 7 May 2016. http://thestudyofvalue.org/wp-content/uploads/2013/11/WP3-Sullivan-2014-Natural-Capital-Myth.pdf

Sullivan, S. 2015. "Wild Game Or Soul Mates? On Humanist Naturalism and Animist Socialism in Composing Socionatural Abundance." Paper Presented at Conference Landscape, Wilderness and the Wild, Newcastle University, March 2015. Accessed 7 May 2016. http://tinyurl.com/Sullivan-wild-game-soulmates

Sullivan, S., and M. Hannis. 2015. "Nets and Frames, Losses and Gains: Value Struggles in Engagements with Biodiversity Offsetting Policy in England." *Value Struggles In Engagements With Biodiversity Offsetting Policy In England.* *Ecosystem Services* 15: 163–172. doi: 10.1016/j.ecoser.2015.01.009.

Sullivan, S., and M. Hannis. 2016. *Relationality, Reciprocity and Flourishing in an African Landscape: Perspectives on Agency Amongst ‖Khao-A Dama, !Narenin and ‖Ubun Elders in West Namibia.* Future Pasts Working Paper No. 2. Accessed 7 May 2016. http://www.futurepasts.net/fpwp2-sullivan-hannis-2016

The Economist. 2015. "The 169 Commandments." *The Economist*, March 28. Accessed 7 May 2016. http://www.economist.com/news/leaders/21647286-proposed-sustainable-development-goals-would-be-worse-useless-169-commandments

Truman, H. 1949. "Inaugural Address of US President Harry S. Truman. January 20. Accessed 7 May 2016. http://www.bartleby.com/124/pres53.html

UNFCCC. 2015. *Paris Agreement on Climate Change.* http://unfccc.int/resource/docs/2015/cop21/eng/l09r01.pdf

United Nations. 2015. *Sustainable Development Goals: Seventeen Goals to Transform Our World.* Accessed 7 May 2016. http://www.un.org/sustainabledevelopment/sustainable-development-goals/

Visvanathan, S. 1991. "Mrs Brundtland's Disenchanted Cosmos." *Alternatives: Global, Local, Political* 16 (3): 377–384. doi:10.1177/030437549101600306.

WCED. 1987. *Our Common Future (The Brundtland Report).* Oxford: Oxford University Press.

Wilkinson, R., and K. Pickett. 2009. *The Spirit Level: Why Equality is Better for Everyone.* London: Penguin.

Wissenburg, M. 2006. *"Liberalism."* In *Political Theory and the Ecological Challenge*, edited by A. Dobson and R. Eckersley. Cambridge: Cambridge University Press.

Response to 'After development? In defence of sustainability'

Lawrence Wilde

This is a reply to:

Hannis, Mike. 2017. "After development? In defence of sustainability." *Global Discourse.* 7 (1): 28–38. http://dx.doi.org/10.1080/23269995.2017.1300404

It was no mean feat of diplomacy to secure the agreement of 195 states to adopt a legally binding commitment to tackle climate change, so news of the Paris Agreement was widely greeted as a significant move forward. The deal, according to the *Guardian*, 'has proven that compromise works for the planet' (15 December 2015), and this reflected a widespread feeling that, finally, the particular interests of competing economic powers had been subordinated to the greater good. Unfortunately, as 'After Development?' argues convincingly, Paris amounts to a paper compromise that promises what it cannot deliver, hobbled by a continued commitment to further economic growth and a highly speculative faith in the development of 'sinks' to remove emissions. In other words, the agreement acquiesces to the failure to control gross emissions, and the headline aspiration to limit warming to 1.5 per cent flouts the real-world likelihood of a 3 per cent increase, rendering the goal of sustainability chimerical. Previous failures to reach agreement on targets for reducing emissions at least exposed the contradiction between the consequences of unlimited economic growth and the need to protect future life, but now the contradiction is simply ignored. In striving to allay the concerns of all parties, Paris conceals the blatant inadequacy of the proposals with a rhetorical gloss.

A similar problem haunts the document specifying the 2030 Sustainable Development Goals (SDGs). Progress on achieving the Millennium Goals had often been obstructed by 'free-market' economic policies imposed by the World Trade Organization (WTO), the International Monetary Fund (IMF) and the World Bank. However, in the 2030 SDGs, the contradiction between human development goals and neoliberal economics has been magically dissolved, as is vividly shown by the explicit commitment to high growth without any acknowledgement of its threat to sustainability. In Weberian terms, the past revealed the contradiction between the substantively rational goal of sustainable development and the instrumental rationality practised by the dominant economic actors, while the present simply denies the very existence of this contradiction. In the face of this, it is understandable that many critics declare the entire paradigm of sustainable development to have failed, but 'After Development' argues for the retention of sustainability as a normative goal, quite rightly in my view. I am also sympathetic to the suggestion that sustainability can best be justified by some form of virtue ethics, as I argue in my book, *Global Solidarity* (Wilde, 2013). There are, of course, difficulties in neo-Aristotelian approaches to global ethics, surrounding the delineation of universal needs and the goal of human flourishing, but engagement with these issues would be, in itself, a welcome development in the struggle to establish global norms. Importantly, it is a theoretical approach that can lend itself to the development of criteria to assess and prescribe policies in key areas of global governance, as well as exposing the calamitous nature of the status quo.

But if sustainability can be rescued, must we abandon 'development' as 'a highly disingenuous term'? I would be reluctant to go along with this part of the argument of 'After Development', for although the concept has undoubtedly been abused, it is not inherently flawed, but rather may be contested on two grounds. First, even when 'development' is considered in narrowly economic terms, the priority of high economic growth needs to be questioned. The fixation with this single indicator is, historically, a relatively recent phenomenon, and the numerous instances of soaring growth rates accompanying persistent severe poverty show how misleading an indicator it is when considering what is good for society as a whole. Indeed, the conditions for stimulating maximum growth are also the conditions that reproduce increasing inequality and social exclusion. Second, if the focus is shifted to 'human development', then it allows for the emergence of the sort of virtue ethics approach that the author would like to see in relation to sustainability. In this respect, I think that the 'human capabilities' approach adopted by Nussbaum (2006, 2011) has much to commend it, despite certain objections. She has been criticised for projecting Western liberal values as universal needs, and for failing to appreciate the extent to which neoliberalism dictates the structural reproduction of global warming and poverty. Nevertheless, the demand for the provision of the means to enjoy a fulfilling existence for all, and for the generations to come, is something that can speak to the concerns of all who are appalled by the injustice and myopia of the status quo.

In the concluding paragraph of 'After Development', the author quite reasonably points out that a coherent argument for a worthwhile ethical objective must be articulated even when it is difficult to imagine how the political transformation required to carry it forward might be accomplished. However, as the article reveals the extent to which worthy normative goals are being subverted by diplomatic legerdemain, it is surely right, as the author indicates, to raise the demand for the radical reconstruction of the institutions and processes of global governance. Global politics was closer to addressing this issue in the 1990s than it is now, and yet the need to do so is more pressing than ever.

Disclosure statement

No potential conflict of interest was reported by the author.

References

Nussbaum, M. 2006. *Frontiers of Justice: Disability, Nationality, Species Membership*. Cambridge, MA: Belknap Press.
Nussbaum, M. 2011. *Creating Capabilities: The Human Development Approach*. Cambridge, MA: Belknap Press.
Wilde, L. 2013. *Global Solidarity*. Edinburgh: Edinburgh University Press.

Post-capitalism, post-growth, post-consumerism? Eco-political hopes beyond sustainability

Ingolfur Blühdorn

ABSTRACT
As a road map for a structural transformation of socially and ecologically self-destructive consumer societies, the paradigm of *sustainability* is increasingly regarded as a spent force. Yet, its exhaustion seems to coincide with the rebirth of several ideas reminiscent of earlier, more radical currents of eco-political thought: liberation from capitalism, consumerism and the logic of growth. May the exhaustion of the sustainability paradigm finally re-open the intellectual and political space for the big push beyond the established socio-economic order? Looking from the perspective of social and eco-political theory, this article argues that the new narratives (and social practices) of post-capitalism, degrowth and post-consumerism cannot plausibly be read as signalling a new eco-political departure. It suggests that beyond the exhaustion of the sustainability paradigm, we are witnessing, more than anything, the further advancement of the *politics of unsustainability* – and that in this politics the new narratives of hope may themselves be playing a crucial role.

1. Introduction

Since the 2012 Rio+20 Summit, at the latest, the paradigm of sustainability is widely regarded as exhausted – categorically unable to deliver any profound structural transformation of capitalist consumer societies. To be sure, actual policy-making, from the local to the international level, firmly holds on to the sustainable development promise that consumer capitalism can actually be reconciled with values of social justice, political equality and ecological integrity. Yet, as modern societies' crises continue to tighten, such promises are becoming ever less plausible. In view of accelerating climate change, the unrestrained exploitation of natural resources, the precariousness of the global financial system, the public and private debt crisis, ever higher levels of social inequality, rapidly eroding trust in political elites, the challenges of mass migration, proliferating movements of populism and so forth – all feeding into a multi-dimensional sustainability crisis that leaves politicians (as well as the market) utterly helpless – there is an anxious awareness that present social and economic arrangements simply cannot be sustained, and that before long some kind of cataclysmic event must and will trigger major change.

In this situation of disoriented anxiety, a number of discourses have (re)emerged which, although not necessarily connected to each other, may generate some considerable hope. They rehearse the hypotheses that the demise of capitalism is now both foreseeable and inevitable (e.g. Streeck 2011, 2014a, 2014b; Mason 2015, 2016); that a new citizens' revolution is emerging to self-organise the departure from the fossil growth economy which mainstream politics has so far failed to deliver (e.g. Prinzen 2005, 2010; Muraca 2013); that a shift in social value preferences is about to take modern societies beyond the consumer culture (e.g. Soper 2007, 2008; Jackson 2009; Schlosberg and Coles 2015); that technological innovation increasingly enables communities to unplug from industrial mega-circulation and develop decentralised, needs-oriented and resource-efficient local economies (e.g. Petschow et al. 2014); and that the arrival of the Anthropocene may finally take modern societies into a new era where nature and society can be developed symbiotically (e.g. Crutzen and Schwägerl 2011; Arias-Maldonado 2012, 2013, 2015).

Thus, the exhaustion of the sustainability paradigm seems to coincide with the rebirth of several ideas reminiscent of earlier, more radical currents of eco-political thought which the reformist sustainability paradigm had pushed into the very margins. And at the latter's demise, the sociocultural conditions for radical change – beyond capitalism, growth and consumerism – in many respects, actually seem more favourable than at any earlier point in time. So, might the exhaustion of the sustainability paradigm, in that it finally re-opens the intellectual and political space, be a blessing rather than a reason for despair? Are we witnessing the emergence of a new, much more genuinely transformative eco-politics? How should we interpret these new initiatives and narratives? In order to shed light on eco-politics beyond the paradigm of sustainability, this article relates them to recent sociological and eco-political theory. It suggests that they remain strangely ignorant of the distinctive conditions and key dilemmas diagnosed, for example, by the theorists of *liquid modernity* (Bauman) and *post-ecologism* (Blühdorn) and that they can, therefore, not offer any plausible perspective for a structural transformation of liberal consumer societies. But despite this striking blindness, these practices and narratives should, arguably, not simply be interpreted as further evidence of the 'pervasive culture of denial' that Foster and many others have attributed to contemporary consumer societies (Foster 2015, 35ff; also see; Hamilton 2010; Norgaard 2011; Dunlap and McCright 2011). Instead, this article will argue that the discourses and experimental practices of post-capitalism, post-growth and post-consumerism are more suitably interpreted within the model of the *politics* and *governance of unsustainability* (Blühdorn 2000, 2011, 2013b, 2014, 2015; Blühdorn and Welsh 2007): as *discourses of simulation* (Blühdorn 2007, 2013a, 2016b) they help to organise – quite contrary to their own self-perception and declared intentions – modern societies' journey towards ever more social inequality and ecological destruction.

In the past decades, environmental sociologists have contributed quite significantly to the 'pervasive culture of denial'. They have forcefully promoted strategies of *sustainable development* and *ecological modernisation* which have, despite their undeniable successes, always been known to be very limited, and hence problematic. Their promises of technological fixes and environmental-economic win–win scenarios could easily be sold to academic funders, governments, businesses and many others who, more than anything, wanted to leave the core principles of liberal consumer capitalism untouched. Thus, environmental sociologists have helped to provide cover under which the socially and ecologically destructive order could continue to flourish and deplete the cultural resources which are essential to even imagine, let alone implement, any alternative to the status quo. But as these narratives are collapsing and emergent social conflicts are becoming unmanageable, environmental sociology may have an opportunity to redress this complicity. Rather than nurturing new narratives of hope, it may now fully focus on its academic task to investigate the prevailing politics of unsustainability. Indeed, looking beyond sustainability is not just a matter of looking for a new eco-political master-frame! Bearing this in mind, the present article proceeds in four steps: it next very briefly reviews the argument that the sustainability paradigm has become exhausted. Section 3 provides a more detailed account of the new narratives of hope. Section 4 explores whether and how these narratives relate to recent sociological and eco-political theory. And the last substantive section then outlines why interpretations of these narratives in terms of *denial* fail to capture the distinctive quality of eco-politics beyond sustainability. It reinterprets these narratives and practices as *exercises of simulation* which help to manage the challenges of sustained unsustainability.

2. Sustainability and ecological modernisation

When in the late 1980s the Brundtland Report (WCED 1987) kick-started the comet-like career of the notions of sustainability and sustainable development, the great eco-political promise of these concepts was that they would address the new social and ecological concerns voiced in some sections of advanced consumer societies and at the same time accommodate the interests of those who were hoping for further economic development and growth. The Brundtland Report acknowledged the problem of Third World poverty and the unsuitability of the industrialised countries' path of development as a model for the global South. It promised to take the concern for environmental integrity seriously and recognised the existence of bio-physical limits. It conceded that in the industrialised North structural change to the established logic of development was required in order to stay within 'the bounds of the ecologically possible' (WCED 1987, 55). Yet, it also provided reassurance that this would neither have to entail a wholesale departure from liberal consumer capitalism, nor a radical critique of the established western logic of modernisation, or even 'the cessation of economic growth' (40). Indeed, the Brundtland commission demanded that the international 'economy must speed up world growth' (89), and it portrayed the advancement of scientific knowledge, accelerated technological innovation, improved monitoring and management, and the internalisation into the market of social and environmental costs as effective tools to 'avert economic, social and environmental catastrophes' (WCED 1987). Put differently, it suggested that modern societies might *grow beyond* and *modernise themselves out of* the social and ecological problems to which the traditional pattern of modernisation had given rise. A new form of *ecological* modernisation (Mol 1995, 1996; Spaargaren 1997; Mol and Sonnenfeld 2000) would now address these problems and put industrialised societies, and the world at large, onto a trajectory of sustainable development. In terms of sociological theory, Ulrich Beck's concept of a *second* or *reflexive* modernity provided the foundations for this new eco-modernist approach which would remedy the unforeseen side effects of traditional, first modernity and fulfil those promises of modernity which had so far remained unfulfilled (Beck 1992, 1997).

Three decades later, the terms sustainability, sustainable development and ecological modernisation are ubiquitously present, but they are, more than ever, fuzzy concepts which, rather than mapping an agenda for, and signalling any commitment to, a structural transformation of liberal consumer capitalism, seem to be tools for artificially extending its life expectancy: as national governments and international institutions are signalling 'little political appetite for anything but very modest change' (Linnér and Selin 2013, 983), 'both sustainability governance and the sustainable development concept are under growing pressure' (Bulkeley et al. 2013, 958). Not only has in contemporary eco-politics the comprehensive package of concerns, which environmental movements had once raised, apparently shrivelled to the single issue of climate change, but in light of international political instability, economic turmoil, populist uprisings and the paralysis of political institutions (such as the European Union) which once spearheaded the sustainability project, there is little evidence of any 'genuine pursuit of serious change' (Foster 2015, 2). 'Mainstreamed as sustainability or sustainable development', Foster notes, 'environmentalism has failed to reduce, even remotely adequately, the impact of humans on the biosphere' (Foster 2015). Hence, the paradigm that for a long time has been beacon of international eco-politics is increasingly regarded as 'an irretrievably misconceived framework and a delusive policy goal' (Foster 2015, Preface).

Apart from the fact that – at least in those *weak* mainstream varieties which have always been dominant (Baker 2006) – the sustainability paradigm had never really intended to suspend the established understanding of progress and development, the prime reason why today it 'no longer exerts the pulling power it once had' (Bulkeley 2013, 959) is, arguably, that it consistently evaded all normative issues and insisted that environmental issues can more effectively be addressed by the means of science, technology, the market and professional management. Trying to bypass the notorious conflicts of values which had previously often obstructed environmental policy-making, the proponents of the new paradigm aimed to detach environmental policy from *soft* subjective and cultural criteria (tradition, aesthetics, religion and ethics) and place it, instead, on *hard* objective scientific foundations. The scientific diagnosis of bio-physical limits was assumed to facilitate agreement about the issues to be addressed, and appropriate technologies – supported by depoliticised 'new environmental policy instruments' (Jordan, Wurzel, and Zito 2003) – were to secure that consensual objectives would actually be achieved.

Yet, in their fixation on science, technology and management, the related policy approaches not only failed to address many of the emancipatory eco-movements' concerns, which were, although they often crystallised around the condition of the bio-physical environment, to a significant extent about non-material issues of identity, integrity and self-determination (Inglehart 1977, 1997; Inglehart and Welzel 2005), but they also failed to recognise that, as a matter of principle, environmental problems are never objectively identifiable conditions *out there* in the natural environment, but always *perceived violations of socio-cultural norms*. For effective environmental policy-making, the accumulation of scientific knowledge and the development of new technologies can, undoubtedly, be extremely helpful, but however sophisticated such knowledge and these technologies might be, they can never substitute for normative judgement. As it were, the shift from thinking in terms of an *environmental crisis* – a concept that explicitly externalises the problem and locates it in the environment – to the frame of the *sustainability* crisis might actually even have placed additional emphasis on the irreducibly normative core of all eco-politics: *What* is to be sustained, *for whom, for how long, in what condition* and *for what reasons*? And the lively debate throughout the 1990s about the *end of nature*, the *culturalisation of nature* and the *naturalisation of culture* (e.g. McKibben 1990; Eder 1996; Beck 1997; MacNaghten and Urry 1998) could actually have provided a very favourable framework for this. But the sustainability paradigm, instead, promoted a strongly techno-managerial perspective and agenda. It failed to define progress and development in terms pointing beyond the established notions of economic growth and material accumulation. It did not provide an attractive vision of a substantially different modernity and, ultimately, it boiled down to the technocratic pursuit of uninspiring goals such as *resource efficiency* or *decarbonisation* – as if these were intrinsically meaningful and desirable. Hence, the sceptical view that this 'would-be scientific model of environmental concern isn't actually part of the solution' but a 'deeply embedded part of the problem' (Foster 2015, 35) does not come as a surprise.

3. Narratives of hope

The 'end of sustainability' (Benson and Craig 2014), it has been suggested, will trigger a 'deep crisis within environmentalism itself' (Foster 2015, 1), force an 'end of pretending' (Foster 2015, Chapter 1) and move capitalist consumer societies beyond their 'current state of denial' (Benson and Craig 2014, 778). For the time being, such predictions do not seem to materialise: not only do recent developments, for example, in the provision of (renewable) energy, geo- and climate-engineering, electric mobility or smart cities provide rich evidence that policy makers continue to have much confidence in technological fixes and Green growth, but even if the sustainability paradigm really has become exhausted, there is no shortage of narratives of hope to counterbalance any 'inner crises of environmentalism' (Foster 2015, 1). The most important one of these – given that capitalism itself has by so many, and for so long, been regarded as the root cause of modern societies' social and ecological problems – is probably that the collapse of capitalism is now imminent and unavoidable, and that this provides a unique opportunity for the transition towards a socially and ecologically more benign socio-economic order. In the wake of the international banking crisis and the subsequent politics of austerity, 'there is now a widespread sense that capitalism is in a critical condition, more so than at any time since the end of the Second World War' (Streeck 2014a, 35). In fact, the crash of 2008/2009 and the economic and political upheaval since have called to mind that, rather than being eternal and without alternatives, 'capitalism has a beginning, a middle and an end' (Mason 2015, xiii) and that, in the course of this lifecycle, instability and crisis have by no means been the exception, but 'the normal condition' (Streeck 2011, 6). And whilst a few decades ago the early Greens' diagnosis that 'the system is bankrupt' (Kelly 1984) had, obviously, still been premature, there is now a widespread feeling that today it really is, and the further 'prospects for capitalism are bleak' (Mason 2015, x).

Streeck focuses specifically on *democratic* capitalism which, he suggests, has always been inherently instable and destined to fail because the two logics, or principles, of resource allocation which it promised to reconcile ultimately remain incompatible. In the post-war era, he argues, the conflict between these two logics – 'one operating according to marginal productivity, or a free play of market forces, and the other based on social need or entitlement, as certified by the collective choices of democratic politics' (2011, 7) – could initially be patched over by high economic growth. But as growth rates began to decline, a range of different strategies were employed to pacify the conflict: high inflation in the 1970s was followed first by lavish government deficit spending and then, since the 1990s, by waves of public asset privatisation, deregulation and increases in private debts (Streeck 2011, 2014a, 2014b). In each case, the objective was to stabilise the inherently instable system by drawing on 'additional money, as yet uncovered by the real economy' (Streeck 2011, 12). However, none of these strategies, Streeck suggests, could be sustained for any significant length of time, and the 'sequential displacement' (Streeck 2011, 23–24) of the irresolvable conflict steadily built up a triple problem of persistently low economic growth, increasing indebtedness (public and private) and ever rising social inequality. The monetary policies of *quantitative easing* and minimal (or indeed negative) interest rates, one might add, are the most recent such displacement strategies, and yet another attempt to mine the resources of the future for consumption in the present. But today even these measures are failing to jumpstart the economy, while the imposition of harsh austerity policies are causing political upheaval and 'pervasive government instability' (Streeck 2014a, 41) not just in Europe, but also in the USA and elsewhere. And as there is nothing to suggest that economic growth may catch up any time soon; as 'even capitalism's master technicians have no clue how to make the system whole again' (Streeck 2014a, 46); and as the limits to the political manageability of ensuing social conflicts seem almost exhausted, the collapse of capitalism does indeed appear a plausible scenario.

Streeck does not explore what may evolve in its aftermath. In fact, rather than conceiving of the end of capitalism as a cataclysmic event, he believes that for the foreseeable future modern societies will remain caught up in 'a long and painful period of cumulative decay: of intensifying frictions, of fragility and uncertainty, and of a steady succession of *normal accidents*' (Streeck 2014a, 64). Paul Mason, in contrast, in *Postcapitalism* (2015) boldly announces the 'beginning of something radically new' and is convinced that 'we can now build a fairer and more sustainable society' (Mason 2016, 45). Mason does not just talk about *democratic* capitalism, but diagnoses the end of capitalism more generally. And the societal order that is emerging to succeed it, he suggests, is no longer based on the logic of competition, profitability and wealth accumulation but on new forms of 'non-market production and exchange' (Mason 2015, 265). Already now, he notes, 'we're seeing the spontaneous rise of collaborative production: goods, services and organizations are appearing that no longer respond to the dictates of the market and the managerial hierarchy' (xv) but are geared towards collective use and social efficiency. We are seeing the rise of 'horizontally distributed peer-production networks' generating 'goods that are either completely free, or which – being Open Source – have very limited commercial value' (143). To this new order he refers as 'Project Zero – because its aims are a zero-carbon energy system; the production of machines, products and services with zero marginal costs; and the reduction of necessary labour time as close as possible to zero' (266). Furthermore, this project will, supposedly, also deliver the eradication of social inequality: 'Because its precondition is abundance, postcapitalism will deliver some form of social justice spontaneously' (144); because 'as much as possible is produced free, for collaborative common use', it offers an opportunity for 'reversing the tide of inequality' (212).

Mason predicts that the new order 'can be global' and will bring 'a future substantially better than the one capitalism will be offering' (2015, xiii). It comes about, he believes, because technological change gives rise to a 'new fault-line' in modern capitalism that runs 'between the possibility of free, abundant socially produced goods, and a system of monopolies, banks and governments struggling to maintain control over power and information' (144). Everything then 'comes down to the struggle between the network and the hierarchy, between old forms of society moulded around capitalism and new forms of society that prefigure what comes next' (xix). In the current interim phase, he notes, the old capitalist structures and the emerging collaborative economy are existing side by side, but eventually capitalism will lose out because technological development 'has created a new agent of change' (xvii) that will 'be its gravedigger' (212). And this ongoing transition 'is not just about economics', he insists, but also entails a 'human transition' (267) in the wake of which a 'new kind of person' (144), 'a new kind of human being' (xiv), is emerging. For Mason, 'the values, voices and morals' of these new 'bearers of the postcapitalist society' are 'obvious' (xvii, 144). Their interests, he notes, are diverse, but they 'converge on the need to make postcapitalism happen' (212).

Mason's optimism is remarkable but, in fact, many of the same ideas also figure prominently in the recent literature on new degrowth and sufficiency movements which are widely portrayed as a promising 'project for a radical transformation of society' (Muraca 2013; Petridis, Muraca, and Kallis 2015; also see e.g. Prinzen 2005; Jackson 2009; Paech 2012; Alexander 2013; Dietz and O'Neill 2013). Many of these authors share Mason's belief in a new collaborative economy that will no longer be profit-driven but non-commercially cater to social needs (Botsman and Rogers 2010). Technological developments such as 3D printing (Petschow et al. 2014) are expected to empower *makers' movements* (Anderson 2012) for decentralised and needs-oriented forms of production and consumption which respect the limits of ecological sustainability and promote environmental justice (Martínez-Alier 2012). Yet, when Mason, following the socialist tradition, explicitly aims for productivity growth and abundance, this literature refreshes the post-materialist belief in degrowth and sufficiency. The former is supposed to re-embed the economy into non-negotiable ecological boundaries; the latter is believed to complement – from the perspective of needs and desires – the supply-side attempts to increase the resource efficiency of production processes (Muller and Huppenbauer 2016, 105). The 'liberation from excess' (Paech 2012) and the embrace of 'voluntary simplicity' (Alexander 2013) are believed to facilitate a lifestyle that is 'more satisfying and would leave us happier' (Jackson 2009, 148). An 'alternative hedonism' (Soper 2007, 2008) is predicted to push the liberation from the false promises of wealth accumulation and mass consumption and to provide much stronger motivation for categorical change than any ethics of 'altruistic compassion and environmental concern' possibly can (Soper 2008,

571–572). And just like Mason believes that already in the present 'whole swathes of economic life are beginning to move to a different rhythm' (Mason 2015, xv), this literature, too, suggests that environmental movements and activism are already in the midst of a shift towards new practice-based forms of action which orchestrate societies' *self-transformation* as part of everyday politics (Forno and Graziano 2014). The 'disconnect between political and ecological values', on the one hand, and 'the everyday and large-scale political, cultural and industrial landscape', on the other, is said to have triggered 'a growth of new groups and movements with a different – much more embodied and applied – idea of appropriate and necessary political action' (Schlosberg and Coles 2015, 8). This proliferation of seemingly disparate initiatives is portrayed as a 'new environmentalism of everyday life', as evidence of 'new growths of radical democracy' and as 'representative of a new and sustainable materialism' (1–2).

And this confidence in a new transformative dynamics at the micro-level is, actually, complemented by a significant macro-level optimism that needs to be addressed here as well: 'the beginning of a new geological epoch', the Anthropocene, which at least some observers enthusiastically welcome as being 'ripe with human-directed opportunity' (Ellis 2011; also see: Crutzen 2002; Crutzen and Steffen 2003; Steffen, Crutzen, and McNeill 2007; Crutzen and Schwägerl 2011; Schwägerl 2012). The concept of the Anthropocene remains contested, and there are very different – indeed incompatible – interpretations of what exactly its arrival may imply (Hamilton 2015, 2016; Lewis and Maslin 2015). Also, the Anthropocene debate differs from the ones explored above in that it is an elite discourse and not rooted in social practices of everyday life. Still, it has been argued very powerfully that in the Anthropocene there is huge potential for human ingenuity to finally overcome the deep rift between nature and society that has marred modernity so far. In this new epoch, humans themselves are said to have become 'a force of nature' changing 'the functioning of the Earth System' (Hamilton 2015, 2), and the old distinction between human society (social systems) and the bio-physical system (nature) as the much larger, self-stabilising context into which the former is embedded becomes obsolete. In this 'age of human kind' (Schwägerl 2012), it has been suggested, the traditional idea of a nature/civilisation dualism is outdated: 'It's no longer us against *Nature*', but it is 'we who decide what nature is and what it will be' (Crutzen and Schwägerl 2011). As Lynas put it: 'Nature no longer runs the Earth', but 'we do' (Lynas 2012, 8). Accordingly, *environmental politics* turns – at least for some contributors to the debate – into *planetary management*, and it no longer implies respecting the laws, imperatives, boundaries and integrity of a superior system which is human civilisation's host, but means that the human 'god species' (Lynas 2012) must make full use of its knowledge, creativity, technology and industry to 'steer nature's course' (Crutzen and Schwägerl 2011). Radicalising the ecological modernisation belief in technological fixes, *good stewardship* now becomes even more Promethean than before and 'may well involve [...] large-scale geo-engineering projects, for instance to *optimize* climate' (Crutzen 2002, 23). Sustainability then no longer means identification of, and subordination to, ecological limits and imperatives, but it is 'an inherently open principle' that frames the debate on the kind of nature and society 'we wish to have' (Arias-Maldonado 2013, 17).

4. Beyond reflexive modernity

So rather than for a 'crisis of environmentalism' modern societies seem set for, or are already witnessing, a powerful 'renewal of environmentalism' (Arias-Maldonado 2013, 17). Admittedly, this brief survey has bulked together diverse literatures and brushed over significant differences within the respective debates. It brings together discussions which are, in practice, not necessarily interlinked and, at times, based on very different ideological positions. But even if they do not add up to one single overarching storyline, and even though, many of these debates' key ideas are, in fact, not particularly new (Muraca 2013, 147, 150–153), these narratives are incredibly attractive, popular and eagerly embraced. Indeed, at a juncture where a radical transformation of the established order of unsustainability seems more urgent than ever, yet the old paradigm of sustainability seems exhausted and unable to signpost the way, they seem to address – and resolve! – a whole range of problems which have obstructed eco-politics so far:

- The end of capitalism, which time and again had been identified as the core problem, no longer appears as a demand and hope for the distant future, but now appears as a thoroughly realistic – indeed, real – scenario;
- It no longer depends on the availability of a – notoriously difficult to identify – revolutionary subject, but capitalism seems to be 'dying, as it were, from an overdose of itself' (Streeck 2014a, 55), quite irrespective of established power relations;
- A profound transformation towards a new socially and ecologically benign order is underway even without anyone being able to offer any consistent vision, utopia or grand master plan;
- Political equality, social justice and democratic governance are core principles of the newly emerging structures;
- Science and technology facilitate needs-oriented production at the micro-level and for macro-level planetary management;
- And the new 'age of human kind' finally enables humanity to 'shift our mission from crusade to management, so we can steer nature's course symbiotically instead of enslaving the formerly natural world' (Crutzen and Schwägerl 2011).

Thus, much of what political ecologists had already been demanding well before sustainable development and ecological modernisation came to dilute, delay and obstruct their agenda may now eventually be coming true. But are these predictions plausible?

Proliferating transformation research is undoubtedly right in suggesting that modern societies, and the global order, are in the midst of profound and very rapid structural change, which political leaders and established political institutions no longer control and co-ordinate. In addition to the problems of the economic system and global warming, the refugee crisis, the spread of terrorism or the rise of rogue politicians such as Donald Trump, Recep Erdoğan or Nigel Farage provides unmistakable evidence. But any attempt to conceptualise this change – as the above narratives of hope are doing – in terms resembling Ulrich Beck's 'reinvention of politics' and his *second* or *reflexive* modernisation that will bring the emancipatory project to fruition and fulfil, finally, the promises of modernity (Beck 1997) seems misdirected. In fact, with regard to both the ecological as well as the democratic dimension of this project, factual developments seem to suggest that the emancipatory agenda – rather than being fulfilled – is in the process of being radically redefined. In this situation, environmental sociologists are well advised to bear in mind that 'social science can do little, if anything, to help resolve the structural tensions and contradictions underlying the economic and social disorders of the day' (Streeck 2011, 28). But what it can – and must – do is provide careful analyses and conceptualisations of these tensions and contradictions. In particular, those raising expectations about a 'renewal of environmentalism', a 'new sustainable materialism' and 'new growths of radical democracy' may be expected to engage with recent debates about *post-ecologism* and *post-democracy* and explain how their activist narratives of hope relate to these socio-theoretical diagnoses.

Crucially important in this context is the hypothesis already touched upon above that the ongoing process of modernisation continuously chips away at its own foundations and incrementally exhausts – not only in *material* but also in *cultural* terms – the very resources on which it rests: democratically, ecologically and economically (Beck 1997; Greven 2009). Talking about capitalism, Streeck refers to the 'non-capitalist foundations – trust, good faith, altruism, solidarity with families and communities' on which the 'stability and survival of capitalism depends', but which it continuously destroys (commodifies) without being able to reproduce them (Streeck 2014a, 50). As regards the emancipatory project, as it had been articulated first by enlightenment philosophy, then by a succession of democratic movements and then by ecological movements campaigning for the liberation, integrity and dignity of nature, this crucial resource is the specifically modernist idea of the *autonomous subject*, which is – further elaborating on what has been said in Section 2 – the ultimate norm of reference wherever social movements are identifying political problems, politicising societal conditions, critiquing prevalent power relations and mobilising political protest, be it with regard to democratic self-determination or in relation to the natural environment (Blühdorn 2000). Addressing the evident failures of traditional modernity and modernisation, Ulrich Beck's *second modernity* was supposed to fulfil the promises inherent in this norm; and the above narratives of hope are suggesting we may be closer to achieving this than ever before. Yet, in the wake of a process which elsewhere I have conceptualised as *second-order emancipation* (e.g. Blühdorn 2013b, 2014, 2016a) the logic of modernisation itself, i.e. the logic of individualisation, differentiation, pluralisation, acceleration, commodification and so forth, has profoundly reshaped prevalent understandings of this norm and thus undermined the normative foundations of the emancipatory project as the new social movements of the 1970s and 1980s had still conceptualised it. This does not necessarily endanger the emancipatory project's overall 'stability and survival', yet it does imply that this project has been comprehensively reformulated and, in a sense, changed direction (Blühdorn 2016b).

Second-order emancipation implies the critical review of, and partial liberation from, the particular norms of subjectivity and identity which, for a long time, had underpinned the emancipatory agenda, but which under the conditions of advanced post-industrial society are experienced as unduly restrictive and a burden to be unloaded. More specifically, the Protestant-rationalist, the Marxian as well as the bourgeois tradition had conceptualised the truly autonomous subject as (a) unitary, consistent, principled, stable and identical, and (b) composed of *innate* qualities of character and *inner* values as opposed to anything external, material, ephemeral and superficial. The new social movements of the 1970s and 1980s – whilst also challenging the rigidity of traditional norms – had once again emphatically renewed the commitment to these ideals. In contemporary societies, however, they now appear ever less appropriate: for purposes of their self-realisation, self-articulation and self-experience, modern individuals rely ever more confidently on material accumulation and consumption, and on the product- and lifestyle-choices provided by the market. And as contemporary societies are becoming ever more differentiated and subject to accelerated innovation; as the life-worlds of modern individuals, the opportunities they want to make use of and the pressures to which they have to respond are becoming ever more multi-faceted, the traditional ideal of the homogenous and unitary identity has given way to more flexible, versatile, plural and dynamic notions of identity: *liquid identity* for *liquid life* in *liquid modernity* (Bauman 2000, 2005). Despite their firm belief in solid, non-negotiable ecological and social imperatives, the libertarian, identity-focused new social movements had, in many respects, themselves initiated this *liquefaction* process. In today's world of information, communication and virtuality, the requirements of image-production, ego-marketing and (social) media resonance have much accelerated this transformation of traditional ideals of subjectivity and identity. It is not only a requirement of the labour market and its continuous pressure on the Self to be *entrepreneurial* and *self-responsible*, but in the private realm, too, *liquid* identity and *liquid* lifestyles promise a richer experience of life and more personal fulfilment.

Thus, the emancipatory project can no longer be conceptualised just as the political struggle for ideals of autonomy and subjectivity which are themselves immutable, but the ongoing process of modernisation remolds these norms themselves (Latour 1993). Second-order emancipation then implies, firstly, the rejection of earlier ideals of subjectivity which are now experienced as too restrictive and, secondly, a much more open-minded reassessment of aspirations, practices and lifestyles which had formerly been portrayed as corrupting character, mutilating the authentic Self, repressive or as *false consciousness*. In eco-political terms, this second-order emancipation erodes the normative validity of any ecological critique: it has induced a pluralisation of understandings of nature and the natural, a diversification of what is being perceived as environmentally problematic or desirable, and a liberation from what activists portray as *categorical ecological imperatives*. Furthermore, it also mainstreams notions of identity, patterns of identity construction and lifestyles which are inherently – by design – unsustainable, in that (a) they are not meant to be sustained, but to be reconstructed as and when required, (b) they are based on patterns of consumption which are well-known to be socially exclusive and ecologically destructive and (c) in that the liberation from social or ecological commitments which may restrict flexibility and mobility is one of the core principles. And beyond that, the new ideals of subjectivity and identity install their own categorical imperative: as ever expanding needs in terms of, for example, mobility, technology, travel opportunities and shopping outlets have become a constitutive and essentially non-negotiable ingredient of freedom, quality of life and wellbeing, ways *must* be found to meet them. I have conceptualised this modernisation-induced value- and culture-shift as the *post-ecologist turn* and the rise of the *politics of unsustainability* (Blühdorn 2000, 2011, 2013b). Ironically, it delivers exactly what sustainable development and ecological modernisation had always aimed for and promised: modern societies are modernizing themselves out of their sustainability crisis. Yet they are doing so not (just) by developing technological solutions to supposedly objective environmental problems, but (ever more importantly) by updating their subjective modes of problem perception, and shifting the boundaries of the socially acceptable, so as to accommodate the particular ways in which modern individuals are interpreting their basic needs, inalienable rights and non-negotiable form of self-realisation.

In the democratic-egalitarian dimension of the emancipatory project, second-order emancipation has no less significant implications: on the one hand, the increasing fixation on self-realisation, self-determination and self-experience, paired with declining confidence in existing political institutions, leads to ever more vociferously articulated demands for more direct democracy, better representation and authentic sovereignty of the people. At the same time, however, the participatory social movements' failure to reverse the continuous rise of political inequality, growing concerns about the unsuitability of democratic processes for conditions of high differentiation and complexity, the neoliberal instrumentalisation of democracy and civil society, and economic growth rates too low to sustain established notions of social equality and policies of redistribution trigger profound democratic disillusionment. *Anti-democratic feelings* (Rancière 2006) and *anti-political sentiments* (Mair 2006) are proliferating. As the limits to growth are more evident and uncontested than ever before, whilst prevalent forms of self-determination, self-realisation and self-experience are more than ever based on expanding and accelerating consumption, egalitarian and redistributive notions of democracy are turning into a serious problem – not only for the privileged, but in virtually all sections of society. Ordinary citizens as well as elites, although for different reasons, 'are losing faith in democratic government and its suitability for reshaping societies' (Mair 2006, 44). Thus, the *post-ecologist* turn is complemented by an equally important *post-democratic turn* (Blühdorn 2013a, 2013b, 2014). Indeed, there is good reason to speak of a profound *legitimation crisis of democracy* (Blühdorn 2016b).

In both of its dimensions, this fundamental value- and culture-shift have major implications for any envisaged socio-ecological transformation. Activists may themselves not share the increasingly prevalent value-orientations and lifestyle ideals. They may campaign individually or within social movement networks against the developments sketched above. Still, the post-ecologist and post-democratic turn, and the prevailing determination to sustain the established order of unsustainability affect the ways in which, and the extent to which, their efforts may have societal resonance and develop transformative potential. Furthermore, these changes in the societal conditions into which such activism is embedded also impact the ways in which such action and the related narratives can plausibly be interpreted. Yet, in the narratives of hope sketched above, these fundamental shifts essentially do not figure. These narratives not only ignore the fact that capitalism has proved, time and again, to be infinitely adaptable and malleable, but in terms of their critique and vision, they remain firmly within the 1970s and 1980s imaginary and thus offer amazingly simplistic interpretations of today's forms of anti-politics. For political activists such social-theoretical deficits may be perfectly acceptable – or even helpful; for political and environmental sociologists, they are not.

Quite clearly, the traditional norms of *solid* subjectivity and identity have never been more than what Kant called *regulative ideas of reason*. Also, the shift towards *liquid* ideals of subjectivity, identity and lifestyles has, undoubtedly, not affected all sections of modern societies to the same degree. Yet, the trend towards ever more differentiation, mobilisation, flexibilisation, innovation, virtualisation and so forth, is uncontested; and the popular embrace of these trends provides evidence that what Beck once critically conceptualised as the *risk society* (Beck 1992) is today much more commonly experienced as an *opportunity society*. Against this background, the old narratives of alienation and repression seem strangely out of date, and so do the promises of sufficiency and post-consumerism. Whilst the sketched value- and culture-shift goes a long way to explain the low appetite for any significant eco-political change, the widely perceived crisis of democracy, the desperate attempts to reinvigorate economic growth, the proliferation of aggressive populism, the continuous increase in social inequality and exclusion, or the unyielding resolve – ritually reconfirmed after every terrorist attack – to *do whatever is necessary to defend our values, our freedom, our culture*, the above narratives of hope are at best 'wishful thinking' (Spash 2015, 13), and at worst a political tranquilliser helping to manage the 'long and painful period of cumulative decay' predicted by Streeck.

Indeed, if there is any truth in the above suggestions about emancipatory progress, the prospects of these narratives and the related social practices developing any transformative potential are – despite the evident crisis of capitalism and the multi-dimensional sustainability crisis – even less favourable today than at earlier points in time. And far from paving the way for a renewal of environmentalism, the arrival of the Anthropocene actually radicalises the normative problems which have always plagued environmental politics: the collapse of the nature–society dualism, which had been essential for any attempt to find an *objective* normative point of reference for eco-political prescriptions, renders environmental policy, once and for all, self-referential (Blühdorn 2015). Already at the turn to the 1990s, McKibben had, in *The End of Nature*, warned that without nature, in the 'post-natural world', there will be 'nothing but us' (McKibben 1990, 55). In the Anthropocene there is, indeed, nothing left that might provide non-subjective, solid, foundations upon which to base environmental politics. More evidently than ever before, environmental policy is now exclusively about prevalent norms of subjectivity: the kind of nature and society 'we wish to have'. Yet, beyond second-order emancipation this is less likely than ever to imply any significant deviation from the established order.

5. Denial or simulation?

Thus, the narratives of hope which are emerging as the paradigm of sustainability seems exhausted are strikingly illusory and blind. Second-order emancipation and the arrival of the Anthropocene clearly take capitalist consumer societies beyond Ulrich Beck's second or reflexive modernity – yet, the prophets of the great transformation unwaveringly hold on to the narratives of this bygone era. In a sense, the Anthropocene is a radicalised global risk society. More than ever it is an 'age of side-effects' and crises (Beck 1997, 11–60). Hence, it might appear that now, as Beck had believed already in the 1990s, 'action [really] has to be taken, immediately, everywhere, by everyone and under all circumstances' (92). Yet, as second-order emancipation has radically redefined the emancipatory project in both its ecological and its democratic dimensions, the progressive emancipatory agenda of societal *metamorphosis* is being superseded by a new agenda of *metastasis*: the ever more ecstatic production of variations of the extant (Baudrillard 1983, 141–142). In fact, in the emerging *third modernity* – which moves beyond the old narratives of alienation and the traditional-style emancipatory project – it remains uncertain whether Beck's kind of action really *must be* taken at all. After all, this only applies if, and to the extent that, social norms are being violated and this translates into political grievances and mobilisation. If, however, in major parts of society patterns of problem perception and thresholds of acceptability are updated to accommodate the implications of now prevalent notions of freedom, wellbeing and the good life, environmentalist appeals for rapid and transformative action will find even less positive resonance than before. And whilst activist movements might continue to campaign for what Michel Serres called *the natural contract* (Serres 1995), or an advisory committee to the German Bundestag a *new social contract for sustainability* (WBGU 2011), the reality of eco-politics is being shaped by a stronger than ever *social contract for sustaining the unsustainable*.

John Foster has conceptualised this as a politics of *denial* and suggested that the above narratives of hope, as well as the related social practices, ought to be interpreted as 'a form of refusal to see' (Foster 2015, 7). Denial, Foster notes, 'isn't just something the bad guys do' (5), but 'the characteristic structures and practices of denial are also fully exhibited by environmental activists' (Foster 2015, 41, also see Hamilton 2010, 95ff). Environmental activists – and their academic division can probably be added in – are well aware, Foster argues, that the window of opportunity to stop climate change and achieve a structural transformation of modern societies has essentially closed, but they keep campaigning 'as if this crucial window for effective action had not closed' (Foster 2015, 5). And the more scientific evidence that environmental and climate change 'are real, unignorable and increasingly imminent' (41) undermines any environmental optimism, the stronger, Foster believes, does the 'desperate need to reassert and reinforce it' (31) grow. He describes this variety of denial as 'willed optimism' (29–33) which, he suggests, is indispensable for activists because, from their perspective, admitting that it is too late 'is taken to mean despair, which would paralyse us' (8).

Foster is right in pointing out that in modern societies eco-political practices of denial are much more widely spread than much of the activist literature (e.g. on the climate change denial industry) suggests. Furthermore, he is right in saying that willed optimism 'warps thought' (Foster 2015, 30) and obfuscates the capacity for sober analysis – which in the academic context is even more detrimental than in political campaigning. And what he describes as the 'pervasive culture of denial' (35) bears striking similarities to the above *social contract for unsustainability* and what I have conceptualised as a *broad societal alliance* for *sustaining the unsustainable* (Blühdorn 2007, 2011, 2016b). Still, for a number of reasons, this thinking in terms of *denial* is, arguably, unable to capture the specific character of contemporary eco-politics. Most importantly, Foster holds on to the belief in undeniable truths and objective ecological threats or crises which those engaging in practices of denial willingly refuse to see. Conceptualisations in terms of denial imply the distinction between facts and illusions and thus fall back into the eco-political positivism which had already marred the paradigm of sustainability and which the arrival of the Anthropocene renders fully untenable. In a sense, Foster's attempt to expose and destroy 'the pervasive culture of denial' is based on – an ever thinner – residue of the belief that it might not be too late, after all, and that enlightenment about *objectively existing environmental problems* might provide us with a very, very last opportunity to turn things round. Yet, such constructions not only themselves tap into *the pervasive culture of denial*, but they also fail to recognise the normative void of eco-politics in the Anthropocene.

Furthermore, Foster's diagnosis of a 'refusal to see' sits uneasily with the fact that in modern information societies, knowledge about climate change, biodiversity loss, resource over-use, environmental refugees, etc. is more readily available than ever before and is, actually, literally being *imposed* on people. Hence, further enlightenment about denial and illusions is ever less likely to effect any significant behaviour change. Instead, a distinctive feature of the prevailing politics of unsustainability is that people are, more than ever, well aware of the social and ecological implications of their lifestyles, but their commitment to these values and lifestyles is at least as strong as any commitment to environmental and egalitarian values resonating from the tradition of first-order emancipation and reflexive modernity. And far from getting politically 'paralysed' or 'despair', as Foster suggests, contemporary individuals and societies – quite realistically recognising that their values and lifestyles cannot be generalised and necessitate social exclusion – are, in fact, taking commensurate action: the manifold ways in which social contracts are being redefined and ties of solidarity severed, the diverse facets and effects of populist mobilisation (also against *green elites trying to impose lifestyle changes*), or the indefatigable efforts of governments to secure further growth at least for some sections of society provide rich evidence that, rather than being paralysed, modern societies are catapulted into action and are, individually and collec-tively, fully engaged in the competitive scramble for limited resources and the pole position in the race for social exclusion. Thus, action is in fact being taken, everywhere, by everybody, under all circumstances! Yet, it is not the kind of action radical ecologists or the believers in reflexive modernisation had had in mind.

The distinctive feature of the new eco-politics is, indeed, as signalled above, the coincidence of (a) an unprecedented level of scientific understanding and public aware-ness of the social and ecological implications of modern lifestyles and patterns of self-realisation and (b) an equally unprecedented determination to defend and further develop these values, lifestyles and emancipatory achievements. When Foster points to the 'the inadmissible awareness' of the ecological and social realities that 'has been growing more and more painfully insistent' (2015, 5); when he notes that modern societies 'are well-placed to see that our newly globalized civilization is now irreversibly committed to a trajectory into climate jeopardy and massive ecological damage' (Foster 2015, 35); and when he states that 'contemporary environmentalists are caught in a tragic bind' (Foster 2015) in that they have to pursue their practices of willed optimism 'with increasing stridency against the clear evidence of facts that they nevertheless increasingly recognize' (Foster 2015, 115), he actually captures this distinctive feature of contemporary eco-politics – and implicitly acknowledges that it cannot really be conceptualised in terms of denial. This simultaneity of awareness and determination shifts the focus of contemporary eco-politics from the attempt to change social values, patterns of behaviour and lifestyles so as to bring them in line with planetary bound-aries, categorical eco-imperatives or norms of equality towards managing the inevitable implications of, and promoting societal *adaptation* and *resilience* to, the sustained violation of these boundaries, imperatives and norms (Blühdorn 2011, 2016a). This crucial shift and new core concern, the concept of denial cannot capture.

Adaptation and building resilience to the apparently non-negotiable conditions of sustained unsustainability entails, in particular, the development of coping strategies for ever increasing levels of social inequality, injustice and exclusion. Norms of social acceptability change only incrementally, and to the extent that the values of first-order emancipation continue to retain validity – at the individual as well as the collective level – the social and ecological implications of the non-negotiable commitment to modern value preferences and lifestyles continue to be perceived as problematic. Alongside the development of effective security policies, the politics of unsustainability therefore requires forms of communication and arenas for social practices in which the commitment to values of ecological integrity and social equality can be articulated and experienced without the values, achievements and further trajectory of second-order emancipation coming under threat. And as the continuous acceleration of innovation and change is a constitutive principle of modern societies, the need for such experiential arenas is considerable. Unsurprisingly, therefore, a wide range of such discourses and arenas have emerged and are being sustained. And they are not simply a tool controlled by manipulative elites, but they are societal tools for the self-management, at the individual and collective level, of irresolvable conflicts between mutually incompatible values. I have conceptualised these forms of communication and practice as *discourses of simulation* (Blühdorn 2007, 2011). They engage a wide and diverse range of societal actors from across the ideological spectrum and all sections of society (Blühdorn 2014, 2016a, 2016b). Adapting Foster's phrase: *simulation is not something just the bad guys do*, but a collective societal practice for managing the implications of the commitment to sustain the unsustainable.

From a functionalist point of view, exactly this is, arguably, where the above narratives of hope find their place. They articulate values and tell stories of transformation which, corresponding to the substantial societal need, are 'heavily marketed and endorsed as path-breaking' (Spash 2015, 13), and enthusiastically embraced by all kinds of actors but which, as regards their transformative potentials, are, sociologically speaking, rather implausible. Like 'sustainability before them', these discourses are indeed 'another servant of powerful interest groups' (14) – which are, however, not just a small social elite, but a rather inclusive alliance of interested parties determined to defend our freedom, our lifestyles, our values and collectively organise the politics of exclusion. Supplementing these purely communicative forms of simulation, the new local initiatives of alternative production, distribution and consumption provide arenas for the real-life exercise of alternative values, practices and social relations. These practices may be highly selective, situated in tightly limited contexts and firmly embedded into macro-structures of unsustainability. Remaining purely *experimental* and *experiential*, they are neither designed to really unhinge the logic which they appear to be challenging, nor are they likely to ever achieve this. Still, they provide opportunities to practically enact and experience ecological and social commitments and self-descriptions. At the same time they also mitigate the inevitable implications of sustained unsustainability: they help the marginalised to self-organise the cost-effective and self-responsible management of their own exclusion. The narratives of the liberation from capitalist power, consumption and alienation, then provide the moral ennoblement of the exclusion which the winners of second-order emancipation regard as inevitable and the losers somehow have to make bearable. This, too, is part of societies' adaptation and building social resilience to sustained unsustainability.

6. Conclusion

So, by way of conclusion we may note: as a road map for the structural transformation of contemporary capitalist consumer societies, the eco-political paradigm of sustainability has indeed become exhausted. Also, critical observers are right in saying that the established order of consumer capitalism has become more fragile and crisis-ridden than ever before. Furthermore, advanced modern societies are indeed post-growth societies – which is not to say that the logic of growth has been abandoned but that – in light of economic stagnation – the demands for further growth which are resolutely articulated by virtually all parts of society can be realised only for some, and at direct expense of others. Fourth, in contemporary capitalist consumer societies, the dualist patterns of thought which are characteristic for modernist thinking have indeed become implausible, both from a social-theoretical and an eco-theoretical perspective. Yet, the hope and claims that any of this might open up new avenues for a societal transformation towards the realisation of eco-egalitarian ideals seem entirely unjustified. Instead, a value- and culture-shift, conceptualised here as second-order emancipation, has taken advanced modern societies into a post-ecologist and post-democratic constellation where unsustainability is a constitutive principle of prevalent ideals of subjectivity, identity and notions of the good life. And these prevailing ideals, in turn, underpin a new social contract for sustaining the unsustainable.

It is from this particular perspective, this article has suggested, that the new social practices and narratives of post-capitalism, post-growth and post-consumerism, need to be interpreted. Yet, the popular narratives of hope, which portray these new practices as the beginning of a great societal transformation towards a socially and ecologically more benign society, do not take account of these major socio-cultural shifts. Just as the exhausted narratives of sustainability before them, they remain within the realm of Ulrich Beck's second or reflexive modernity and refuse to acknowledge that modern societies have moved on – into a third modernity. Within this third modernity, governed by the values of second-order emancipation, these narratives of hope, therefore, only contribute to the construction and maintenance of societal self-descriptions which perform the ongoing validity of the old eco-emancipatory project. Or, put differently, they contribute to the stabilisation of the order which they intend to attack. The objective of making this argument is not to question the commitment and sincerity of social movement actors. But a clear distinction ought to be made between such actors and their sociological observers. Whatever the latter may suggest in terms of interpretations of the former's endeavours can claim only restricted validity because it invariably remains contingent on the assumptions, reach and plausibility of the socio-theoretical models which frame the observers' perspective. Yet, this does not absolve environmental sociologists from their responsibility to critically investigate and interpret the new activists' practices and self-descriptions, rather than simply reproduce them. At present, however, it seems that many observers are, once again, more inclined to promote popular and convenient – albeit implausible – narratives of hope. If environmental sociology can do anything to nurture transformative energies at all, exploring the prevailing politics of unsustainability – and its own contribution to it – is its most promising strategy.

Acknowledgements

I would like to thank Andrew Dobson, Clive Hamilton, Fred Luks and the anonymous reviewers of *Global Discourse* for their constructive comments on an earlier version of this article.

Disclosure statement

No potential conflict of interest was reported by the author.

References

Alexander, S. 2013. "Voluntary Simplicity and the Social Reconstruction of Law: Degrowth from the Grassroots Up." *Environmental Values* 22 (2): 287–308. doi:10.3197/096327113X13581561725356.
Anderson, C. 2012. *Makers: A New Industrial Revolution*. New York: Crown Business.
Arias-Maldonado, M. 2012. *Real Green: Sustainability after the End of Nature*. London: Ashgate.
Arias-Maldonado, M. 2013. "Rethinking Sustainability in the Anthropocene." *Environmental Politics* 22 (3): 428–446. doi:10.1080/09644016.2013.765161.
Arias-Maldonado, M. 2015. *Environment & Society: Socionatural Relations in the Anthropocene*. Heidelberg: Springer.
Baker, S. 2006. *Sustainable Development*. London: Routledge.
Baskin, J. 2015. "Paradigm Dressed as Epoch: The Ideology of the Anthropocene." *Environmental Values* 24 (1): 9–29. doi:10.3197/096327115X14183182353746.
Baudrillard, J. 1983. *Der Tod Der Moderne: Eine Diskussion*. Tübingen: Konkursbuchverlag.
Bauman, Z. 2000. *Liquid Modernity*. Cambridge: Polity.
Bauman, Z. 2005. *Liquid Life*. Cambridge: Polity.
Beck, U. 1992. *Risk Society: Towards a New Modernity in the Global Social Order*. Cambridge: Polity.
Beck, U. 1997. *The Reinvention of Politics: Rethinking Modernity in the Global Social Order*. Cambridge: Polity.
Benson, M., and R. K. Craig. 2014. "The End of Sustainability." *Society and Natural Resources* 27 (4): 777–782. doi:10.1080/08941920.2014.901467.
Blühdorn, I. 2000. *Post-Ecologist Politics: Social Theory and the Abdication of the Ecologist Paradigm*. London: Routledge.
Blühdorn, I. 2007. "Sustaining the Unsustainable: Symbolic Politics and the Politics of Simulation." *Environmental Politics* 16 (2): 251–275. doi:10.1080/09644010701211759.
Blühdorn, I. 2011. "The Politics of Unsustainability: COP15, Post-Ecologism and the Ecological Paradox." *Organization & Environment* 24 (1): 34–53. doi:10.1177/1086026611402008.
Blühdorn, I. 2013a. *Simulative Demokratie: Neue Politik Nach Der Postdemokratischen Wende*. Berlin: Suhrkamp.
Blühdorn, I. 2013b. "The Governance of Unsustainability: Ecology and Democracy beyond the Post-Democratic Turn." *Environmental Politics* 22 (1): 16–36. doi:10.1080/09644016.2013.755005.
Blühdorn, I. 2016b. "Das Postdemokratische Diskursquartett: Diskursive Praxis in Der Simulativen Demokratie." *Psychosozial* 39 (1): 51–68.

Blühdorn, I. 2016a. "Sustainability, Post-Sustainability, Unsustainability." In *The Oxford Handbook of Environmental Political Theory*, edited by T. Gabrielson, C. Hall, J. M. Meyer, and D. Schlosberg, 259–273. Oxford: OUP.

Blühdorn, I. 2015. "A Much-Needed Renewal of Environmentalism? Eco-Politics in the Anthropocene." In *The Anthropocene and the Global Environmental Crisis: Rethinking Modernity in a New Epoch*, edited by C. Hamilton, F. Gemenne, and C. Bonneuil, 156–167. London: Routledge.

Blühdorn, I. 2014. "Post-Ecologist Governmentality: Post-Democracy, Post-Politics and the Politics of Unsustainability." In *The Post-Political and its Discontents: Spaces of Depoliticisation, Spectres of Radical Politics*, edited by E. Swyngedouw and J. Wilson, 146–166. Edinburgh: University Press.

Blühdorn, I., and I. Welsh. 2007. "Eco-Politics beyond the Paradigm of Sustainability: A Conceptual Framework and Research Agenda." *Environmental Politics* 16 (2): 185–205. doi:10.1080/09644010701211650.

Botsman, R., and R. Rogers. 2010. *What's Mine is Yours: How Collaborative Consumption is Changing the Way We Live*. London: HarperCollins.

Bulkeley, H., A. Jordan, R. Perkins, and H. Selin. 2013. "Governing Sustainability: Rio+20 and the Road Beyond." *Environment and Planning C: Government and Policy* 31: 958–970. doi:10.1068/c3106ed.

Crutzen, P. 2002. "Geology of Mankind." *Nature* 415: 23. doi:10.1038/415023a.

Crutzen, P., and C. Schwägerl. 2011. "'Living in the Anthropocene: Toward a New Global Ethos". *Yale Environment* 24: 360. Accessed 11 August 2016 Available at http://e360.yale.edu/feature/living_in_the_anthropocene_toward_a_new_global_ethos/2363/

Crutzen, P., and W. Steffen. 2003. "How Long Have We Been in the Anthropocene Era?" *Climatic Change* 61: 251–257. doi:10.1023/B:CLIM.0000004708.74871.62.

Dietz, R., and D. O'Neill. 2013. *Enough is Enough: Building a Sustainable Economy in a World of Finite Resources*. New York: Routledge.

Dunlap, R., and A. M. McCright. 2011. "Organized Climate Change Denial." In *The Oxford Handbook of Climate Change and Society*, edited by J. Dryzek, R. Norgaard, and D. Schlosberg. Oxford: Oxford University Press.

Eder, K. 1996. *The Social Construction of Nature*. London: Sage.

Ellis, E. 2011. "The Planet of No Return." *Breakthrough Journal*, no. 2: 37–44.

Forno, F., and P. R. Graziano. 2014. "Sustainable Community Movement Organisation." *Journal of Consumer Culture* 14 (2): 139–157. doi:10.1177/1469540514526225.

Foster, J. 2015. *After Sustainability*. Abingdon: Earthscan.

Greven, M. T. 2009. "War Die Demokratie Jemals *Modern?*" *Berliner Debatte Initial* 20 (3): 67–73.

Hamilton, C. 2010. *Requiem for a Species: Why We Resist the Truth about Climate Change*. London: Earthscan.

Hamilton, C. 2015. "Getting the Anthropocene So Wrong." *The Anthropocene Review* 2: 102–107. doi:10.1177/2053019615584974.

Hamilton, C. 2016. "The Anthropocene as Rupture." *The Anthropocene Review* 2 (1): 59–72.

Hamilton, C., C. Bonneuil, and F. Gemenne, eds. 2015. *The Anthropocene and the Global Environmental Crisis*. London: Routledge.

Inglehart, R. 1977. *The Silent Revolution: Changing Values and Political Styles among Western Publics*. Princeton, NJ: Princeton University Press.

Inglehart, R. 1997. *Modernization and Post-Modernization: Cultural, Economic, and Political Change in 43 Societies*. Princeton, NJ: Princeton University Press.

Inglehart, R., and C. Welzel. 2005. *Modernization, Cultural Change and Democracy: The Human Development Sequence*. Cambridge: Cambridge University Press.

Jackson, T. 2009. *Prosperity without Growth: Economics for a Finite Planet*. London: Earthscan.

Jordan, A., R. Wurzel, and A. Zito, eds. 2003. "New Environmental Policy Instruments." *Environmental Politics* 12 (1): 179–200.

Kelly, P. 1984. *Fighting for Hope*. London: Horgarth Press.

Latour, B. 1993. *We Have Never Been Modern*. Cambridge, MA: Harvard University Press.

Lewis, S., and M. Maslin. 2015. "Defining the Anthropocene." *Nature* 519: 171–180. doi:10.1038/nature14258.

Linnér, B. O., and H. Selin. 2013. "The United Nations Conference on Sustainable Development: Forty Years in the Making." *Environment and Planning C: Government and Policy* 31: 971–987. doi:10.1068/c12287.

Lynas, M. 2012. *The God Species: How Humans Can Really Save the Planet*. London: Harpercollins.

MacNaghten, P., and J. Urry. 1998. *Contested Natures*. London: Sage.

Mair, P. 2006. "Ruling the Void? The Hollowing of Western Democracy." *New Left Review* 42: 25–51.

Martínez-Alier, J. 2012. "Environmental Justice and Economic Degrowth: An Alliance between Two Movements." *Capitalism Nature Socialism* 23 (1): 51–73. doi:10.1080/10455752.2011.648839.

Mason, P. 2015. *Post-Capitalism: A Guide to Our Future*. London: Allen Lane.

Mason, P. 2016. "Nach Dem Kapitalismus?!" *Blätter Für Deutsche Und Internationale Politik* 5 (16): 45–59.

McKibben, B. 1990. *The End of Nature*. London: Penguin.

Mol, A. 1995. *The Refinement of Production: Ecological Modernisation Theory and the Chemical Industry*. Utrecht: van Arkel.

Mol, A. 1996. "Ecological Modernisation and Institutional Reflexivity: Environmental Reform in the Late Modern Age." *Environmental Politics* 5 (2): 302–323. doi:10.1080/09644019608414266.

Mol, A., and D. Sonnenfeld. 2000. *Ecological Modernisation around the World*. London: Routledge.

Muller, A., and M. Huppenbauer. 2016. "Sufficiency, Liberal Societies and Environmental Policy in the Face of Planetary Boundaries." *Gaia* 25 (2): 105–109. doi:10.14512/gaia.25.2.10.

Muraca, B. 2013. "Décroissance: A Project for a Radical Transformation of Society." *Environmental Values* 22: 147–169. doi:10.3197/096327113X13581561725112.

Norgaard, K. 2011. *Living in Denial: Climate Change, Emotions, and Everyday Life*. Cambridge, MA: MIT Press.

Paech, N. 2012. *Befreiung Vom Überfluss: Auf Dem Weg in Die Postwachstumsökonomie*. Munich: oekom.

Petridis, P., B. Muraca, and G. Kallis. 2015. "Degrowth: Between a Scientific Concept and a Slogan for a Social Movement." In *Handbook of Ecological Economics*, edited by J. Martínez-Alier and R. Muradian, 176–200. London: Edward Elgar.

Petschow, U., J. Ferdinand, S. Dickel, H. Flämig, M. Steinfeldt, and A. Worobei. 2014. "Dezentrale Produktion, 3d-Druck und Nachhaltigkeit: Trajektorien und Potenziale Innovativer Wertschöpfungsmuster Zwischen Maker-Bewegung und Industrie 4.0." In *Institut Für Ökologische Wirtschaftsforschung*, 206 (14). Berlin: Schriftenreihe des.

Prinzen, T. 2005. *The Logic of Sufficiency*. Cambridge, MA: MIT Press.

Prinzen, T. 2010. *Treading Softly: Paths to Ecological Order*. Cambridge, MA: MIT Press.

Rancière, J. 2006. *Hatred of Democracy*. London: Verso.

Schlosberg, D., and R. Coles. 2015. "The New Environmentalism of Everyday Life: Sustainability, Material Flows and Movements." *Contemporary Political Theory* 15: 1–22.

Schwägerl, C. 2012. *Menschenzeit*. München: Goldmann.

Serres, M. 1995. *The Natural Contract*. Ann Arbor: University of Michigan Press.

Soper, K. 2007. "Rethinking the Good Life: The Citizenship Dimension of Consumer Disaffection with Consumerism." *Journal of Consumer Culture* 7 (2): 205–229. doi:10.1177/1469540507077681.

Soper, K. 2008. "Alternative Hedonism, Cultural Theory and the Role of Aesthetic Revisioning." *Cultural Studies* 22 (5): 567–587.

Spaargaren, G. 1997. *The Ecological Modernisation of Production and Consumption: Essays in Environmental Sociology*. Wageningen, NL: Wageningen Agricultural University.

Spash, C. 2015. "The Future Post-Growth Society." *Development and Change* 46 (2): 366–380.

Steffen, W., P. Crutzen, and J. McNeill. 2007. "The Anthropocene: Are Humans Now Overwhelming the Great Forces of Nature?" *Ambio* 36 (8): 614–621.

Streeck, W. 2011. "The Crisis of Democratic Capitalism." *New Left Review* 71: 5–29.

Streeck, W. 2014a. "How Will Capitalism End?" *New Left Review* 87: 35–64.

Streeck, W. 2014b. *Buying Time: The Delayed Crisis of Democratic Capitalism*. London: Verso.

WBGU, German Advisory Council on Global Change. 2011. *World in Transition. A Social Contract for Sustainability*. Berlin: WBGU.

WCED, World Commission Commission on Environment and Development. 1987. *Our Common Future*. Oxford: Oxford University Press.

REPLY

There never was a categorical ecological imperative: a response to Ingolfur Blühdorn

Daniel Hausknost

This is a reply to:

Blühdorn, Ingolfur. 2017. "Post-capitalism, post-growth, post-consumerism? Eco-political hopes beyond sustainability." *Global Discourse*. 7 (1): 42–61. http://dx.doi.org/10.1080/23269995.2017.1300415

With his analysis of eco-political 'narratives of hope' as 'exercises of simulation which help to manage the challenges of sustained unsustainability', Ingolfur Blühdorn offers a powerful diagnosis of contemporary environmental politics in affluent consumer democracies. His description of contemporary eco-politics as a de-facto *social contract for sustaining the unsustainable*' (Blühdorn 2017, original emphasis) is compelling. However, his *explanation* of the phenomenon of simulation as resulting from 'second-order emancipation' is less convincing. In this brief response, I will point out why a focus on cultural and value change *alone* seems insufficient to understand why late-modern societies are unable or unwilling to transform into something more sustainable. I will argue that a systemic perspective on political legitimacy and coping strategies of the state is helpful to complete the picture and to understand the comprehensive structural constraints of modern societies.

For Blühdorn, second-order emancipation implies the 'partial liberation from the particular norms of subjectivity and identity which, for a long time, had underpinned the emancipatory agenda'. These norms are based on the conception of a 'truly autonomous', unitary and consistent subject that originates from the Protestant-rationalist, bourgeois and Marxian traditions of thought. Crucially, this subject is 'composed of *innate* qualities of character and *inner* values as opposed to anything external, material, ephemeral and superficial' (Blühdorn 2017, original emphases). Blühdorn then argues that all emancipatory movements, including the ecology movements of the 1970s and 1980s, were premised on this rigid conception of the subject. From the 1990s onward, he claims, this monolithic subject had been liquefied, leaving the emancipatory project a hollow and empty discourse that is kept alive only to secure the normative integrity of modernity.

Although Blühdorn's description of the post-modern subject as inconsistent in its environmental behavior and moral standards is undeniably accurate, his storyline of second-order emancipation can be challenged on two grounds: one is the mono-lithic construction of the subjectivity of first-order emancipation, which might never have empirically existed in its purported form. The second is the implicated claim that the 'eco-political imperatives' of the emancipatory project had ever been socially dominant and have only now been overcome. In both cases, I offer a somewhat different reading of contemporary environmental politics.

As regards my first challenge, it is questionable to assume that any (let alone all) of the eco-activists of the 1970s and 1980s would have subscribed to Blühdorn's rigid conception of the subject. Many green activists and thinkers of that defining era were influenced by the general move toward holistic thinking and 'New Age' philo-sophy. Some emerged out of the Hippie movement or the anti-authoritarian projects of the 1960s. Others were engaged in the peace or feminist movements, which both worked to unhinge 'modern' (i.e. Eurocentric, male) subjectivity. The common denominator of all these influences is precisely the urge to liberate society from the shackles of modern rationalism and the Cartesian subjectivity that they blamed to be the root cause of much contemporary evil, not least the ecological crisis. Thus, the emancipation these early ecology movements sought was precisely an emanci-pation from the 'iron cage' of rationalist progressivism (including orthodox Marxism), with which they associated the very type of subjectivity Blühdorn portrayed as 'emancipatory'.

Consequently, either of two conclusions must be drawn: (a) the entire ecology movement from its very inception in the 1960s has always already been part of 'liquid modernity', which would disable Blühdorn's main argument that second-order emancipation 'erodes the normative validity of any ecological critique'. Or (b) the eco-movement is indeed to be counted toward the first-order emancipatory project, but then Blühdorn's monolithic definition of the emancipatory project as 'the poli-tical struggle for ideals of autonomy and subjectivity which are themselves immu-table' would become problematic and his main argument inconsistent.

Already in 1961, sociologist David Riesman in his book *The Lonely Crowd* (2001) introduced a distinction between an 'inner-directed' social character that domi-nated much of the nineteenth and half the twentieth century and which resonates with Blühdorn's 'autonomous subject', and an 'other-directed type', which appears after World War II and relies on conspicuous consumption, reassurance by and competition with others, and leisure as a means of identity formation. This type resembles the 'liquid' subject in Blühdorn and is associated with the completion of the industrial transition. It may thus be argued that the liquefaction of the modern subject started much earlier than in Blühdorn's account and that the eco-movement was a *result* of it rather than its first victim. Was not the emergence of the eco-movement(s) premised precisely on the dissolution of traditional modern standards of authority (the party, the revolutionary vanguard, the state) that were typical for the first-order emancipatory project (i.e. the bourgeois and socialist revolutions)?

This directly leads to my second challenge: the claim that second-order emanci-pation involves a 'liberation' from 'categorical ecological imperatives' implies that such imperatives ever existed as a socially dominant standard that would warrant an act of 'liberation'. Again, I would like to offer an alternative reading: the fact that the environmental movement gained some political influence in the 1980s in advanced capitalist democracies was not due to any power to impose categorical ecological imperatives (nor due to the willingness of the public to accept these), but due to the fact that it capitalized on severe *local* environmental problems that started to undermine the state's legitimacy at that time: acid rain, dying lakes and rivers, obstructive smog, toxic chemicals, etc. While the eco-movement's motivation to fight these instances of industrial self-destruction was *antisystemic*, the state's *systemic* response was to integrate the management of these environmental problems into its administrative core (known as the emergence of the 'environmental state' – Duit, Feindt, and Meadowcroft 2016) and to solve most of them within one or two decades by means of regulative measures in the techno-scientific sphere (known as 'ecological modernization' – Mol, Sonnenfeld, and Spaargaren 2009). Most of these problems were solved at the level of industrial production and design, without requiring any significant behavioral changes on the part of the general public. The consumer-citizen could continue to increase their levels of consumption without feeling any environmental pain. This systemic response by the capitalist democratic state dispossessed the eco-movement of its antisystemic edge and forced it into a mode of compliance (focusing on participative problem resolution) that is henceforth known as 'environmental governance' (Newig and Fritsch 2009).

The global, systemic and ultimately existential issues like climate change, mass species extinction, resource depletion and deforestation, on the other hand, were a complete failure then and now, as they require systemic change and not just technological solutions. Although part of the campaigning repertoire of eco-activists from the beginning, they were and are lost causes in an uphill battle against economic growth and consumer choice. This means, and here is where my storyline differs significantly from Blühdorn's, that even in the purported golden age of emancipatory (new social) movements, the vast majority of the population was *not* willing to change their lifestyles or to comply with any eco-political imperatives. The priority of the mainstream consumer-citizen since the 1950s has always been (I claim) to maximize their material standard of living and to trust in the state to deal with the ensuing environmental problems in terms of technological and regulatory solutions. The 'limits to growth' challenge remained unresolved both in 1972 and in 2016.

The consequence is – here I concur with Blühdorn – that now that the global problems have become the pressing ones in the public perception of advanced consumer democracies, no further progress in environmental reform seems possible, precisely because reform would not suffice to solve them. The radical transformations required are out of the question – both for the state as a system dependent on economic growth and capital accumulation and for the consumer citizen insisting on choice and affluence (Hausknost 2014). The only program available is thus to simulate the change most of us agree is necessary in order to sustain that which we all know is unsustainable and to hope that technological progress (i.e. further ecological modernization) might save us from having to give up consumer society.

To sum up: eco-politics is locked into a mode of simulation not because we have liberated ourselves from alleged *categorical ecological imperatives* of the past, but because the global environmental problems of today would require radical transformations that by far exceed the repertoire of ecological modernization the capitalist democratic state is used and able to deploy. This would have been the same 30 years ago, but back then climate change and biodiversity loss were sidelined in favor of more 'pressing' local problems that were amenable to techno-managerial solutions. The bleak prospect implied here is that public support for radical change will emerge only once the global problems turn into painful local ones that severely affect the quality of life in affluent societies. Needless to say that at that point it will be too late to solve them.

Disclosure statement

No potential conflict of interest was reported by the author.

References

Blühdorn, I. 2017. "Post-capitalism, post-growth, post-consumerism? Eco-political hopes beyond sustainability." *Global Discourse* 7 (1). http://dx.doi.org/10.1080/23269995.2017.1300415.

Duit, A., P. H. Feindt, and J. Meadowcroft. 2016. "Greening Leviathan: The Rise of the Environmental State?" *Environmental Politics* 25 (1): 1–23. doi:10.1080/09644016.2015.1085218.

Hausknost, D. 2014. "Decision, Choice, Solution: "Agentic Deadlock" in Environmental Politics." *Environmental Politics* 23 (3): 357–375. doi:10.1080/09644016.2013.874138.

Mol, A. P. J., D. A. Sonnenfeld, and G. Spaargaren, eds. 2009. *The Ecological Modernisation Reader: Environmental Reform in Theory and Practice.* London; New York: Routledge.

Newig, J., and O. Fritsch. 2009. "Environmental Governance: Participatory, Multi-Level – and Effective?" *Environmental Policy and Governance* 19 (3): 197–214. doi:10.1002/eet.509.

Riesman, D. 2001. *The Lonely Crowd: A Study of the Changing American Character.* Abridged and rev. Yale Nota Bene, ed. New Haven, CT: Yale University Press.

On the obsolescence of human beings in sustainable development

Ulrike Ehgartner, Patrick Gould and Marc Hudson

ABSTRACT

In 1956, the Jewish-German philosopher Günther Anders developed a philosophical anthropology on the technological and moral challenges of his time. Anders suggested the societal changes that arose with the industrial age opened a gap between the capability of individuals to produce machines and their ability to imagine and deal with the consequences caused by this capability. He argues that a 'Promethean gap' manifests in academic and scientific thinking and leads to an extensive trivialization of societal issues. In the face of climate change, Anders' philosophical anthropology contributes substantially to our attempts to fight climate change with innovation. Anders' description of 'apocalyptic blindness' helps us to explain why we cannot help pairing our belief in historical progress and growth with our ideas on social and environmental justice. With that said, this paper contributes to the debate on humanity 'after sustainability' by calling to mind Anders' historical theory on the outdatedness of humankind and his thoughts on our lack of imagination.

And how do we respond to it?
Just in the same way we respond to newspaper reports: not at all.
And why do we not react? Out of courage? Out of stoicism? [...]
Out of the lack of imagination. Because we are apocalyptically blind.'
                          Günther Anders (1961 [1956], 263)[1]

Introduction

Sustainability is dead. Long live the sustainability. Since the 1970's, crisis has been the defining theme for environmentalists. Biodiversity crisis, oil crisis, nuclear crisis, drought crisis, flood crisis, warming crisis, extinction crisis – a multitude of crises coalescing in a 'nexus' of threats. As such, visions of the apocalypse, and 'end-times', have come to form another central component for the environmental movement. The underlying critique of late capitalist society has been 'If we carry on this way, the world as we know it will be destroyed'. Indeed, visions and predictions of judgment and apocalypse are not new phenomena; but what has interested scholars of environmental history is the specific representation and identification of the apocalypse in contemporary Western society around climate change (Buell 2003; Michael and Barr 2014).

But what if the apocalypse or end-time was not some point over the horizon, a future event yet to be experienced, but what if it was now, in this moment? This idea, a realignment of the apocalypse to envelope the present, to take our gaze away from the past and future and develop an understanding and philosophy of the present was the central idea of Günther Anders. Not another obscure German philosopher we hear you cry. But what is peculiar about Anders' relative anonymity in English-speaking academic work is his importance and standing in German-speaking scholarship, where his stature was gained through his philosophies on technology, environmental politics and culture (Liessmann 2002; Bahr 2012; Dries 2014).

This article seeks to contribute to existing moves that 'close the case' on the sustainable development paradigm (Foster 2015; Benson and Craig 2014). Through the lens of Günther Anders' main ideas, *promethean shame* and *apocalyptic blindness*, this article suggests ways of developing a 'post-sustainability' approach to include a more robust understanding of how we may come to frame and understand widespread denial and confusion in '*Endzeit*' (end-time) and '*Zeitende*' (end-of-time).

The first section of this article frames Anders' main positions and perspectives in relation to international policies surrounding sustainability and economic development. Locating Anders in the academic landscape with reference to his personal and philosophical history, the recently agreed UN Sustainable Development Goals (SDGs) will be discussed.

This will bring the discussion on to two more salient developments in sustainability: sustainable consumption and the citizen-consumer. Again these will be explored and investigated through Anders' main philosophical contributions, giving way to a more general outline on the morality of economic liberalism in Western societies.

Finally, we will argue that bringing Anders' philosophical anthropology into play will help us to understand that the 'sustainability' paradigm has failed. We argue that developing a philosophy of the present through education and personal morality to end the 'promethean shame' of our current malaise can aid research and understandings on the difficulties and possibilities of a world after sustainability.

Condemned to freedom

In a special issue that dedicated to exploring themes around denial, sustainability and climate change, the growing interest in Anders' work in Anglophone countries[2] provides particular purchase to explore these issues. Born in 1902, the consequences of the Industrial Revolution as well as the catastrophes of the twentieth century were crucial aspects in Günther Anders' life. While Hiroshima and the nuclear threat are at the core and probably the most obviously influential historical conditions of Anders writing, events such as Auschwitz and the Vietnam War, as well as his life periods in exile in

France and the USA crucially influenced Anders' thinking and provided the key element of his philosophical anthropology (Bahr 2012; Van Dijk 2000).

Given his positioning – historically, as well as intellectually – Anders can be aligned with many other intellectuals and activists of his time who expressed concerns about technology and popular culture and made the destructive potential of modern technology and the omnipresent potential for mass destruction the focal point of their historical, social and moral analyses. Nevertheless, it would be a disservice to the importance and influence of Anders' work to dismiss him as just another moralizing critic of modernization and technology. As Christopher Müller (2015) argues in his recent mapping of what he calls 'desert ethics' – inaccessible spaces of human agency – 'it is to this attempt to think machines "differently" that Anders' reflections on the obsolescence of moral sentiments can make an important contribution'.

In post-war time, the vast impact of machines was widely welcomed in society, while various philosophers warned of their threats and consequences. Thus, in many ways, Anders reminds us of more famous contemporaries such as Lewis Mumford, Jacques Ellul or Norbert Wiener.[3] However, Anders' thinking is notable for his persistence in recognizing the twentieth century not only as a new historical era but also as an 'end-time'. His prognostic hermeneutic of a world of machines (Anders 2002, 424–426) and his ability to argue that the reproduced reality reflects back on to the actual reality (Anders 1961, 165–170) are just a few aspects that should not be disregarded in contemporary research.

An early and significant moment in Anders' life was his lecture on 'The Unworldliness of the Human Being' in 1929,[4] where he opposed the philosophical attempt to establish the essence of the human being as such. Carrying all anthropological questions on who or what human beings are to their grave,[5] this moment of academic positioning can be marked as the beginning of Anders' lifelong dispute with Heidegger.[6] More than this, it can be claimed that this lecture marks out the moment Anders broke with academia. He could not return to Heidegger and Husserl and the Frankfurt School scholars followed another school of thought (Bahr 2012).

Regardless of the formal consequences that Anders' early positioning on the essence of the human being might have had, it provided the foundations to his philosophical anthropology (Bahr 2012). Anders elaborated his perception of the human being by placing his philosophical anthropology within Nietzsche's animal that is not yet adapted to his environment (Nietzsche 1907, 82), when he argued that the course of conduct of human beings is not determined as it is for animals.[7] Unlike animals, humans are not adjusted to the world they live in. Thus, they are not forced to follow a given path and given their promethean freedom, they have to find their own way and are, consequently, doomed for self-creation: '(A)rtificiality is the nature of man and his essence is instability' (Anders 2009, 279).[8]

As humans do not simply react to the world around them but are forced to make it theirs, they do not have to use the given resources only, but they can invent, produce and use things. Thus, they are free and they are not (Anders 1961, 15–16); they are, to put it in the famous words, 'condemned to freedom'.[9] Anders argues that not humans are the subject of history in our times, but the machines that they created. Being in an inferior position in relation to machines, human beings have lost their freedom as they are forced to use and consume the machines' products (Bahr 2012; Liessmann 2002).

We know but we cannot comprehend

In late September 2015, falling leaves gathered in the drains and the gutters of New York City; a street cleaner busied along sweeping them into his black bag. Not far away, a similar exercise was taking place. In the conference hall of the UN, the upper echelon of suited global street cleaners ratified a set of 17 SDGs to clear our world of detritus and decay by 2030.

In the tradition of summits that date back to the 1972 Stockholm Conference on the Human Environment, major stakeholders took part in a widely discussed debate on sustainable development (Death 2015). Again, international agreements emphasize the importance of tackling the challenge of climate change. The agreements made both hold a reformist approach and have ambitious aims; being well aware of our own unsustainability, the urgency to radically change our ecological policies is being recognized.

However, these agreements carry either no legal obligations or weak ones with few, if any, enforcement mechanisms (Spash 2016). Facing societal and environmental change, we carry on as usual rely on technology that might or might not yet exist. All attempts for adaptation seek to defend, secure and reinforce our existing technological and managerial systems, not touching the mechanisms of the modern market economy (Blühdorn 2008; Barnett et al. 2011; Blühdorn 2015). Even though we acknowledge that the issue is serious, we are – in Anders' words – 'apocalyptically blind' (Anders 1961, 235–306).

'Apocalyptic blindness', according to Anders, is the mindset of humans in the Age of the Third Industrial Revolution[10]; it determines a notion of time and future that renders human beings incapable of facing the possibility of a bad end to their history. The belief in progress, persistently ingrained since the Industrial Revolution (see also Popper 1957), causes the incapability of humans to understand that their existence is threatened, and that this could lead to the end of their history.[11] We are unable to understand, because we have lost our ability to relate conduct and consciousness to the same matter. In other words, we face a gap between our ability to produce and our ability to imagine; a gap between knowledge and comprehension – a 'Promethean gap' (Anders 1961).

Even though Anders is often referred to as a moralist, he did not attempt to reason morally, neither was he seeking to appropriate a new moral to the twentieth century. Essentially, he attempted to explain how technology and the division of labour *eliminate* morals, or more precisely, moral imagination. This is a crucial point, since Anders believed that it is ultimately the lack of moral imagination that made omnicide – the extermination of all life – not an unlikely event to happen. The lack of moral imagination becomes apparent in the way that processes of work consist of so many steps of various instances, so that none of these steps could be identified as *the* one-step. Thus, in relation to the atomic bomb, in the end, no one could be blamed for having caused the apocalypse (Anders 1961, 245).

According to Anders, it is the moral situation that determines whether we are able to comprehend a matter; whether something concerns us or not.[12] There are numerous examples of matters which concern us, but subjectively they do not. We are concerned with issues such as oil spills, rising sea levels and the suffering caused by intensive animal husbandry. These are things we either may or may not comprehend; things we are excluded from interfering with, given the division of responsibilities, ownership structures and political forces. Anders says that if the possibility to create and command over matters is taken from us and we do not explicitly offer resistance, it will soon lose any real concern for us. We are blind to whatever we are forced to refrain from.[13] It is not that we do not know. We know, but we do not comprehend. Therefore, we carry on life as if we would not know (Anders 1961, 285–286).

Universal mechanization and the identity crisis

Global mechanisms for bringing about environmental change and human progress have been on the UN's agenda since the late 1960s, and came to an early head at the United Nations Conference on the Human Environment in 1972 at Stockholm. In the midst of the Cold War, heightening concerns around nuclear war and environmental destruction prompted action on creating international treaties on the protection of the environment.[14]

As years passed and damage accumulated, the solution amongst policymakers and statesmen was ever greater integration through the global economy, and the construction of a universal mechanism that can bring about a more peaceful, just and sustainable world; in the famous words of the Brundtland Commission (United Nations 1987), 'meeting the needs of the present without compromising the ability of future generations to meet their own needs'. The sustainability paradigm that emerged back then did recognize the limits to growth and the need for a shift of focus from Western consumerist needs to global fundamental human needs and made, initially, no pretence of having a deep-rooted relation to environmental movements.

However, as soothing as the still well-cited words from the UN's early days sustainable agenda are for the 'soul' in our age (Anders 1961, 15), given the Zeitgeist of this age, they were – as Anders would undoubtedly say – never seriously considered to be more than symbolic statements. Aesthetic norms such as the preservation of the beauty of the nature, religious imperatives to protect divine creation and ethical principles to respect the integrity and dignity of nature (Blühdorn 2015, 158) are not applicable in a society in which technology is the subject of history (Anders 2002, 271). The construction of a universal discourse around environmental sustainability is condemned to be paired with development plans based on principles and measures of science and economics.

The human being of the twentieth century, says Anders, manifests as a faulty piece of machinery within machines of a set design (Anders 1961, 32–34). The sustainable development paradigm has seen the continued functionalization of man, the subordination of human will to the will of the machine, a techno-totalitarian apparatus with 'the human being condemned to freedom' (Van Dijk 2000, 29). The shift of responsibility to an entity that we constructed silences our last remaining call of consciousness. This entity is represented by electronic machines, the epitome of science and progress; with humankind right beside it – half grateful and half triumphant. Understanding that the machines are achieving better performances than ourselves, we accept that we are less competent and shift, consequently, the responsibility for the outcomes of actions on to the object. In that way, personal responsibility is replaced with mechanic 'responses' (Anders 1961, 246).

Goals as phantoms

Anders' perspective on apocalyptic blindness rests on the future-orientated activities of man – 'looking, listening and living away' (Anders 1961, 236). Nothing represents this view better than the creation of 'goals' as a way to measure and achieve progress in global development and sustainability. In our inability to fear,[15] the formulation of goals gives us hope that we are preparing aims for the future. In that way, we approach the historical catastrophe as a part of our history and are blind to its true meaning: signifying the end of our history and as such something that cannot go down in history (Anders 1961, 262–263). Despite our planning for the future, from 'the World in 2050' reports to pension schemes and frozen food, Anders argues we are always drawn back to the present and the future is always in a state of 'not yet' (Müller 2015, 53).

Replacing the Millennium Development Goals (MDGs) that expired at the end of 2015 amid controversy and debates over their effectiveness (Rieff 2015, 48–51); the SDGs provide 17 antidotes to prescribe to a sick patient. Like an overused New York taxi that has chugged its way to the garage, a band of mechanics gleefully waits with a toolbox in one hand and a card machine in the other. Except the planet is neither a human being nor a car. 'An immense industrial network cannot be managed', Georges Bataille (1988, 19) wrote of the Marshall Plan, 'in the same way that one changes a tire'.

When one reads through the 'Transforming our world: the 2030 Agenda for Sustainable Development', the level of scope and aspiration is considerable. From the 91 subsections, there are constant references to the '5 P's': people, planet, peace, prosperity and partnership. Yet there is something contradictory, careless and excessive about the number points and the topics they cover.

The sheer number of aims and promotions can situate individuals in a quagmire of policy interventions – where to start? What to do? Like a child writing their Christmas list to Santa, the policymakers couldn't help themselves in just putting one or two more in. Here is a small selection:

3.6 By 2020, halve the number of global deaths and injuries from road traffic accidents

4.4 By 2030, substantially increase the number of youth and adults who have relevant skills, including technical and vocational skills, for employment, decent jobs and entrepreneurship

12.8 By 2030, ensure that people everywhere have the relevant information and awareness for sustainable development and lifestyles in harmony with nature

14.b Provide access for small-scale artisanal fishers to marine resources and markets

(United Nations 2015, 12-23)

For all the fine verbs such as "ensuring," "committing," "providing," "aiming" and "ending," in 2030 will anyone have performed these verbs to the level needed to arrive at the promised sustainable nirvana? Making use of a jargon of consideration and ambition, the list of goals remains vague in declaring what the actual contents and means of their implementation would be. This indeterminacy, a goal attainment followed by another goal attainment, is particularly relevant to Anders' view on our apocalyptic blindness. The 'end-time' we find ourselves in, an epoch of which there is no other to come, mobilizes the future only to blind us to its possibilities. The calculation of time is a product of the machine; through the setting of goals as a pillar of sustainable development that calculates the future as a concrete space, one that is set but at the same time in need of constant work and adaptation.

The SDGs 'will be voluntary and country-led … and will respect [national] policy space and priorities' (United Nations 2015, 27). Indeed, the SDGs are not ensured by any legal bindings or sanctions. This means that the UN will have to rely on self-commitments. Aiming to accomplish such a universalizing consensus, Ban Ki-Moon's idea on role allocation seems clear – 'Governments must take the lead in living up to their pledges'. At the same time, he is 'counting on the private sector to drive success' (Moon 2015 [26 September]).

Based on the success of previous 'voluntary-led' and 'self-regulating' schemes, strategies, pacts, acts and goals should we be wary of such promises? The UN implores us not to be, for the SDGs are argued to take a different course from the MDGs in taking a 'people-centred' approach; that is, responsibility is for one and all – 'as we embark on this great collective journey, we pledge that no one will be left behind' (United Nations 2015, 2). The UN promises us that the SDGs are the blueprints, but we, 'the people', are the builders. Except we are not the builders. And this is the trick; the great sleight of hand of international development and progress. Behind the language of global responsibility, intra-species solidarity and shared values exists a sociotechnical apparatus grand in design yet unmoored from its consequences – that is, apocalyptically blind.

The language used in the context of sustainable development creates the idea that we are all complicit. Voluntary self-commitment should transform our 'unsustainable lifestyles' into 'more sustainable lifestyles'. The narrative that we are all part of it, that we, the majority of humans, wanted, planned and made it, however, is absurd; not only absurd, but dangerous. This perception only suits the unlucky ones who happen to be the immediate 'subjects' of the machines, who command over their production and application. Thus, talking about the 'suicide of mankind' provides an ideally broad basis for responsibility, a 'superb alibi', where everybody is virtually complicit but nobody immediately guilty (Anders 1961, 255–256).

The (un-)sustainable consumer: guilty of the lack of responsibility

The horrifying character of the current situation of humankind, although it is our work, is not our fault. We can only perceive, as Benjamin famously wrote of Paul Klee's Angelus Novus 'a chain of events', even though the Angel, looking at the same events 'sees one single catastrophe which keeps piling wreckage upon wreckage and hurls it in front of his feet' (Benjamin 1969, 257–258). Not only are we not culpable, but also we are not even permitted to be culpable anymore. Being irresponsible for our own actions, humans find themselves as a 'miserable' resource: they are perishable – a product of nature, a body that is so rigid and unfree that it could never keep up with the changes of technology. Given that situation, the human being suffers from feelings of inferiority in the face of their machines (Anders 1961, 49–50).[16]

The twentieth century taught us to disregard the human being as an integrated whole, and separate the individual as an actor from its quality as a sentient being.[17] Being all successors of a history of schizophrenic beings when one person could work for a death camp and be a loving father at the same time, Anders would argue, we certainly have a hard time to find a contradiction between doing a nine-to-five job to make a living and advocating for environmental and human rights issues. As both fragments are not related to each other, they are not getting in the way of each other (Anders 1961, 272).

In academic research, in policy papers, as well as in marketing strategies for sustainable consumption, it is often claimed that global, social and environmental problems such as working conditions of farmers in the global south or children in textile factories are too abstract for our imagination. Anders would agree with these findings in that our power for imagination does not stand up to the system of the global production of goods and the economic interrelation with the world. More importantly, however, he would ascribe the call for and implementation of sustainable consumption to the manifestation of promethean shame.

Dealing with sustainability, many businesses, policymakers, campaigners, lobbyists and academics, take the socially and environmentally caring consumer or citizen – or citizen-consumer (Sassatelli 2007; Trentmann 2007), as they are habitually called, building on the naïve faith in promethean freedom – as a matter of fact. Based on that, ways are explored to 'nudge' this attitude of concern towards actual behaviour (Richard and Sunstein 2008; Barr and Prillwitz 2014). In response to these attempts that try to determine mechanisms of sustainable behaviour, Anders would argue that in contemporary times, examining whether people care or not is futile. In an age where people cannot be responsible for their own actions, 'care' is an irrelevant indicator for human behaviour, regardless of whether they are acting as consumers or as citizens.

Moreover, as opposed to the notion of the ethically concerned consumer,[18] Anders would claim that a couldn't-care-less attitude is determining the behaviour of the contemporary human. This is not because we lost all our morals, but due to our attempts to hide the shame for not being responsible for our actions,[19] *the shame about our shame*. Having feelings of inferiority towards our machines, we are hiding our shame behind gestures of concealment; in order to fool others and also ourselves. Taking up a couldn't-care-less-attitude is a likely strategy here, as it stands in opposition to shame. Shame is invisible as long as it is covered with confidence: 'The one who is not hiding, who keeps visible, is not under the suspicion of shame – and therefore stigma (Anders 1961, 29).

Thus, in the face of climate change, nominating ethical consumerism to a saviour perfectly fits into the concept of concealment; we can comfort ourselves in maintaining the means of production and consumption, which we learnt to take as a given. Any attempts to change patterns related to these means would put us at risk to humiliate ourselves. Hence, as long as we produce and consume with the confidence of doing something good, we do not get into the shameful situation of being forced to confess that there might be something faulty about the system we are living in, of which we are responsible for while we are not.

The moral schizophrenia of the citizen-consumer

How do we know that we have reached the end of sustainability? Anders would answer this question by saying that we know it when supporting 'sustainable economic growth' appears to be the morally legitimate way to commit to sustainable development.

In 'The Obsolescence of Human Beings', Anders describes a society in which con-sciousness was replaced with conscientiousness. Anders identifies enterprises as institu-tions in which people are expected to join the given processes with 100% and so are the birthplaces of the conformist (Anders 1961, 289–291).[20] No matter whether individuals know what they are doing or not – there is no consciousness required for it, as product and production, morally speaking, are torn apart: 'The moral status of a product does not cast a shadow on the moral status of the one who works and therefore participates in its production. No matter whether he knows or does not know, what he is doing; he does not need a consciousness for what he is doing' (Anders 1961, 289). And so we do welcome ideas on sustainable development today and try to make the 'right choices' in the supermarket. And it is not even difficult. In fact, one would struggle to find a company that does not claim to favour a sustainable economy.

Today's citizen-consumers show conscientiousness in relation to sustainable devel-opment, when they are in fact supporters of the current system and the market economy. We have learnt not to question taking historical progress and growth as the substrate of humanity (Anders 1961, 277–278). To a wide extent, we cannot even imagine to scrutinize our current system: A world without economic growth exceeds our imaginative power – we are blind to it. Defining sustainable development in a way that leaves the primacy of markets untouched, we bring evidence to our blindness. 'No situation is more evil than the one in which the evil became such an integral part of the situation that the individual can spare to be the evil' (Anders 1981, 88),[21] as Anders put it once.

So why is it that we still hold on so strongly to a language around responsibility? Why do we not let go of the ideas raised by the environmental movement of the early 1980s, whose critique was mainly concerned with corporations in a way that has not got much in common with the ideals of a sustainable development today? Why do we speak about the ethical, political and emancipated consumers? A look at Anders' analysis of the situation of the workers in the age of the Second Industrial Revolution can explain this. While being expected to demonstrate conscientiousness by showing a sense of duty for the system they are operating in on the one hand, they are, on the other, expected to be absolutely themselves in what they do outside of their working life. They are, for Anders, caught in a moral dilemma (Anders 1961, 291).

It can be said that the impossibility of balancing between compliance and emancipa-tion reveals the schizophrenic character of the citizen-consumer that is in no way less schizophrenic than the character of the modern factory workers. For the latter, Anders claimed, there is no such thing as a sphere outside of the enterprise, because all crucial tasks are done inside the enterprise. Expected to embody two different types of being, a conformist in work and a nonconformist in private, the worker remains indolent; they expect a continuation of the process that is beyond their responsibility. Their own actions, however, are limited and are not involving any planning for time periods (Anders 1961, 291–294).

It is within his 'philosophical considerations on radio and television' (Anders 1961, 97–212) when Anders elaborates on how consumption is a force, in particular in the way it replaces leisure and manifests in daily life. The force to consume elides the world outside of the system of production. Leisure time, as opposed to working time, does not exist anymore as such; it is an inbuilt and necessary component to maintain the system.

Thus, being given a 'choice' can be subjectively perceived as freedom but this is bound to the force of consumption, which is just another aspect of the force of production (Ribolits 1997).

Defining 'boycott' and 'buycott' as the common means of political participation, indeed, every individual can join in and do their part for a better world at any time, if they want to – by voting with their money. Facing the decline of gatherings, formations and social movements, shopping for the good cause became the new and defining type of political engagement, participation and change (Micheletti, Stolle, and Berlin 2012). The 'shopping for change' paradigm demands us to be responsible individuals that consider complex social and environmental problems and develop own values and norms. The means to express this responsibility, however, are limited to the market – a system so deeply ingrained that we are blind to the restrictions it imposes on us.

Ethical consumerism reproduces the assumption that the consumer is the key agent for social change (Barnett et al. 2011). Ethical consumers are informed, reflexive and emancipated when they exercise choice and thereby pick the products that, as they have been told, are the 'right choice'. The paradigm of the informed and emancipated consumer creates the idea of individual freedom; a freedom whose limitation to economic liberalism we are blind to realize. It is the one we are used to, as the classical market theory taught us that 'the market is a democracy where every penny gives the right to vote' (Frank Fetter quoted in Dickinson and Carsky 2005, 25). However, '… the fact that the lack of freedom appears natural to us, that we do not notice the lack of freedom or, should we notice it, we do so tranquilly and with equanimity, does not make the situation any less disastrous. To the contrary: since the terror is delivered in the form of a thousand little cuts and eliminates imagination of a possible alternative situation, or any idea of opposition, it is in a way more fatal than any recognizable deprivation of liberty' (Anders 1961, 198). Therefore, consumer choice, which promises to give us freedom within consumerism (Slater 1997), functions as a powerful tool to maintain our blindness. To quote Anders: 'no type of disempowerment of individuals is more successful than the one that seemingly safeguards their freedom' (Anders 1961, 104).

Combating future-blindness – learning to predict the after

The term 'sustainability' originated in the forest management of the early eighteenth century. In 1713, mining administrator Carl von Carlowitz published 'Sylvicultura Oeconomica' in which he argued that a continuously stable and sustainable utilization of forests was demanded (Ott and Döring 2004). Thus, it was in reaction to a period of crisis and scarcity caused by the mining industry's immensely increased demand of wood that had consumed whole forests, that the term 'sustainability' was used for the first time. Thus, the concept of sustainability came up in reaction to a development in which long-termism was replaced with short-termist profitability and the utilization of resources increased exponentially.

In the 1980s, the term was revisited and the ecological focus was expanded to economic and social aspects. Sustainability initially held strong links to environmental movements that acknowledged limitations of growth and advocated for an awareness of the resource intensity of Western lifestyles. However, the inclusion of 'development' gave way to a conceptualization of sustainability that is adapted to the conditions it was intended to combat. Sustainability, consequently, remains an ideological promise to make some green technological adaptations while carrying on as usual. As such, it becomes apparent that the apocalyptical blindness that Anders attested 60 years ago in relation to the nuclear threat has been equally manifested in relation to the threat coming along with the resource consumption of today.

The launch of SDGs, yet again, demonstrates how apocalyptical blindness bears upon future-related blindness. The bourgeois belief in progress, Anders argues, makes humans future-blind. Having been transformed into beings forced to use the machines we produced, we accept the situation as a given: It is the only possible scenario of the world that we can imagine for us and we take it with enthusiasm. Certain questions about practices do not – indeed cannot – even come up, because the technologies determine what we have to want (Liessmann 2002, 156). Short-sighted, we run into the world of progress, while the horizon of the future, or what we could grasp from it, remains provincially narrow (Anders 1961, 282–284).

We are *'inverted utopists'*. While utopists are incapable of creating what they imagine, we are incapable of imagining what we created (Anders 1981, 96). We are so habituated to this state that we are able to content ourselves with actions such as ethical consumption. We know about the interconnectedness of societal and environmental issues and we do 'our bit' when we make informed choices as consumers, or so we tell ourselves. Corporations do their bit too, because they enable the individual to make these informed choices. Protected by the 'alibi of the alleged knowledge' we can seclude ourselves in our state of not knowing (Anders 1961, 270).

As such, the Promethean gap between knowledge and comprehension becomes ever more obvious. Concepts like sustainable development and ethical consumption focus on the knowledge that humans need to keep up with the requirements of the market and with its innovations. For Anders, however, the key lies in the comprehension of technological developments in relation to the self-perception of humanity. Thus, Anders demands that we have to learn to interpret technological developments in relation to ourselves as well as that we have to identify ourselves in relation to the world we are living in. We have to overcome the fact that our spiritual state at any given time only ever reflects the technical state of the past. That means we have to move on to a 'prognostic interpretation' (Anders 2002, 428).

This does not mean a sole fascination with the future though, for Anders it rests on our ability to overcome our concept of time: 'Time should not lie ahead of us, but captured by us, with us', in our presence' (Anders 1961, 284). That is, technology needs to be integrated into the self-interpretation of humanity rather than humanity integrated into technology. This is a moral task to all of us: '(I)f it is our fate to live in a (self-created) world of excess that eludes from our imaginations and feelings and in this way endangers us fatally, then we have to try to catch up with this excess' (Anders 1961, 274). Thus, '…we have to learn to do what the seers of antiquity did (or were convinced they were doing): predict the future. The guts that we have to learn how to read as prognostic signs are not those of sacrificial animals, but those of machines. The machines reveal the world of the future to us and what our grandchildren will be like, provided they will exist. And if they will not do this themselves, we have to force them to do it' (Anders 2002, 428).

The Prussian educational reformer Wilhelm von Humboldt once stated that it should be *the ultimate purpose of the human entity* to enable ourselves to grasp as much of our world as possible and to connect with it as close as we can; to become free from immaturity, self-confident, emancipated and to actively take part in our environment and community; in short: to stand in interaction to the world around us (Von Humboldt 1980). In that sense, Anders end-time philosophy has rightly been interpreted as humanistic and educational, rather than apocalyptic (Bahr 2012). Having reached the last epoch of humanity, increasing our ability to imagine our productive capacity is, according to Anders, the only way to interrupt the course towards the doom that threatens us (Anders 2002, 428–429). The knowledge to use or consume the products that we produced and to adapt to the institutions we created has to be accompanied by a comprehension of ourselves in our world.

Conclusion

'Our end of the world is sung from the rooftops even by sparrows; the element of surprise is missing; it seems only a question of time.' (Enzensberger 1978)

We have written this article with the feeling and opinion that some aspects of Anders' work are vital to an historical understanding of the twenty-first century and in particular, anthropogenic climate change and catastrophe. In the debate on options for political and personal action for sustainable development, Anders' cultural critique has been long required.

The 1950s, if they are thought of at all, are remembered as a time of technological optimism and *Vorsprung durch Technik*. Keynesian economic growth and technological prowess promised electricity too cheap to meter, the obsolescence of work and the notion of 'holidays on the moon' Anders was an early voice warning that this moment would not last. Many people reading this article will still be alive in 2050. Our visions for that time are bleaker – acidified oceans, scorched land, drowned cities and relentless extreme weather events. In 100 years, a geological blink of an eye, we will have passed from promethean power to powerlessness, from control to contingency. Voices like Anders deserve to be heard as we chart an uncertain path.

Uncertainty, passivity and denial – these are themes drawn out across this special issue and things we have sought to address in this article; highlighting the value of Anders' work on these themes. In particular, why do we not act? How are we able to think but not feel? Why are we, as Paul Gilroy (2012) argues, 'zombies … who exist in the context of a neo-liberal order that thrives on the brutal division of the world into two great teams: winners and losers'. Anders' philosophical anthropology dealt with these issues at length. In particular, the 'pluralization' or 'splitting' of man. Humanity is not a single-headed object, but 'a pair of men; the individual (who, as a metaphysical self-made man, had fought a Promethean struggle against the Gods) has now been replaced by men who fight each other for domination' (Anders 1965, 149). The sustainable development paradigm has reinforced this pairing; we fight each other for domination, for control and for power.

For decades, one of the most widespread arguments from environmental groups has been the uneven ecological and social consequences of climate change; how poor nations and groups are to suffer first. As such, the apocalyptic vision of catastrophic climate change is not 'a bolt from the blue' but 'insidious and torturingly slow in its approach, the apocalypse in slow motion' (Enzensberger 1978, 75). The apocalypse of catastrophic climate change has itself been subject to division, plurality and machination; each part a section that can be fixed in itself – planetary climate change moves forward not as a whole but as fragments of destruction and annihilation.

And here we come back to Anders' (not Sartre's) notion that we humans are 'condemned to freedom'. We are free to engage in the world economy and sustainable development but under specific rules. Nations and groups at risk of climate change, also at risk of becoming losers in the global economic race for sustainable development, can supposedly become winners. They can play the game, they are free to choose, but they are condemned to that freedom under particular rules and laws. The first law we can establish of this game is: there will be winners and losers.

In order to overcome this dialectic between winners and losers, master and slave, proletariat and bourgeoisie, Anders offers us some suggestions in order for us to 'catch up' with our creations. Catching up is very different from 'reconnecting' or 'realigning' or other such 're's' that have dominated narratives on how to develop a more sustainable world such as 'reconnecting with nature' or 'realigning our values'. Anders is not a conservative, or someone who believes in a romanticized past of pre-technological innovation, rather he sees technology and machines as overtaking us, and we need to move forward, not backwards.

In a remarkable series of letters between Günther Anders and Claude Eatherly, a pilot of a scout plane during the Hiroshima bombing, we are offered a rare moment of instrumentalism and succinctness from Anders (Eatherly 1962, 11-15) in a section titled 'Commandments in an Atomic Age' that we still find applicable today. We will leave you with these.

'First Thought: *Atom*
(The world around us is not stable.)
Second Thought: *The possibility of the apocalypse is our work. But we know not what we are doing.*
(The gap between action and imagination.)
Third Thought: *'Widen your sense of time.'*
(Stretch your moral fantasy.)
Fourth Thought: *'Don't be a coward.'*
(It is *our* business, it is our turn to worry, we are equally incompetent.)'

Notes

1. All quotations of Anders' German contributions used in this paper (Anders 1961, 1964, 1981, 2002) have been translated by the author.
2. See, for example, Dawsey (2012, 2013); Babich (2012, 2013a, 2013b); Müller (2015) as well as the recent translation of Anders' essay on 'The world as phantom and as matrix:

Philosophical considerations on radio and television', as well as a complete translation of 'The Outdatedness of Human Beings 2' available online (Libcom.org 2014, 2015).

3. This is particularly evident for his analysis of the human being. Reading about the 'meta-morphosis' in the industrial age (Anders 1961, 15–16), for example, inevitably provokes associations with Lewis Mumford's 'transformation' (Mumford 1957).

4. In German orig: 'Die Weltfremdheit des Menschen' (Liessmann 2002, 30–52). This speech is not available in German original. However, a French essay version based on this speech was published 6 years later, of which there is an English translation available ('The Pathology of Freedom: An Essay on Non-Identification', 2009).

5. 'For Anders, such attempts to separate and single out the human being from the aggregate of beings, and therefore all forms of anthropocentrism, are typical of the metaphysics of the Western world. Such an elevated position of the human being leads to degradation of all other beings to mere means and must ultimately lead to exploitation and destruction of nature' (Van Dijk 2000, 102).

6. Having been a student of Heidegger in his earlier life, he later on claimed that he had been fallen under his 'demonic spell' (Dries 2014). On Anders' standpoint to the question 'what is man' and his critique of Heidegger in that context see also Anders (2002, 128–130).

7. Further to this anthropologist tradition, Anders could be denominated as Gehlens' anti-pode in the context of the twentieth century. Despite the similarities in both their analyses, Anders substantially distanced himself from the conservative anthropologist Gehlen, refer-ring to his words as 'darkest provincialism' (Greffrath 1989, 48–50). On Gehlen and his explanations of the human as a deficient being (Mängelwesen), see Gehlen (1940).

8. Anders' philosophical anthropology explains how humans are set to not look towards a certain end: If human history is made for experimenting and designing, there is no end of it to be seen (Anders 1961). The notion of humans being sacrificed to the demands of the machinic world, however, was current at the time. See Charlie Chaplin's, 'Modern Times', in which he becomes quite literally a cog in the machine. See also Fritz Lang's dystopic, 'Metropolis' for a similar account. Earlier, the English novelist E.M Forster wrote a short story, 'The Machine Stops' about humans who had become dependent upon machines for every aspect of their lives.

9. Note that, even though it was Sartre, who adopted fundamental thoughts of this piece and made the quote of the man condemned to be free famous, it was Anders' who stated this claim about the human existence in his 'Pathology of Freedom' already 'a few years before Sartre', as emphasized by Anders (Anders 2002, 130).

10. The first volume of Anders' major work was originally published in Germany in 1956, given the title: 'Die Antiquiertheit des Menschen. Über die Seele im Zeitalter der zweiten indus-triellen Revolution. [The Outdatedness of Human Beings 1. On the Soul in the Era of the Second Industrial Revolution]'. This was followed by a second volume in 1980, titled 'Die Antiquiertheit des Menschen: Über die Zerstörung des Lebens im Zeitalter der dritten industriellen Revolution. [The Outdatedness of Human Beings 2. On the Destruction of Life in the Era of the Third Industrial Revolution]'. In the second volume, Anders explains that epochs no longer change after 1945, as with the atomic bombing of Hiroshima notions of a continuation of history and a succession of other epochs became invalid. The current epoch, in any event, is the last one. The third revolution is, therefore, the last age of humanity (Anders 2002, 15–33).

11. The faith in progress and the trust in new technological solutions to recurring issues define the thinking in the twentieth century, when nobody would think, as Heidegger (1976) had put it, that 'only a god can save us'.

12. Though of course, social and financial benefits can accrue to those who are able not to see, a point made forcefully in pre-bomb literature such as Hans Christian Andersen's 'The Emperor's New Clothes' and Henrik Ibsen's 'An Enemy of the People'. For a more recent, and scholarly exposition of this, see Stanley Cohen's 'States of Denial: Knowing about Atrocities and Suffering' (Cohen 2001).

13. See in that context the existentialist thought on the self-deceiving attitude of humans and that '(b)ad faith … is a social disease rather than an individual failing, in Sartre's view, and is

an ongoing condition rather than a sporadic activity' (Webber 2010, 188). Also note the more recent literature on 'willful blindness' in the context of short term economic interest (Heffernan 2011).

14. For discussion see Howe (2014)

15. Anders argues that anxiety got converted into a commodity. These days, he says, everybody speaks about anxiety, but just a few speak out of anxiety (Anders 1961, 264).

16. Perhaps Anders would see this continuation of 'universal mechanization' as an unavoidable tendency from the division of labour and specialization in the late eighteenth century. This would be quite a deterministic interpretation of Anders' thoughts though, and while he was highly influenced by Marx's analysis of dialectical materialism, he also provides the space for the reclamation of the human 'soul' from the processes of modernization and an eventual apocalypse.

17. The similarity to Arendt's famous observation about the banality of evil is unmistakable (Arendt 1963).

18. 'Alternative', 'ethical', 'critical', 'radical' or 'political' consumption typically implies a notion that critically questions the contemporary consumption patterns such as in particular over-consumption, less in a sense of a renunciation of consumption, but more as active political participation through the marketplace (Sassatelli 2007, 186–188).

19. Anders explains that the identity crisis of the human being is strongly related to shame. In the given situation, humans are forced to identify themselves with something that is part of them, even though they cannot identify themselves with it. Thus, humans are not ashamed *even though* it is not their fault, but *because* it is not their fault. They cannot deal with the contradiction, and they can also not deal with their shame (Anders 1961, 69).

20. 'Every epoch gets the prophets it deserves' (Anders 1964).

21. In that effect, Anders explains how for NS war criminals their actions were morally right. Back then, it was morally legitimate to take part in the operations of a death camp. The circumstances changed and moral legitimation shifted after the war, but back then, they did not act very different to what they were committed to by work organization (Anders 1961, 287–288). 'As long as we do not face the fact and do not realize that contemporary enterprises are the forge, the modus operandi and the prototype of gleichschaltung, we will remain incapable to understand the figure of the conformist. We will remain incapable to understand what it is all about the obdurate men who refused to regret or take the responsibility for co-conducting in atrocities'. The atrocities were not 'erratic incidences' of history that only happened once will ever happen again (Anders 1961, 290).

Acknowledgements

We would like to thank both reviewers Nina Isabella Moeller and John Martin Pedersen for their positive and enriching comments on the paper. Their helpful remarks led to a great improvement of the work, in particular in terms of language and clarity. Thanks also to Joachim Gruber, Abdulla Adel and Chloe Jeffries for their constructive comments on this article.

Disclosure statement

No potential conflict of interest was reported by the authors.

References

Anders, G. 1961. *Die Antiquiertheit des Menschen. Band I: Über die Seele Im Zeitalter Der zweiten industriellen Revolution*. Munich: C.H. Beck.

Anders, G. 1964. "Der sanfte Terror." *Theorie des Konformismus. Merkur* 18 (193): 209–224.

Anders, G. 1981. *Atomare Drohung. Radikale Überlegungen zum atomaren Zeitalter*. Munich: C.H. Beck.

Anders, G. 2002. *Die Antiquiertheit des Menschen. Band II: Über die Zerstörung des Lebens im Zeitalter der dritten industriellen Revolution*. Munich: C.H. Beck.

Anders, G. 1965. "Being without Time: On Beckett's Play *Waiting for Godot*." In *Samuel Beckett: A Collection of Critical Essays*, edited by M. Esslin. Englewood Cliffs: Prentice-Hall.

Anders, G. 2009. The Pathology of Freedom: An Essay on Non-Identification. translated by, K. Wolfe. *Deleuze Studies* 3 (2): 278–310. doi:10.3366/E1750224109000658.

Arendt, H. 1963. *Eichmann in Jerusalem*. New York: Viking Press.

Babich, B. 2012. "On Machines as the Masters of Humanity: Martin Heidegger, Günther Anders, and the Singularity of Digital Technology." *Journal of the Hannah Arendt Center for Politics and Humanities at Bard College* 2: 122–144.

Babich, B. 2013a. "Angels, the Space of Time, and Apocalyptic Blindness: On Günther Anders' Endzeit–Endtime." *Ethics Politics* 2: 144–174.

Babich, B. 2013b. "O, Superman! or Being Towards Transhumanism: Martin Heidegger, Günther Anders and Media Aesthetics." *Divinatio* 83–99.

Bahr, R. 2012. *Günther Anders: Leben und Denken im Wort*. Berlin: epubli.

Barnett, C. et al. 2011. *Globalizing Responsibility: The Political Rationalities of Ethical Consumption (RGS-IBG Book Series)*. Chichester: Wiley-Blackwell.

Barr, S., and A. Prillwitz. 2014. "A Smarter Choice? Exploring the Behaviour Change Agenda for Environmentally Sustainable Mobility." *Environment and Planning C* 32 (1): 1–19. doi:10.1068/c1201.

Bataille, G. 1988. *The Accursed Share: Volume 1*. London: Zone Books.

Benjamin, W. 1969. *Illuminations, Edited with an Introduction by Hannah Arendt*. Translated by H. Zohn. New York: Schocken.

Benson, M., and R. Craig. 2014. "The End of Sustainability." *Society & Natural Resources: An International Journal* 27 (7): 777–782. doi:10.1080/08941920.2014.901467.

Blühdorn, I. 2008. "Sustaining the Unsustainable: Symbolic Politics and the Politics of Simulation." In *The Politics of Unsustainability: Eco-Politics in the Post-Ecologist Era*, edited by Blühdorn, Ingolfur, and Ian Welsh. 67–91. London: Routledge.

Blühdorn, I. 2015. "A Much-Needed Renewal of Environmentalism? Eco-Politics in the Anthropocene." In *The Anthropocene and the Global Environmental Crisis: Rethinking Modernity in a New Epoch*, edited by C. Hamilton, F. Gemenne, and C. Bonneuil, 156–167. London: Routledge.

Buell, F. 2003. *From Apocalypse to Way of Life: Environmental Crisis in the American Century*. London: Routledge.

Cohen, S. 2001. *States of Denial: Knowing about Atrocities and Suffering*. London: Polity Press.

Dawsey, J. 2013. *The Limits of the Human in the Age of Technological Revolution: Günther Anders, Post-Marxism, and the Emergence of Technology Critique*, Dissertation, University of Chicago http://gradworks.umi.com/35/68/3568370.html

Dawsey, J. 2012. "Where Hitler's Name is Never Spoken: Günther Anders in 1950s Vienna." In *Austrian Lives (Contemporary Austrian Studies, Vol. XXI)*, edited by G. Bischof, F. Plasser, and E. Maltschnig, 212–239. New Orleans/Innsbruck: University of New Orleans Press/Innsbruck University Press.

Death, C. 2015. "Disrupting Global Governance: Protest at Environmental Conferences from 1972 to 2012." *Global Governance: A Review of Multilateralism and International Organizations* 21 (4): 579–598.

Dickinson, R., and M. Carsky. 2005. "The Consumer as Economic Voter." In *The Ethical Consumer*, edited by R. Harrison, T. Newholm, and D. Shaw. Thousand Oaks, CA: Sage.

Dries, C. 2014. "Vita Günther Anders (1902-1992). Internationale Günther Anders Gesellschaft." http://www.guenther-anders-gesellschaft.org/vita-guenther-anders/

Eatherly, C. 1962. *Burning Conscience: The Case of Hiroshima Pilot, Claude Eatherly, told in letters to Gunther Anders*. New York: Monthly Review Press.

Enzensberger, H. M. 1978. Two Notes on the End of the World. *New Left Review* 110. 74–80.

Foster, J. 2015. *After Sustainability: Denial, Hope, Retrieval*. Abingdon, Oxon, New York: Routledge.

Gehlen, A. 1940. *Der Mensch, Seine Natur und Seine Stellung in Der Welt*. Berlin: Junker & Dünnhaupt.

Gilroy, P. 2012. "'My Britain is Fuck All' Zombie Multiculturalism and the Race Politics of Citizenship." *Identities: Global Studies in Culture and Power* 19 (4): 380–397. doi:10.1080/1070289X.2012.725512.

Greffrath, M. 1989. "'Wenn ich verzweifelt bin, was geht's mich an?' Gespräch mit Günther Anders." In *Die Zerstörung einer Zukunft – Gespräche mit emigrierten Sozialwissenschaftlern*, edited by M. Greffrath, 17–55. Frankfurt am Main: Campus.

Heffernan, M. 2011. *Wilful Blindness: Why We Ignore the Obvious at Our Peril*. New York: Simon and Schuster.

Heidegger, M. 1976. ""Nur noch ein Gott kann uns retten," Der Spiegel 30 (Mai, 1976): 193-219, Trans. by W. Richardson as "Only a God Can Save Us"." In *Heidegger: The Man and the Thinker*, 2010 edited by T. Sheehan, 45–67. New Brunswick, New Jersey: Transaction Publishers.

Howe, J. 2014. *Behind the Curve: Science and the Politics of Global Warming*. Seattle: University of Washington Press.

Libcom.org. 2014. The Obsolescence of Man, Vol I, Part 2: The World as Phantom and as Matrix: Philosophical Considerations on Radio and Television. https://libcom.org/library/obsolescence-man-volume-i-part-two-%E2%80%9C-world-phantom-matrix-philosophical-considerations-r

Libcom.org. 2015. *The Obsolescence of Man – Volume 2*. https://libcom.org/library/obsolescence-man-volume-2-g%C3%BCnther-anders

Liessmann, K. P. 2002. *Günther Anders: Philosophieren im Zeitalter der technologischen revolutionen*. München: C.H. Beck.

Michael, Y., and J. Barr. 2014. "(Mis)Reading Revelations: Apocalyptic Visions and Environmental Crisis & Augury: Elegy." *Undercurrents: Journal of Critical Environmental Studies* 18: 7–17.

Micheletti, M., D. Stolle, and D. Berlin. 2012. "Habits of Sustainable Citizenship: The Example of Political Consumerism." In *The Habits of Consumption*, edited by A. Warde and D. Southerton, 141–163. Helsinki: Helsinki Collegium for Advanced Studies.

Moon, B.-K. 2015. Secretary-General's Remarks at the United Nations Private Sector Forum New York, 26 September. http://www.un.org/sg/statements/index.asp?nid=9020

Müller, C. 2015. "Desert Ethics: Technology and the Question of Evil in Günther Anders and Jacques Derrida." *Parralax* 21 (1): 42–57. doi:10.1080/13534645.2014.988910.

Mumford, L. 1957. *The Transformations of Man*. London: G. Allen & Unwin.

Nietzsche, F. 1907. *Beyond Good and Evil*. translation by H. Zimmern. New York: Macmillan.

Ott, K., and R. Döring. 2004. *Theorie und Praxis starker Nachhaltigkeit*. Marburg: Metropolis.

Popper, K. 1957. *The Poverty of Historicism*. London: Routledge.

Ribolits, E. 1997. *Die Arbeit hoch?* Munich: Profil.

Richard, T., and C. Sunstein. 2008. *Nudge: Improving Decisions about Health, Wealth and Happiness*. Yale: Yale University Press.

Rieff, D. 2015. *The Reproach of Hunger: Food, Justice and Money in the 21st Century*. London: Verso.

Sassatelli, R. 2007. *Consumer Culture: History, Theory and Politics*. Los Angeles: Sage Publications.

Slater, D. 1997. *Consumer Culture and Modernity*. Cambridge, UK: Polity Press.

Spash, C. 2016. "This Changes Nothing: The Paris Agreement to Ignore Reality." *Globalizations* 13 (6): 928–933, doi:10.1080/14747731.2016.1161119.

Trentmann, F. 2007. "Introduction: Citizenship and Consumption." *Journal of Consumer Culture* 7 (2): 147–158. doi:10.1177/1469540507077667.

United Nations. 1987. *Our Common Future – Brundtland Report*. Oxford: Oxford University Press.

United Nations. 2015. Transforming Our World: The 2030 Agenda for Sustainable Development. http://www.un.org/pga/wp-content/uploads/sites/3/2015/08/120815_outcome-document-of-Summit-for-adoption-of-the-post-2015-development-agenda.pdf

Van Dijk, P. 2000. *Anthropology in the Age of Technology: The Philosophical Contributions of Günther Anders*. Amsterdam: Rodopi.

Von Humboldt, W. 1980. "Theorie der Bildung des Menschen." In *Wilhelm von Humboldt. Werke in fünf Bänden, Bd 1*, edited by A. Flitner and K. Giel, 234–240. Darmstadt: Wissenschaftliche Buchgesellschaft.

Webber, J. 2010. *Reading Sartre: On Phenomenology and Existentialism*. London: Routledge.

Apocalyptically blinded

Nina Isabella Moeller and J. Martin Pedersen

This is a reply to:

Ehgartner, Ulrike, Patrick Gould and Marc Hudson. 2017. "On the obsolescence of human beings in sustainable development." *Global Discourse*. 7 (1): 66–83. http://dx.doi.org/10.1080/23269995.2017. 1300417.

'There is a crack in everything/that's how the light gets in'
Leonard Cohen, Anthem.

As admirers of Anders' uncompromising vision and wit, we are delighted to have been invited to respond to Ehgartner et al.'s (2017) contribution to this special issue, in which they argue that Anders' concepts of 'promethean shame' and 'apocalyptic blindness' can help explain humanity's current situation and shed new light on the psychology of business-as-usual.

Anders writes in the foreword to the 1979 edition of '*Antiquiertheit des Menschen*'[1] (Anders 2009) that his main theses had – in the face of growing environmental threats – become even more relevant than they originally were. This lasting relevance had, in his own words, less to do with the quality of his analysis and more to do with the unfortunate state of the world and its humans. The evolution of his thought, however, is sorely missed as the Earth races past the 400 ppm mark, deeper into the anthropocene, and climate change disasters are no longer empty threats, but full-blown realities.

In this short response, we will raise some questions with regard to (1) apocalyptic blindness and (2) the apocalyptically blind. Firstly, as compelling as Anders' critique is with respect to the atomic bomb, one needs to ask whether it holds in the same way with respect to climate change. We think that something has changed in recent decades, which is also captured in debates centred on the concept of 'the anthropocene', which we take to denote a vision of our capacity to self-destruct – certainly a capacity to profoundly change our environment to a degree that registers on geological and evolutionary scales. In 2016, the problem is not that we cannot imagine the apocalypse, it is that we cannot imagine a way out of it.

While social movements have been warning about ecological destruction and lamenting widespread inertia at least since the 1960s, the mainstreaming of environmentalism with the Brundtland Report (WCED 1987) has spelled a commercialization of eco-threats. The dominant framing of humanity's current predicament emphasizes 'planetary limits' and impending environmental collapse: the apocalypse makes it into our consciousness daily. We are force-fed resource shortages, hurricanes, droughts, floods, wildfires and, say, Zika.

Yet the only proposal for a 'way-out' that gets onto the agenda is 'further in': sustainable development (or the now increasingly common 'green growth', a term with the sole redeeming feature that it does not hide its aspirations). 'Sustainability' as necessary response to environmental doom has become a global, post-political consensus (see Swyngedouw 2011) – managing technological and behavioural transformations while leaving the organizing principles of the capitalist market and liberal state incontestably in place, indeed consolidating them.[2] Electric cars, photovoltaic roof tiles, bioplastics and zero carbon holidays get sold by peddling dystopian imaginaries. Hence we could say that, rather than being blind *to* the apocalypse, we are now blinded *by* it; blinded so we cannot see a way out.

Our imagination has been stretched to the breaking point. Increasingly, democratic political processes are suspended in order to protect us from doom:[3] we have entered a permanent state of exception (Agamben 2005), which the narrative of constant crisis serves to legitimate (Skilling 2014). Conveniently, a sense of pervasive unease and anxiety permits the machine of accumulation unfettered acceleration.

Ehgartner et al. (2017) point out that Anders' answer to the predicament he identifies centres upon the development – the 'widening' – of our moral imagination: we must 'stretch' our imagination to begin grasping the consequences of our doing more fully. Instead, we argue that as our apocalyptic imagination is about to explode, we need to dream up visions for new/better/more appropriate/other forms of life. Given that there is widespread acceptance that ecological disaster is already with us now, we need to develop ways of coping with the fallout that makes human life worth living; terms like mitigation and adaptation sound hollower yet than the long co-opted 'sustainability'.[4]

How could we live together – with other humans as well as non-humans – in a world even more ravaged by extreme weather, pollution and consequent shrinking of habitable and fertile land? How would we feed, shelter, heal, enjoy? How would we raise our young? Without other visions, real or fictitious examples of other 'worlds', other ways of life, and the willingness to let them guide and inspire experiments in collectivity that do not rely on petroleum, rare earth metals or the commodity form, such questions might just remain unanswered.

We need to ask fundamental questions. We need to examine the way we metabolize the world, the way we reproduce our everyday every day. In other words, we need to ask such questions as philosophers once asked, before professionalism and library dust rendered their actions irrelevant.[5] Alternatively, we might get stuck in a scenario of authoritarian managerialism, concomitant social collapse and unreined violence wreaking more havoc than floods and desertification.

But who is this 'we' whom we summon, who continues to shepherd gadgets along the road to omnicide? Using the generic 'we' is especially problematic when human beings are meant. Critics of technology are, somewhat unsurprisingly, mostly deeply embedded in technological culture themselves, sometimes unable to see that humanity is (still) more variegated than that. Indeed, those social movements whose ideas were later co-opted for the sustainable development agenda, have been reacting to the industrial machine's threatening disasters by going back to the land, already for more than a century.[6]

It is crucial to realize that 'we' are not *all* apocalyptically blind(ed). 'We' are not only citizen-consumers in over-industrialized countries; 'we' are also subsistence farmers, indigenous forest dwellers, nomadic pastoralists and fisherpeople, neo-rural activists and others whose lives purposefully or inadvertently contribute to the continued existence of a world 'outside' of capitalist technocracy.[7]

We suggest that it is in 'their' spaces, through 'their' practices and relations that 'we' may find guidance on how to proceed towards a world in which humanity has a future. Dialogue is not enough. Complete immersion might be.

Notes

1. Vol 1, originally published in 1956.
2. Although Brexit, Trumpism and the general post-truth tendencies threaten with the kind of eco-fascistic future that an apocalypse might just 'justify'.
3. This varies between environmental, economic or terrorist doom.
4. 'Degrowth' might be one of the few 'goals' that is resistant to co-optation, and one we hold worth exploring as an alternative to 'sustainability'. Thanks to John O'Neill for pointing out this particular value of the term.
5. We also need to address a new and fundamental question: how can live in harmony with the microbiome, rather than wage a losing war on bacteria?
6. Needless to say, the Romantics went for walkabouts in disgust of the Satanic Mills in Engels' rendition of Blake's Christian critique. More specifically, however, the late nineteenth century saw the formation of *Lebensreform* (Life Reform) communes, such as Himmelsbach and Monte Verita in and around the German and Swiss alps, which clearly prefigured the 1960s and 1970s hippies (cf. Barlösius 1997). Particularly the work and followers of Rudolf Steiner have stood the test of time. These movements rejected urbanization, toxic medicine and food, while constructing viable alternatives still in existence. Certain philosophers at the time, notably Henri Bergson, also rejected the progressivist, teleological lemming-like march into the abyss and sought to push humanity in new and promising directions. Curiously, or paradoxically, Bergson's first public lecture in the U.S. caused the first traffic jam on Broadway in New York City (Henri Bergson, *Stanford Encyclopaedia of Philosophy*: http://plato.stanford.edu/entries/bergson/). It took two world wars and the advent of artificial insulin and antibiotics to 'restore faith' in the industrial machine, which admittedly gave some of us, in Euro-America, a few decades of prosperity. In other words, before we could arrive at the dismal scenario described by Anders as our inability to imagine the apocalypse, the more profound and genuinely original attempts at developing imaginaries for the purposes of avoiding precisely such an endpoint had to first be marginalized or destroyed. Are we going round in circles?
7. In Anders' sense of the word as 'the rule of machines'.

Disclosure statement

No potential conflict of interest was reported by the authors.

References

Agamben, G. 2005. *State of Exception*. Chicago: University of Chicago Press.

Anders, G. 2009. *Die Antiquiertheit Des Menschen Bd. I: Über Die Seele Im Zeitalter Der Zweiten Industriellen Revolution*. München: Beck.

Barlösius, E. 1997. *Naturgemäße Lebensführung: Zur Geschichte Der Lebensreform Um Die Jahrhundertwende*. Frankfurt a: M. Campus.

Ehgartner, U., P. Gould, and M. Hudson. 2017. "On the Obsolescence of Human Beings in Sustainable Development." *Global Discourse* 7 (1). doi:10.1080/23269995.2017.1300417.

Skilling, P. 2014. "Everyday Emergency: Crisis, Unease and Strategy in Contemporary Political Discourse." *Critical Policy Studies* 8 (1): 61–77. doi:10.1080/19460171.2013.862504.

Swyngedouw, E. 2011. "Depoliticized Environments: The End of Nature, Climate Change and the Post-Political Condition." *Royal Institute of Philosophy Supplement* 69: 253–274. doi:10.1017/S1358246111000300.

WCED (World Commission on Environment and Development). 1987. *Our Common Future*. Oxford: Oxford University Press.

Beyond sustainability: hope in a spiritual revolution?

Rachel Bathurst

ABSTRACT

A multi-disciplinary discourse on post-sustainability requires the entry of theology as a crucial element because, in presupposing a creator God who created the universe, it allows exploration of humanity's condition in relation to the natural environment in the context of a transcendent yet present divine otherness, a perspective unique to theology. This article draws on relevant theological literature to offer an emerging theology on sustainability and a fresh perspective for debate. It specifically addresses sustainability as perceived by the United Nations and accepted by governments in which global capitalism goes unchallenged and questions the plausibility of such an approach from a theological perspective. It does this by exploring the human condition shaped by the capitalist system, especially desire and the pursuit of freedom and how this interacts with the natural environment and compares this with God's purposes for humanity, nature and the world as his creation. An argument emerges in this paper which suggests that theology can offer the tools of hope in the shape of spiritual transformation and in the face of a failing illusory concept of sustainability.

The causes of irreversible anthropogenic environmental damage, such as that caused by climate change and biodiversity loss, are most often associated with economic growth and development (Adams 1991; Northcott 1996). The United Nation's (UN) sustainability agenda, herein simply the 'sustainability agenda', which is largely centred on the notion of sustainable development, attempts to address these issues by integrating human economic activity and social concerns with the natural environment. This approach is quickly becoming globally accepted as the panacea to the planet's sustainable future. Yet there is a growing concern that sustainability measures associated with sustainable development and other 'green' agendas are not succeeding in halting biodiversity loss (CoP 10 of the CBD 2010) or reducing greenhouse gas emissions (IPCC 2014). What happens when the present sustainability paradigm fails? This paper attempts to unravel the potential failure of the sustainability agenda from a Christian theological perspective, before going on to establish the foundations of a post-sustainability theology which can offer tools of hope for a renewed Earth in a paradigm beyond sustainability, and in doing so show the importance of a coherent Christian theology in a post-sustainability discourse.

However, the first question to ask is what can theology bring to a world beyond sustainability that has not already been tried? Historically, Christian socialist and liberal thought have brought with them social reform in various contexts and with varying degrees of success and failure. For example, the liberalist progression towards a welfare system in Britain brought Christian ethics successfully into a capitalist society providing care for the impoverished and less able. Wogaman (e.g. 1988) and Preston (e.g. 1991) are, according to Atherton (1992), the key proponents of Christian liberalist thinking in the last century found in Western society. On the other hand, the Christian socialism of the liberation movements, rooted in the abhorrence of social poverty created by a capitalist order, has perhaps had less longevity around the world but no less success at social transformation (Gutiérrez 1988).

In today's context humanity is facing an uncertain future, one that has the potential to see change in the political economy if the sustainability agenda fails. As Atherton (1992) suggests, we are in an interim era and as such it is 'precisely the time and the place for developing and testing provisional frameworks for living' (204). This is where Christian theology is of use as a new paradigm beyond the sustainability agenda emerges, as it not only has a history of social reform and transformation to draw on, whilst learning from mistakes, but it speaks through the different social paradigms that the world has seen throughout its 2000 year history. Although I do not propose an alternative political economy in this paper, I am convinced that a Christian theological perspective holds the fundamental elements upon which to base hope in a post-sustainable world, and from which a new world order will develop through a spiritual revolution, whether essentially socialist, liberal or another in nature.

In a contemporary context, the complexities of the social order require not just the liberation of the oppressed and those in poverty from the injustices of the capitalist system towards a social revolution as in the way of Marxism, but forces examination of the vast environmental concerns facing the planet. This twofold exploration is the concern of many ecotheologians who in their attempt to understand ways to respond to the environmental crisis also apply critique of the capitalist system and its effects on the natural and social orders, although their aim is to favour redeveloping a theology which can be a robust help to respond to the environmental crisis rather than proposing alternative political economies. For example, Hall (2006) has recently re-established the motif 'stewardship' as a means for a Christian response towards caring for the world in a more holistic way, despite historical biblical connotations towards advocating domination over nature (White 1967; Santmire 1985), which has led to wide discourse over the use of the term 'dominion' in Genesis 1 (Berry 2006; Hiebert 2011). The re-emergence of the term 'stewardship' in Christian circles might provide a useful connection with the use of stewardship outside of Christianity, especially in policy circles where it is widely recognised as humanity's duty to care for the Earth (Osborn 2006; Patten 2006) or in interfaith connections such as with a Muslim ethos of humanity being entrusted by God to safeguard his Earth (Omar Naseef 1986). However, critics of Hall's (2006) model claim that his focus on the servanthood of Jesus' life does not fully reflect the relational aspect of a life in God through the redemption of Christ and has been rejected (e.g. Scott 2003;

Page 2006; Deane-Drummond 2008) in favour of redeveloping doctrine towards solving the issue of sustainability.

The Christian doctrines of creation, through which the origins of the universe are ascribed to God, and of the Trinity, through which God is understood as the three persons of Father, Son and Holy Spirit, are often seen as an appropriate place to start for authors choosing this approach because it allows the fundamental relationships between nature, humanity and God to be explored (Bouma-Prediger 2001; Scott 2003, 2004; Ayre 2014). Eschatology, the study of the time of Christ's future return, is also seen as 'the key to an adequate ecological anthropology' (Conradie 2005, 13), which some pursue with the idea of the seventh day of creation (the Sabbath) described in Genesis 1, as being a significant factor in an eschatological understanding of creation (Moltmann 1985; Santmire 2006; Deane-Drummond 2008). Systematic Christian theology makes use of all the important doctrines, and more recently this theological framework has been used to explore single environmental issues more holistically. For example, see Northcott and Scott (2014) for a collection of doctrinal essays exploring the issues surrounding climate change.

Christian or virtue ethics to a theology of nature or specific environmental issue is another avenue taken by Christian ecotheologians attempting to understand the moral role rooted in Christianity of humans towards nature (Northcott 1996; Deane-Drummond 2004; Northcott 2014). However, most theologians have yet to apply a theological critique specifically on the sustainability agenda, or to acknowledge the possibility of a post-sustainability paradigm, although few have gone some way into addressing the need for alternative approaches. For example, Bookless (2007) has proposed an alternative sustainability model based on biblical themes.

Ecotheology also offers a way in for more radical ideas associated with feminism or liberation theologies. Ideas which draw on the interrelatedness of the material and spiritual between humanity, God and nature to counter a society of individualism (McFague 1993; Primavesi 2003) are situated here, whilst other ecotheologians are more concerned with the oppression of women and nature within a patriarchal capitalist society (Merchant 1990; Ruether 1996).

A turn to relevant work outside of ecotheology reveals a range of views engaged with the political economy, and in particular capitalism. Whilst some apply theological critique of capitalism with a view to largely accepting its presence within a global society but with changes according to their recommendations (Weber 1958; Novak 1993; Wogaman 1986), the liberationists draw on biblical insights to bring about a socialist order (e.g. Gutiérrez 1988; Sobrino 1988). More recently, Goodchild critiques the global market economy through the development of a theology of money (2009), whilst other scholars are proposing radical alternative economies based on biblical insight, such as Duchrow (1998), or based on the gift of Christ's sacrifice (Milbank 1996, 2001; Bell 2012).

In my view, in order to explore the sustainability agenda and the aftermath of its failure satisfactorily, a combination of capitalist critique and redevelopment of doctrines is required, which is where this work is located. Firstly, I call on the work of two contemporary theologians, Daniel Bell Jr and William Cavanaugh, who have given recent theological perspectives on the political economy of capitalism (Bell 2012; Cavanaugh 2008). My aim is to understand the underpinning drivers for a general societal acceptance of the sustainability agenda from a theological perspective through their work. I then combine their ideas with a contemporary ecotheolgian, Ernst Conradie, whose primary driver is to respond to the environmental crisis through the knowledge of the Christian faith, ecology and social analysis, and also the influential modern theologian Jurgen Moltmann's doctrine of creation. In this endeavour, I propose that the foundation of a robust theological challenge to the sustainability agenda will be developed, and which will open into a grounding of Christian hope and an establishment of the normative Christian context from which an alternative political economy might develop. I, therefore, assert that Christian theology plays a significant part in the establishment of a discourse on the post-sustainability paradigm. This research forms the first part of a longer postgraduate project which theologically critiques international sustainability policy, funded by the Lincoln Theological Institute at the University of Manchester.

Terminology

Before I begin, clarification on the terminology used is necessary, firstly, in the use of the term 'community'. Life on Earth in Christian theology has recently been ascribed the term 'Earth community' (Rasmussen 1996; Conradie 2005). Community often describes a group of people with similar interests or origins, but it can also mean 'the condition of sharing or having certain attitudes in common' (Oxford Dictionaries 2016). The latter description concerns all who inhabit the Earth, humanity and nature together, and share in the abundance that God provides through the Earth. Community in this sense is about relationships that work so that all members have their share providing what they need, and I shall use this term to mean all members living in solidarity with one another on Earth, including human and non-human.

Clarification of the terms 'creation' and 'nature', and the difference between them is also necessary given the ambiguity around the use of these terms. In a Christian theology God created the entire cosmos, all living and non-living things, and all that is seen and unseen. Although the doctrine of creation is far richer in its discourse about the events in the creation act itself and how God relates to his creation, I will use the term 'creation' here simply to mean that which God created. The term 'nature' is also problematic, being either abstract or actual in meaning. It can mean the world of the non-human (Castree 2005) or as Williams (1983) suggests, the whole material world itself, often including humans. A second meaning of nature is the essence of something with certain physiological or inherent characteristics which give the object of focus its uniqueness, or it can imply an inherent order (Castree 2005) or force directing the world (Williams 1983). What is clear is that the number of alternative meanings to nature illustrates the difficulties that arise when applying nature as a term.

Moreover perspectives of nature are often socially constructed, where cultural perceptions influence our reading of nature. Where Castree (2005) explains this through the de-naturalisation of nature, which views nature as not a 'real' entity, but what is being represented in nature, Habgood (2002) suggests social construction of nature is about what we perceive as natural in relation to the meanings placed on words associated with a digression from our perception of normality, such as 'artificial', 'unnatural', 'non-natural', and 'super-natural'. The opposite view to de-naturalisation is to assume that the world beyond the human is 'real', in terms of a natural order to be studied, regardless of human perception (Castree 2005). It is this 'real' concept of nature that I shall be using in this paper, with the understanding of nature as an order with multiple living and non-living entities beyond the human. God's creation is also 'real' in terms of physical matter to be studied, and includes nature as a real entity. However, it is important to clarify that creation and nature are not interchangeable terms due to their different meanings, as Scott (2003) makes clear.

A broken earth community

In attempting to understand how Christian theology might offer hope in a post-sustainability paradigm, a look at God's original intentions for his creation might help. In a Christian theology, the relational is paramount to God. God has created a community on Earth, both human and non-human, to live in harmonious relationship with each other out of the abundance of the created Earth in order for all members to flourish (Conradie 2005), whilst also being rooted in the relationality of the Trinitarian God (Edwards 2014), the giver and sustainer of life. In other words, in a Christian theology, the relational aspect of this 'common realm' of God–nature–humanity (Scott 2003) is the vital element to the health or flourishing of all life on Earth. This approach has similarities to an Islamic theology which has the Unity of God, reflected in the union of humanity and nature as a central concept. However, whereas Muslims understand that humanity is responsible for upholding the unity and integrity of God's creation and that we will be judged on our actions to keep the balance and harmony of the Earth whilst God himself is set apart from his creation (Omar Naseef 1986), the Christian understands God to be involved in his creation, and it is God who sustains his creation. Either way the significance of harmonious community then to both Earth and God suggests a theology of the post-sustainability paradigm is to be located in the relational.

However, in a contemporary context, the Earth community is broken. This brokenness is historical. The separation of nature and humanity occurred through the interplay of anthropocentric biblical interpretation (White 1967; Santmire 1985) and rising anthropocentric scientific attitudes on cultural values (Santmire 1985; Bauckham 2006), which in turn influenced theology and science. The influence of Christianity's anthropocentric orientation on Western culture is acknowledged by those who practice other religions, especially Buddhism which rejects anthropocentric views towards nature in favour of a more holistic perspective of seeing the whole of human life as a part of nature's cycles (Titmuss 1994).

Into an already broken interrelatedness between humanity and nature therefore, where 'we feel no real affinity for the Earth and no real sense of loss when it is being seriously scarred and impaired' (McDonagh 1986, 60–61), comes the establishment of a global market economy. The culture of the capitalist economy not only makes the nature-humanity divide acceptable by measuring human wellbeing in terms of wealth accumulation without reference to nature (Northcott 1996), it deepens the divide between all members of the Earth community and humanity's relationship with God. The insertion of capitalist values and tools into the humanity-nature divide is best illustrated in the implementation of the UN's Convention on Biological Diversity (CBD), launched in 1992 at the Rio de Janeiro Earth summit, which I will turn to next.

Case study: the CBD

The CBD, a global legal instrument with 196 national and international signatories, was developed as the result of the culmination of effort by the UN and other international conservation bodies in the 1970s and 1980s to integrate the progress of human development and nature conservation aims, especially in the wake of the World Commission on Environment and Development Report, *Our Common Future* (Brundtland 1987) on sustainable development. The CBD marked the first global legal agreement with the threefold aims of conserving biodiversity, sustainably using its components and sharing equitably the benefits arising from the use of genetic resources (United Nations 1992). Its 2050 vision states, 'biodiversity is valued, conserved, restored and wisely used, maintaining ecosystem services, sustaining a healthy planet and delivering benefits essential for all people' (CoP 10 of the CBD 2010, 7). Such vision and aims mark this UN agreement as being the one that holds the torch of hope for biodiversity and the resilience of nature to withstand better the impacts of human development, whilst allowing humanity to continue in its endeavour to pursue its own wellbeing. The 2050 vision continues to envisage all people 'living in harmony with nature' (CoP 10 of the CBD 2010, 7).

Whilst the CBD's operative framework, the *ecosystem approach*, gives a foundation of principles that seeks to integrate adaptive environmental management principles with socioeconomic factors (CBD 2004), national and international Biodiversity Targets, which include actions to reduce the rate of biodiversity loss and also to integrate socioeconomic and nature conservation policies, are to be met by 2020 (CoP 10 of the CBD 2010). The significance of this in relation to the further separation of the Earth community through the use of capitalist tools, is tied in with the launch of the Millennium Ecosystem Assessment (MA) in 2005 (Millennium Ecosystem Assessment 2005), which mapped and assessed the state of the world's ecosystems in terms of ecosystem goods and services[1] for the first time and linked these to human wellbeing. By breaking ecosystems down into units of goods and services it was now possible to evaluate ecosystems in economic terms, and to allocate and distribute the costs and benefits to society of the sustainable use of natural resources (TEEB 2010). In other words, how changes in ecosystems influence the wellbeing of humans could now be measured in economic terms.

The significance for the implementation of the *ecosystem approach* and meeting the 2020 biodiversity targets is that it provides a way to integrate socioeconomic policies with those associated with nature conservation (POST 2011). Nature can be plugged into wellbeing indices or measured in terms of its capital. Decision makers can make informed decisions on which ecosystem goods and services would benefit their communities most, and therefore decide which ones would be worth investing in and conserving and which would not. Capitalist economic incentives in the form of Payment for Ecosystem Services and Biodiversity credits and offsetting are encouraged by the UN to maintain the protection of ecosystems by landowners. The aim is to benefit humans and nature by choosing the 'correct' bundle of services which maintain healthy ecosystems and bring about human wellbeing measured through economic growth (POST 2007).

The concern with the valuation of ecosystem goods and services is that the capitalist model used assumes that ecosystems are 'the constant and stable background for economic activity' (O'Neill and Kahn 2000, 333) rather than understanding that ecosystems are complex and highly dynamic entities. The thousands of interactions between elements of the ecosystem change both spatially and temporally within the ecosystem and with others around it (O'Neill 2001) enabling the functioning of the whole integrative system. However, these crucial interactions are not recognised in such a model making the total economic value of the ecosystem useless (Hussen 2013). As Büscher *et al.* state, valuing ecosystems through capitalist markets breaks the connectivity and relationships that are fundamental to the resilience of ecosystems, and suggest that capitalism has the potential to provoke a 'large-scale ecological crises' (2012, 6), where humans are 'deriving goods and services rather than participating in ecosystem dynamics' (O'Neill 2001, 3279). In theological terms it is the relations between members of the Earth community and their interactions with the non-living parts of God's creation, in the context of relations with God, which maintain the health of the global ecosystem.

Within an already separated Earth community then, the relations between members of the community are being further separated, through the goal of human wellbeing and under the guise of sustainability, as illustrated by the current economic implementation of the *ecosystem approach* to meet the CBD Biodiversity Targets. At a time when climate change impacts are increasing in severity, the UN have potentially unleashed the catalyst for the end of the sustainability paradigm and the hope that goes with it.

In choosing human wellbeing as the ultimate goal, the sustainability agenda has been misled to potentially disastrous consequences. It means that socioeconomic needs have priority over nature in national and international policies, and the dominant utilitarian market economy, which has human wellbeing as the ultimate goal, facilitates the advancement of this priority. The result, as Messer (2006) notes, is that the pursuit of individual desire to attain the goal of human wellbeing becomes our fundamental motivation and priority in decision making. The personal pursuit of wellbeing leads to individualism which fundamentally opposes the relational community that God has intended.

In the pursuit of individual wellbeing each individual decides on his or her own merit what to attain for their own sake and not for the common good. Moreover, even though individual wellbeing is subjective, it becomes the foundation of the social order and, as MacIntyre (2007) notes, societies are unable to agree on solutions when moral judgements are required, such as in an environmental crisis, and where Christian morals previously offered a morality base for decision making in society, now no reference to God exists. However, as Northcott (2001) highlights, leaving God out of such decision making or morality leaves him out of any purpose he may have for his creation. He continues stating that it is left to humanity to transform creation according to their own will, without guidance from God or understanding of the limits of his created order to decide, with humanity claiming the ultimate responsibility for saving the earth. God's creative work and healing of the Earth becomes a human achievement; one that is failing in the guise of the UN's sustainability agenda in which human wellbeing is the goal.

The consequences for an Earth community where humanity and nature are separated through historical and contemporary utilitarian cultural and scientific and theological attitudes towards nature, and in which human society suffers from the pursuing of individualistic goals created by the capitalist culture, is that the dynamic and complex interrelations between ecosystem elements could break apart. That is the non-human members of the Earth community are being separated, and the question remains how much separation can the Earth community take, and will the sustainability agenda be the solution? A theological understanding is important here because when understood in the context of God's intentions for the Earth to live in community with each other, any breakdown in relations is considered damage to the Earth. As separation deepens and spreads across the entire Earth community, a view of a spiritually diseased Earth emerges, with the only remedy being reconciliation. Although some are attempting to understand the Earth's tipping points in order to try to stem the damage (e.g. Steffan et al. 2015), the theological perspective that I propose offers hope through a revolution which will recover the relational aspect of the Earth community which I argue is vital for sustaining the Earth.

In attempting to understand how reconciliation between nature and humanity can be brought about, an understanding of the problem is necessary before consideration of a theological solution is made. In the next section I explore what I believe to be the roots of the problem; that of the work of the individualistic capitalist culture and its consumerist values on humanity's desire which undermines the reconciliation process and also the sustainability agenda, and illustrates the need for a spiritual revolution if the Earth community is to be maintained. The work of two contemporary Christian theologians, Cavanaugh and Bell, is helpful here.

The roots of our problem: distorted desire and a lack of telos

The crisis that we face through anthropocentric damage to the environment is not simply something to put right in the ecological realm, but as Northcott (1996) and Conradie (2005) claim, it is a moral crisis belonging to the 'dominant and increasingly global economic system and the consumerist values supporting it' (Conradie 2005, 2). If Conradie and Northcott are right, it would be appropriate to explore Christian theological perspectives on the drivers and morality of capitalism in the attempt to get to the root of the problem.

Cavanaugh's (2008) comparison of the concept of freedom found through the market economy with that found in God's purposes, or *telos*, is a helpful place to start. The market economy gives freedom of choice to an individual pursuing their own wellbeing. Some authors believe that individual choices can also benefit the common good when enough of the same choices are made and that this is akin to the work of Christian freedom (Novak 1993), a notion which is rooted in Adam Smith's concept of the 'invisible hand' of the market doing the work for the common good by default instead of relying on moral decisions (Smith 1776). However, Cavanaugh's (2008) view is that Christian freedom and the freedom of choice found in the market are not the same. He believes that freedom in a capitalist market is an illusion because it is freedom *from* interference or coercion by others for an individual to pursue their own desire, whereas real freedom is freedom *for* a purpose, or telos. In Christian theology this is freedom towards the ultimate end which God has intended for his entire creation. Cavanaugh claims that telos enables people to judge what is good or not, and in a free market in which there are no moral choices as every choice is subjective and based on the goal of individual wellbeing, there is no telos. According to Cavanaugh where there is no telos, humans are autonomous and cut-off from God and are not free. Humans, he continues, are free when they are participating in the telos of God's grace.

The illusory freedom of the capitalist market, according to Cavanaugh (2008), suggests that human desire is endless and that anything desired can be pursued without any moral decisions having to be made. If true freedom is found in the telos of God, Cavanaugh asserts, it helps us to decide between true desire and false desire, and without which we are not free to make informed choices. He concludes that capitalism cannot therefore produce real freedom, thereby further accentuating individualism over community and undermining the relational intention of God's purposes for his creation. To summarise, Cavanaugh claims that the freedom found in capitalism is illusory, offering no sense of morality, and has no regard for telos. It is a freedom that breaks apart the communal relationship and instead limits the relational human to an individual unit in a society of other individual units with no purpose or morals. The goal of individual wellbeing offered by the free market vastly truncates God's intentions for the human to live in a social dimension for the flourishing of the whole of the Earth community. The unseen limitations imposed by capitalism therefore means its freedom is illusory, as Cavanaugh describes.

Individualism, the largest factor in the cause of the environmental crisis, according to Francis (2015), is created through selfish desire (Long 2000) to consume. In turning to Bell's (2012) work, which draws on Deleuze's writings on desire (Deleuze and Guattari 1983; Deleuze and Parnet 1987), Bell claims that desire is the root motivation of humans through which creativity and productiveness flow. He endorses Deleuze and Guattari's (1987) view that capitalism holds this positive desire 'hostage' transforming it into labour and anonymity through globalised multinational businesses, and into its negative form of consumption, enabling the capitalist economy to grow and succeed. Moreover, Deleuze and Guattari (1987) believe that the power of capitalism is its ability to incorporate diverse social constructions without needing external forces or homogenous modes of production to succeed in any given political economy. Even governments globally have become subservient to the power of capitalism, they claim (Deleuze and Guattari 1983). Bell (2012) summarises this by stating that desire is liberated from its previous context and disciplined by globalised capitalism culminating in human desire becoming subservient to capitalism.

Bell's (2012) development of the discipline of desire by capitalism is a crucial element in understanding how capitalism undermines the process of reconciliation between the members of the Earth community and God. Bell claims that desire orientated towards capitalism is a distortion of human desire blocking our relationship with God, each other and the rest of creation. He insists this is a 'cataclysmic change' (90) and a revolution of a theological nature which forces people to desire something other than that which God has originally intended. This notion also implies that a theological revolution is necessary to return to God, although Turpin (2012) understands the desire that motivates capitalism to be 'spiritual', rather than theological. Seen in a spiritual capacity allows the exploration of the power of the capitalist system to drive spiritual behaviours such as consumerism, the values of which turn human desire into a negative motivation orientated towards self, rather than orientated towards God. It is consumerist values that transform desire to drive the pursuit of individual, but illusory, freedom, which truncates God's intentions for the Earth community.

The idea that consumerism is a spiritual activity is significant to the theology in this paper. Cavanaugh (2008) explains that through consumerism people pursue 'meaning and identity, a way of connecting with other people' (36), which as Turpin (2012) describes brings loyalty and a religious understanding to the capitalist market. Moreover, Miller (2004) views consumer desire and religious desire as similar entities in a pursuit of transcendence and self-transformation. Although apparently similar, they are not the same as Cavanaugh (2008) claims. He proposes that consumerism is a restless activity creating a restless spirit because of the insatiable desire for 'something better'. This restless spirit, Cavanaugh continues, is due to the lack of telos present in the capitalist system. The distortion of desire towards capitalist values, as described by Bell (2012) drives the restless spirit. Both Bell and Cavanaugh believe that as the capitalist system allocates resources under conditions of scarcity this produces an insatiable desire continuously pursuing, but never attaining, human wellbeing. With telos, however, Cavanaugh (2008) claims that human flourishing, as opposed to human wellbeing, and the flourishing of the whole of creation is purposed and will be achieved.

The power of capitalism distorts positive desire orientated towards God, into an inward selfish desire which disregards God and his relational purposes for us. It shapes human behaviour, holding humans captive and making us unable to change or even to want to change. It gives humans the false perception of ourselves as in a better situation than the theologically normative, that is the values that belong to God and were present before humanity entered the world. In actuality, it diminishes social relationships and favours the pursuit of selfish wealth and power to realise one's dreams. Individualism is preferred to community; expression of self is a priority over obedience to God; individuals are encouraged to make choices to benefit one's self alone; relationships are competitive; and others are viewed in terms of how they can serve our self-serving projects (Milbank 1996; Bell 2012). As Turpin (2012) laments, in holding matters of the spirit captive, Christians and non-Christians alike are unable to choose to stand outside the capitalist system which directs spiritual energies into materialism which means, Bell (2012) continues, Christians cannot worship or desire God as they were created to do.

It is pertinent here to note O'Conner's (1988) observations on the inherent weakness of the capitalist system which he attempts to show through Marx's contradiction of capitalism and his own second contradiction between the conditions of production and the productive forces and relations. He asserts that the capitalist system reverts to a socialist form after a time of economic crisis, although he makes clear that what results is a distortion of socialist ideas. However, the implication remains that the default or normative state is a social order tending towards community and cooperation, and one that belies the Christian normative of God's pre-existing and intended social order based on relationships in his creation. On this observance alone, capitalism goes against the Christian theological normative grain, bringing human desire along with it, so that an inherent tension exists in all who are caught up in the capitalist paradigm. Whilst capitalism remains dominant the Earth will remain in tension, never able to flourish. An alternative is paramount if God's intentions for his creation are to be realised. What that might look like is not the subject of this paper, although it might follow from my conclusions, but what is relevant here is how an understanding of God's purposes for the world gives a perspective that can be built on for future hope in a post-sustainability paradigm, the outworking of which is likely to be determined through interdisciplinary dialogue.

To summarise, according to Cavanaugh (2008) and Bell (2012), humans have a God-given condition to desire, but the direction of desire is the crucial factor, and as Cavanaugh implies, a reorientation of this desire towards God and his intended purposes for his creation in order for it to flourish is required if people are to be truly free. Turning to God in this way, both Cavanaugh and Bell suggest, will re-establish relations and individualism will recede whilst the desire to live-in-community will increase. The restless consumerist spirit which lacks telos, will find its home in the telos of God. The proposal that Cavanaugh and Bell allude to is a spiritual revolution which re-orientates humanity with God in order to overcome desire's distortion and find true freedom. But is this what is required to reconcile the Earth community and bring about hope in a post-sustainability paradigm? In order to answer this question from a Christian theological perspective, I will bring the root of the problem as I have perceived it through Bell and Cavanaugh, into the context of a creation theology. The ideas of contemporary ecotheologian, Ernst Conradie, and the modern influential theologian Jurgen Moltmann are of use here.

Reconciliation of the Earth community: re-establishing humanity's worth

Many authors find that the attempt to understand God's intention for his Earth community is an appropriate starting point when entering into a redevelopment of a creation theology. Conradie (2005) picks up on the idea of the Earth community as God's household describing it as the ordering of the household economy, in order to show how this requires humanity to communicate and live within the God given order allowing the whole of it to flourish. He proposes that 'the whole household of God is precious in God's eyes' (80), and he sees no requirement 'to defend a position of special status for humans in God's household on the basis of human uniqueness' (80), as an anthropocentric view might do. Conradie believes that although unique human characteristics are to be treasured, they do not give us special privileges or position in God's household. The distinctiveness of humans to other creatures 'can be affirmed and treasured as long as it enriches the earth community' (Conradie 2005, 81). Therefore according to Conradie every member of God's household is unique and special to God and has a vocation to fulfil. There is inherent value, or worth, in all members of the community.

A note is necessary here to indicate my preference of the term 'worth' over 'value' used in this sense, which is best described by Habgood (2002). He states that 'value implies somebody doing the valuing, whereas worth inheres in the thing itself. In the light of its own nature … every form of life pursues its own good in its own way, and its worth lies precisely in this individual pursuit' (71). I will use worth to mean inherent characteristics of life.

According to Conradie (2005), all creatures in the Earth community, including humans, have worth, because each is precious to God and each is important to the whole community on Earth. Every member has a vocation, and a reason to exist. That is to enable the whole Earth community to flourish. This implies purpose inherent in each member of creation. The bible confirms that God sees his creation as 'good' (Genesis 1), implying a characteristic within each member is goodness, a given quality as Habgood (2002) observes. Indeed theologians, such as Northcott, describe the worth of nature as 'the existence of value and moral significance' (1996, 92–93) in the natural order created by God, and its rediscovery is necessary for human-nature reconciliation. This, in my view is only part of the story as the requirement to understand humanity's worth is also necessary for human-nature reconciliation. Francis (2015) understands it through his assertion that individualism derived from the pursuit of desire for human wellbeing and happiness through material satisfaction, causes not just environmental damage, but also leads to a lack of personal value given to each individual by others. A renewal of human relations with each other is required, Francis continues, before reconciliation with nature happens. This would suggest that the lack of worth placed on nature in our utilitarian culture is also manifested in society, implying that the work of capitalism has increased separation, not just between humanity and nature, but within the human social order as community experiences diminish and as desire of self-fulfilment becomes the normative cultural value.

Cavanaugh (2008) and Bell (2012) show how capitalism limits humans, but the deception offers wellbeing and freedom, which is illusory. Humans are deceived into thinking their worth is located in negative consumptive values, rather than the positive telos of God's love and grace. Humanity may have misunderstood the inherent worth of nature in their utilitarian disregard of its needs and limits, but humans have also misunderstood their *own worth* in relation to nature and God. Humanity has limited the flourishing of nature and the flourishing of itself, by seeking its own wellbeing, rather than that of the Earth community's flourishing through the telos of God's purposes for his creation. *The sustainability agenda is not working because the goal is wrong.* Advocates of sustainable development, in trying to integrate humanity and nature through sustainability measures, are deceived and instead find that the separation between humanity and nature, and also within nature, is deepened.

The importance of telos as a concept for a post-sustainability theology appears to be the key that holds the emerging theology together. What is this telos then that God has intended for the Earth community, and why is it so important for its flourishing? In order to understand this question, a turn to the influential work of Moltmann (1985) is required. Moltmann declared that humans are not the 'crowning glory' of creation, as a traditional anthropocentric Christianity and culture would believe, but that this is the place of the Sabbath, described in the biblical creation account in Genesis 1 where the Sabbath is the biblical seventh day of creation. On the preceding 6 days the Genesis account tells us that God created the Earth and all it needs to function. He created the sea and sky, the land with all sorts of vegetation on it, all kinds of animals to fill the land, sea and sky, including humans which were to fill all parts of the Earth and according to Conradie (2005), have a unique role within the Earth community, but without special status and, therefore, have no reason to dominate nature in a utilitarian fashion because all are precious in God's eyes. Moltmann's (1985) theology, in line with Conradie's view, claims that humanity, created on the same day as the other creatures, is not the reason for God's creative act.

Therefore, the goal of creation, the telos, is not human wellbeing, as it is in the sustainability agenda, but the Sabbath. If this is the case what is it about the Sabbath that brings about the flourishing of the whole of the Earth community and can give hope? Moltmann (1985) states that the clue is found in what God does with the seventh day following his creative activity in the preceding 6 days. It is the seventh day that God blessed. Although God *declared* that his creation in the other days 'was good' (Genesis 1), Moltmann continues, inhering not just the Earth community with goodness and worth, but the entire cosmos, he *blessed* the actual day when it came to the seventh day. Everything that the seventh day, or the Sabbath, represents is blessed. God's telos, and therefore, the flourishing of the Earth community, is associated with all that the Sabbath represents. Moltmann's notion of the Sabbath as telos could be critical in the development of a theology of post-sustainability and requires closer attention.

Firstly, the consideration that God blesses rest within this Sabbath day and what this means for God's creation is warranted. Bratton (2006) suggests that the Sabbath rest is about the work of the Holy Spirit renewing creation. For example, in Leviticus 25.2–1 God gives a Sabbath year of rest for the land every seventh year, which both Moltmann (1985) and Northcott (2006) see as significant for the land in retaining its fertility, and shows that God understands the importance of land for all the creatures that dwell in it. Moltmann (1985) expands this view. He proposes that the Sabbath is the time when God rests from his work of creation so that he can be free *for* his completed creation. He claims that God's work is completed only through this rest, and out of this rest 'spring the blessing and sanctification of the seventh day' (278). Moltmann continues claiming that God rests on the Sabbath allowing his creation to rest from work and 'to exist in his presence' (1985, 279).

Therefore, according to Moltmann (1985), the restlessness of all living creatures in this world finds its blessing of rest with God in the Sabbath, which therefore provides a space of freedom from activity which is not blessed, including striving for happiness and human wellbeing, the bonds of a life held hostage to capitalism. The contrast can clearly be seen between God's restful and joyful purpose for his creation, leading to its blessing, and modernity's striving and consumerist restlessness, leading to the destruction of God's relational purposes for creation.

Therefore, the first thing to notice is that the Sabbath is for rest, praise and worship of God. Without respecting this day, those who desire the values that capitalism maintains are held hostage, unable to be renewed or rested, always striving for happiness. Humans find their place in the context of the Sabbath being the pinnacle of God's creation. They find their true worth beside nature, in solidarity, being blessed in the rest given to us on the Sabbath, and together praising God. On this account then, God's restful and joyful purpose for his creation to flourish is found in the telos that Cavanaugh (2008) describes.

A second theological enquiry into the notion of the Sabbath is of significance to a post-sustainability paradigm. The Sabbath can be seen as a metaphor for an *eschatological* day, which describes a time towards the ultimate goal or end (Santmire 2006). Santmire observes that the Sabbath day in the Genesis account has no evening and therefore no end. The whole of creation is orientated towards this day to come, when Christ will come again to reign and creation will be fulfilled in eternal joy. Moltmann (1985) believes that all of creation is orientated towards an ultimate end in God which can be found in the Sabbath. The eschatological Sabbath is the time when all will be blessed as all rest in praise and worship of God eternally. The fulfilment of all of creation in a renewed Earth through the work of the Holy Spirit, affirms humanity's place within the Earth community (Scott 2003). It orientates humanity towards God, rather than the orientation away from God and distorted desire towards capitalist consumer values (Bell 2012). As Conradie (2005) states, we 'can only understand the place and vocation of humanity in the Earth community if we have a sense of the destiny or telos of creation and of humanity…. Moreover, it is only in the eschatological consummation that the goodness of creation can be affirmed *and* that redemption from sin can be secured finally'. (13)

Rae's (2006) understanding, pertinent to this view, is that by recognising the Sabbath, the telos for creation is understood as that of giving God glory through his relationality of love, which is achieved in Christ's resurrection and through the power of the Spirit. The Sabbath, he states, challenges the use of nature for our own wellbeing as the ultimate aim of human relation with creation, as with the aims of the sustainability agenda, and that the Sabbath is not an ethic or policy but a direction with an ethos and a goal towards which we must be directed.

Moltmann's (1985) and Conradie's (2005) work draw out the need for humanity to re-establish our true worth in the context of the rest of the Earth community, that of nature, and in the context of a relationship with God and his intentions for the whole of his Earth community. Humans have limited themselves and nature by focusing on human wellbeing as the ultimate goal and not on God or his purposes for his creation. Establishing an eschatological Sabbath and all that it represents as the goal of creation, places humanity in its proper context and gives freedom from striving for unattainable human wellbeing based on economic growth. In the Sabbath, the relational aspect of God's intentions, vital for the flourishing of the Earth community, is given its proper context through each member in solidarity with one another orientated towards God. The Sabbath used in this sense is a metaphor, which represents the ultimate intentions of God for his creation and the fulfilment of the flourishing of his creation, and it is from here that a post-sustainability theology emerges.

Conclusion

A Christian theological perspective on the sustainability agenda highlights distorted ambitions and the demise of the relational, vital for God's sustaining purposes for creation. This is corroborated through the illustration of the global implementation of the CBD through the *ecosystem approach*, which facilitates the integration of nature conservation policies with a policy framework orientated towards economic growth and has the potential to be the catalyst along with the impacts of climate change to bring about the post-sustainability paradigm. Payments for Ecosystem Services and other capitalist tools are being endorsed by the UN to achieve the sustainability aims of the CBD, and are being taken up at an unprecedented speed with the potential to deepen the separation of an already broken Earth community. The hope of reconciliation between the members of the Earth community in a Christian theology is through a spiritual revolution which seeks to locate the healing within the relational. To understand how this might be achieved the root of the problem has to be uncovered, which starts with a distorted human desire limiting our freedom.

Humanity has not understood its proper worth and has limited itself by a distortion of desire away from God as the intended focus of our desire, towards the consumerist values of a capitalist culture into an illusion of autonomous freedom without purpose. This illusion gives us a sense of status, meaning and identity. However, in actuality, by not understanding our true worth as members of the whole community of Earth in solidarity with each other, each as precious as each other, we actually rob ourselves of the true freedom found in God's purpose for his whole creation, including humans. It is as though in choosing to pursue the illusions of capitalism with its individualist consumer values giving humanity a sense of significance, humanity has chosen not to enter into the full worth of being human. The pursuit of distorted desire limits the flourishing of humanity and nature in its relentless self seeking of ultimate wellbeing. God's intentions for humanity and nature are for something much more than the broken, distorted and limited life that has been chosen through pursuit of economic growth and human wellbeing, and in the name of sustainability. The environmental crisis that Northcott (1996) and Conradie (2005) both described as a moral crisis pertaining to the capitalist culture is essentially a spiritual crisis. It is the re-orientation of our desire back towards God, as Bell (2012) describes, that brings about our true freedom, away from being held captive by capitalism and into his telos. The freedom that results will produce reconciliation between humans, and with the understanding that humanity, although inherent with unique given characteristics, is also in solidarity with the rest of the Earth community, which when orientated in the same direction towards God and the eschatological Sabbath, will produce reconciliation between humans and nature. The flourishing of the entire Earth community, therefore, is the normative context in the freedom of the telos intended by God.

Christian theology is a crucial element in a discourse about the post-sustainability paradigm because it arguably gives the normative context discovered through understanding the purposes of God for his creation even before the existence of humanity. It allows an understanding of not just how humanity has a distorted understanding of its worth through the direction of human desire orientated towards capitalist values, but also the true worth of humanity in relation to the true worth of nature. When we understand our true worth, away from consumerist values, and find freedom in the telos of God, reconciliation can have a chance and the Earth community can be renewed. In a post-sustainability paradigm, when perhaps measuring human wellbeing in terms of economic growth has lost its appeal and the bonds of capitalism are loosened, a coherent Christian theology, which may have parallels with a Muslim theology of caring for the Earth to connect with an interfaith dialogue as well as with those of no faith, has the potential to bring hope and healing. What is crucial however is that a Christian theology requires a presence within a discourse on post-sustainability in order to bring a normative relational aspect to an emerging socioeconomic and political framework in the aftermath of the failure of the sustainability agenda.

Note

1. Ecosystem services come under four types: (1) provisioning roles (such as food and fuel); (2) regulating roles (such as flood and climate regulation); (3) supporting roles (such as nutrient cycling and soil formation); and (4) cultural roles, or non-consumptive (such as recreational or spiritual benefits). Described in Alcamo and Bennett (2003).

Acknowledgements

Acknowledgements go to Professor Dan Brockington, Director of Sheffield Institute for International Development, University of Sheffield, and Professor Peter Scott, Samuel Ferguson Professor of Applied Theology and Director of the Lincoln Theological Institute, University of Manchester for advice given on an earlier draft of this paper.

Disclosure statement

No potential conflict of interest was reported by the author.

Funding

Funding from the Lincoln Theological Institute, University of Manchester, UK

References

Adams, W. M. 1991. *Green Development: Environment and Sustainability in the Third World*. London: Routledge.

Alcamo, J., and E. M. Bennett. 2003. *Ecosystems and Human Well-Being: A Framework for Assessment. Summary*. Washington, DC: Island Press.

Atherton, J. 1992. *Christianity and the Market: Christian Social Thought for Our Time*. London: SPCK.

Ayre, C. 2014. "Where on Earth Is the Church? Theological Reflection on the Nature, Mission, Governance and Ministry of the Church Amidst the Global Environmental Crisis." In *Christian Faith and the Earth: Current Paths and Emerging Horizons in Ecotheology*, edited by E. M. Conradie, S. Bergmann, C. Deane-Drummond, and D. Edwards, 137–156. London: Bloomsbury.

Bauckham, R. 2006. "Modern Domination of Nature–Historical Origins and Biblical Critique." In *Environmental Stewardship: Critical Perspectives – Past and Present*, edited by R. J. Berry, 32–50. London: T&T Clark.

Bell Jr., D. M. 2012. *The Economy of Desire: Christianity and Capitalism in a Postmodern World*. Grand Rapids: Baker Academic.

Berry, R. J. 2006. *Environmental Stewardship: Critical Perspectives – Past and Present*. London: T&T Clark.

Bookless, D. 2007. "Towards a Theology of Sustainability." In *When Enough Is Enough. A Christian Framework for Environmental Sustainability*, edited by R. J. Berry, 35–49. Nottingham: Apollo, Inter-Varsity Press.

Bouma-Prediger, S. 2001. *For the Beauty of the Earth: A Christian Vision for Creation Care*. Grand Rapids: Baker Academic.

Bratton, S. P. 2006. "Sea Sabbaths for Sea Stewards: Rest and Restoration for Marine Ecosystems." In *Environmental Stewardship: Critical Perspectives – Past and Present*, edited by R. J. Berry. London: T&T Clark.

Brundtland, G. H. 1987. *Our Common Future: Report of the World Commission on Environment and Development*. Oxford: Oxford University Press.

Büscher, B., S. Sullivan, K. Neves, J. Igoe, and D. Brockington. 2012. "Towards a Synthesized Critique of Neoliberal Biodiversity Conservation." *Capitalism Nature Socialism* 23 (2): 4–30. doi:10.1080/10455752.2012.674149.

Castree, N. 2005. *Nature*. Abingdon, Oxon: Routledge.

Cavanaugh, W. T. 2008. *Being Consumed*. Michigan: William B. Eerdmans Publishing Company.

CBD. 2004. *The Ecosystem Approach. CBD Guidelines*. Montreal: Secretariat of the Convention on Biological Diversity.

Conradie, E. 2005. *An Ecological Christian Anthropology: At Home on Earth?* Aldershot: Ashgate.

CoP 10 of the CBD. 2010. "X/2. the Strategic Plan for Biodiversity 2011-2020 and the Aichi Biodiversity Targets." Conference of the Parties to the Convention on Biological Diversity at its Tenth Meeting, Nagoya, Aichi, Japan.

Deane-Drummond, C. 2004. *The Ethics of Nature*. Oxford: Blackwell Publishing.

Deane-Drummond, C. 2008. *Eco-Theology*. London: Darton, Longman and Todd.

Deleuze, G., and F. Guattari. 1983. *Anti-Oedipus: Capitalism and Schizophrenia*. Translated and edited by R. Hurley, M. Seem, and H. R. Lane. Minneapolis: University of Minnesota Press.

Deleuze, G., and F. Guattari. 1987. *A Thousand Plateaus: Capitalism and Schizophrenia*. Translated and edited by B. Massumi . Minneapolis: University of Minnesota Press.

Deleuze, G., and C. Parnet. 1987. *Dialogues*. Translated and edited by H. Tomlinson and B. Habberjam. New York: Columbia University Press.

Duchrow, U. 1998. *Alternatives to Global Capitalism: Drawn from Biblical History, Designed for Political Action*. Translated by E. Griffiths, E. Hicks, K. Archer, and K. Schorah. Utrecht: International Books.

Edwards, D. 2014. "Where on Earth is God? Exploring an Ecological Theology of the Trinity in the Tradition of Athansius." In *Christian Faith and the Earth: Current Paths and Emerging Horizons in Ecotheology*, edited by E. M. Conradie, S. Bergmann, C. Deane-Drummond, and D. Edwards, 11–30. London: Bloomsbury.

Francis, P. 2015. "Laudato Si' (Praise Be to You – on Care for Our Common Home), Encyclical." Accessed July 17 2015. http://w2.vatican.va/content/francesco/en/encyclicals/documents/papa-francesco_20150524_enciclica-laudato-si.html

Goodchild, P. 2009. *Theology of Money*. North Carolina: Duke University Press.

Gutiérrez, G. 1988. *A Theology of Liberation: History, Politics, and Salvation*. 15th anniversary ed. Translated and edited by C. Inda and J. Eagleson. Maryknoll: Orbis.

Habgood, J. 2002. *The Concept of Nature*. London: Darton, Longman and Todd.

Hall, D. 2006. "Stewardship as Key to a Theology of Nature." In *Environmental Stewardship: Critical Perspectives – Past and Present*, edited by R. J. Berry, 129–144. London: T&T Clark.

Hiebert, T. 2011. "Reclaiming the World: Biblical Resources for the Ecological Crisis." *Interpretation* 65 (4): 341–352.

Hussen, A. 2013. *Principles of Environmental Economics and Sustainability. An Integrated Economic and Ecological Approach*. 3rd ed. New York: Routledge.

IPCC (Intergovernmental Panel on Climate Change). 2014. "Summary for Policymakers." In *Climate Change 2014: The Physical Science Basis. Contribution of Working Group I to the Fifth Assessment Report of the Intergovernmental Panel on Climate Change*, edited by T. F Stocker, D. Gin, G. K. Plattner, M. Tignor, S. K. Allen, J. Boschung, A. Nauels, Y. Xia, V. Bex and P. M. Midgley. Cambridge: Cambridge University Press.

Long, D. S. 2000. *Divine Economy: Theology and the Market*. London: Routledge.

MacIntyre, A. 2007. *After Virtue: A Study in Moral Theory*. London: Duckworth.

McDonagh, S. 1986. *To Care for the Earth: A Call to a New Theology*. London: Cassell.

McFague, S. 1993. *The Body of God: An Ecological Theology*. London: SCM Press.

Merchant, C. 1990. "Ecofeminism and Feminist Theory." In *Reweaving the World: The Emergence of Ecofeminism*, edited by I. Diamond and G. Feman Orenstein, 100–105. San Francisco: Sierra Club Book.

Messer, N. 2006. *Christian Ethics. SCM Studyguide*. London: SCM Press.

Milbank, J. 1996. "Socialism of the Gift, Socialism by Grace." *New Black Friars* 77 (910): 532–548. doi:10.1111/nbfr.1996.77.issue-910.

Milbank, J. 2001. "The Midwinter Sacrifice: A Sequel to "Can Morality Be Christian?" *Angelaki: Journal of the Theoretical Humanities* 6 (2): 49–65. doi:10.1080/713650415.

Millennium Ecosystem Assessment. 2005. *Ecosystems and Human Well-Being: Synthesis*. Washington, DC: Island Press.

Miller, V. J. 2004. *Consuming Religion: Christian Faith and Practice in a Consumer Culture*. New York: Continuum.

Moltmann, J. 1985. *God in Creation: An Ecological Doctrine of Creation: The Gifford Lectures 1984-1985*. Translated and edited by M. Kohl. London: SCM Press.

Northcott, M. S. 1996. *The Environment and Christian Ethics*. Cambridge, UK: Cambridge University Press.

Northcott, M. S. 2006. "Soil, Stewardship and Spirit in the Era of Chemical Agriculture." In *Environmental Stewardship: Critical Perspectives – Past and Present*, edited by R. J. Berry, 213–219. London: T&T Clark

Northcott, M. S. 2014. *A Political Theology of Climate Change*. London: SPCK.

Northcott, M. S. 2001. "Ecology and Christian Ethics." In *The Cambridge Companion to Christian Ethics*, edited by R. Gill, 209–227. Cambridge, UK: Cambridge University Press.

Northcott, M. S., and P. M. Scott, edited by. 2014. *Systematic Theology and Climate Change*. Abingdon, Oxon: Routledge.

Novak, M. 1993. *The Catholic Ethic and the Spirit of Capitalism*. New York: Free Press.

O'Conner, J. 1988. "Capitalism, Nature, Socialism: A Theoretical Introduction." *Capitalism, Nature, Socialism* 1 (1): 11–38. doi:10.1080/10455758809358356.

O'Neill, R. V. 2001. "Is it Time to Bury the Ecosystem Concept? (With Full Military Honours, of Course!)." *Ecology* 82 (12): 3275–3284.

O'Neill, R. V., and J. R. Kahn. 2000. "Homo Economus as a Keystone Species." *Bioscience* 50 (4): 333–337. doi:10.1641/0006-3568(2000)050[0333:HEAAKS]2.3.CO;2.

Omar Naseef, A. 1986. "The Muslim Declaration on Nature." In *The Assisi Declarations. Messages on Humanity and Nature from Buddhism, Christianity, Hinduism, Islam and Judaism*, edited by WWF-International. Bath, UK: Alliance of Religions and Conservation.

Osborn, D. 2006. "Environmental Stewardship Needed for the Core Mission of Public Bodies." In *Environmental Stewardship: Critical Perspectives – Past and Present*, edited by R. J. Berry, 228–233. London: T&T Clark.

Oxford Dictionaries. 2016. "Definition of *Community* in English." Accessed March 31 2016. http://www.oxforddictionaries.com

Page, R. 2006. "The Fellowship of All Creation." In *Environmental Stewardship: Critical Perspectives – Past and Present*, edited by R. J. Berry, 97–105. London: T&T Clark.

Patten, C. 2006. "Ethics and Stewardship." In *Environmental Stewardship: Critical Perspectives – Past and Present*, edited by R. J. Berry, 199–207. London: T&T Clark.

POST (Parliamentary Office of Science and Technology). 2007. *Ecosystem Services. PostNote 281*. London: Parliamentary Office of Science and Technology.

POST (Parliamentary Office of Science and Technology). 2011. *Natural Capital Accounting. PostNote 376*. London: Parliamentary Office of Science and Technology.

Preston, R. H. 1991. *Religion and the Ambiguities of Capitalism*. Cleveland, OH: Pilgrim Press.

Primavesi, A. 2003. *Gaia's Gift*. London: Routledge.

Rae, M. 2006. "To Render Praise: Humanity in God's World." In *Environmental Stewardship: Critical Perspectives – Past and Present*, edited by R. J. Berry, 291–311. London: T&T Clark.

Rasmussen, L. 1996. *Earth Community, Earth Ethics*. Geneva: World Council of Churches Publications.

Ruether, R. R. 1996. "Introduction." In *Women Healing Earth*, edited by R. R. Ruether, 1–8. London: SCM Press.

Santmire, H. P. 1985. *The Travail of Nature: The Ambiguous Ecological Promise of Christian Theology*. Minneapolis: Fortress Press.

Santmire, H. P. 2006. "Partnership with Nature according to the Scriptures: Beyond the Theology of Stewardship." In *Environmental Stewardship: Critical Perspectives – Past and Present*, edited by R. J. Berry, 253–272. London: T&T Clark.

Scott, P. M. 2003. *A Political Theology of Nature*. Cambridge, UK: Cambridge University Press.

Scott, P. M. 2004. "Creation." In *The Blackwell Companion to Political Theology*, edited by P. Scott and W. T. Cavanaugh, 333–347. Oxford: Wiley-Blackwell.

Smith, A. 1776. *Wealth of Nations*, 1. London: W. Strahan and T. Cadell.

Sobrino, J. 1988. *Spirituality of Liberation: Towards Political Holiness*. Maryknoll: Orbis books.

Steffan, W., K. Richardson, J. Rockström, S. E. Cornell, I. Fetzer, E. M. Bennett, R. Biggs, et al. 2015. Advance Online Publication. "Planetary Boundaries: Guiding Human Development on a Changing Planet." *Science Express* January. 15: 2015.

TEEB (The Economics of Ecosystems and Biodiveristy). 2010. *The Economics of Ecosystems and Biodiversity: Mainstreaming the Economics of Nature: A Synthesis of the Approach, Conclusions and Recommendations of TEEB.* Prepared by P. Sukhdev, H. Wittmer, C. Schröter-Schlaack, C. Nesshöver, J. Bishop, P. ten Brink, H. Gundimeda, P. Kumar, and B. Simmons. TEEB. Accessed February 27 2017. http://www.teebweb.org/our-publications/teeb-study-reports/synthesis-report/

Titmuss, C. 1994. *The Green Buddha.* Totnes: Insight Books.

Turpin, K. 2012. "Consuming." In *The Wiley-Blackwell Companion to Practical Theology*, edited by B. J. Miller-Mclemore, 70–79. West Sussex, UK: Wiley-Blackwell.

United Nations. 1992. "8. Convention on Biological Diversity". Article 1. United Nations Treaty Collection, Chapter XXVII: Environment. Rio De Janeiro. Accessed 5 June 1992. https://treaties.un.org/Pages/CTCTreaties.aspx?id=27&subid=A

Weber, M. 1958. *The Protestant Ethic and the Spirit of Capitalism.* New York: Charles Scribner's Son.

White, L. 1967. "The Historical Roots of Our Ecologic Crisis." *Science* 155: 1203–1207. doi:10.1126/science.155.3767.1203.

Williams, R. 1983. *Keywords.* New York: Fontana.

Wogaman, P. 1986. *Economics and Ethics: A Christian Inquiry.* Philadelphia: Fortress Press.

Wogaman, P. 1988. *Christian Perspectives on Politics.* Philadelphia: Fortress Press.

REPLY

Response to 'Beyond sustainability: hope in a spiritual revolution?'

Rachel Muers

This is a reply to:

Bathurst, Rachel. 2017. "Beyond sustainability: hope in a spiritual revolution?" *Global Discourse*. 7 (1): 87–105. http://dx.doi.org/10.1080/23269995.2017.1300410.

Lynn White's famous analysis of the pernicious effects of anthropocentric Christian theology on Northern and Western attitudes to non-human nature has cast a long shadow. Many ecotheologies, including many of those cited in 'Beyond Sustainability', have been framed as direct or indirect responses to White – defending or reframing Christian theology as a positive contributor to environmental concern and to responses to the environmental crisis. Alongside this, however, theology is also able to raise critical questions for contemporary environmentalism. As the author of 'Beyond Sustainability' (Bathurst 2017) rightly suggests, theology can provoke and sustain the rigorous interrogation of taken-for-granted value judgements, particularly those of global capitalism. In the light of its perspective on the ultimate *telos* of humanity and non-human nature, theology holds up for critical evaluation any and every set of assumed values, goals or principles of action. Sustainability, as the author of 'Beyond Sustainability' shows – and as I have argued elsewhere, in relation to earlier UN documents – is one contemporary value that calls for theological critique and reformulation (Muers 2008). In particular, insofar as the theory and practice of sustainability relies on and reinforces the values of global capitalism, theology should not allow itself to be co-opted into the search for sustainability. Of particular importance, as again the article demonstrates, is the question of hope. For what is it right to hope, and what constitutes an adequate object and practice of hope? The idea of the Sabbath as *telos*, as developed in Moltmann, Rae and others, provides one example of a theological challenge to the hopes and desires of modernity – hope for an end to work, striving and acquisition and not for the indefinite sustaining of (something like) the status quo. Other recent theological interventions – for example, Sallie McFague's critique of consumerism from the perspective of saintly lives – take different routes through Christian tradition to confront the same deep-rooted assumptions.

This alternative teleology, as the article implies but does not explore at length, is grounded not only in scripture and tradition but also in lived practices, including practices of worship; and, taken seriously, it might be expected to give rise to distinctive forms of ethical and political action. Arguably, as Willis Jenkins' important work suggests (Jenkins 2008), Christian environmentalism is best understood not simply through theology – providing alternative paradigms or grand narratives – but through the lived relationship between theology and practice, worked out in particular cases. Viewed in this way, Christian environmentalism turns out to be rather more diverse, complex and messy, and its mapping of the future rather more provisional and humble, than the present article suggests.

This raises a critical question about the framing of the article within 'a global discourse on sustainability' and about its call for a 'spiritual revolution amongst the capitalist cultures of the world'. Is it possible that the presentation of a single 'global' vision – spoken in a single human voice, while taking what purports to be a God's-eye view – is part of the spiritual and environmental problem, rather than part of the solution? Is it possible that we need to change the form and not merely the content of the global-teleological stories told in the contemporary world? When the article calls for a 'new world order' developed on the basis of 'a Christian theological perspective', we must acknowledge that the history of attempts to re-order the world from Christian perspectives, to implement a vision of 'God's purposes for humanity, nature and the world', is not universally positive. To the extent that calls for a 'spiritual revolution' imply that theology can be disseminated from the top down, as a single alternative framework that offers the 'tools of hope', there is a real risk that it will repeat the errors both of the anthropocentric theology that White critiqued and of the sustainability discourses that force all natural goods and relation-ships into a single framework of value.

In practice, if there is to be a 'spiritual revolution' in response to the environmental crisis it must presumably involve the radical surrender of the God's-eye perspective and the rediscovery of the humility proper to the human. My question is about how this humility can best be reflected in the practices and structures of religion – including the practice of theology – as it seeks to interact with powerful global narratives of sustain-ability. Trying to out-narrate sustainability, or ecosystems thinking, by presenting 'the normative context discovered through understanding the purposes of God for his creation' might on the one hand help to inculcate this humility. On the other hand, especially without a clear account of how this 'normative context' is perceived, related to and lived with, there is a risk that it simply replaces one overweening grand narrative with another.

A further question that follows from this concerns the nature and status of hope. To put it baldly, why should we assume that Christian theology – or any theological work – is going to provide a solution to the environmental crisis? And if we make that assumption, is there a risk that what started out as a theologically founded critique of ideology could be co-opted by that same ideology? As I noted (Muers 2008, 153–155) in relation to the United Nations GEO-3 report (2002), there have been plenty of attempts to put 'the world's religions' to work in the service of globally organised responses to the environmental crisis, and it is not always clear that this is being done with a full understanding of the deep challenge that these 'religions' might pose to the whole framework. More to the point, however, it is at least arguable that the distinctive contribution of Christian theology to political and environmental discourse is found in theologies of the cross and resurrection, as much as in theologies of creation and incarnation. How might the centrality of a story of failure and death to Christian theology – including Christian theological accounts of hope – shape a theology 'beyond sustainability'? I hope that at least some of these questions will be taken further in the critical conversations initiated by this author.

Disclosure statement

No potential conflict of interest was reported by the author.

References

Bathurst, R. 2017. "Beyond Sustainability: Hope in a Spiritual Revolution?" *Global Discourse* 7 (1). http://dx.doi.org/10.1080/23269995.2017.1300410

Jenkins, W. 2008. *Ecologies of Grace: Environmental Ethics and Christian Theology*. Oxford: Oxford University Press.

Muers, R. 2008. *Living for the Future: Theological Ethics for Coming Generations*. London: T&T Clark.

Environmental education after sustainability: hope in the midst of tragedy

Panu Pihkala

ABSTRACT

In this article, I discuss the challenge posed to environmental education (EE; and education for sustainable development) by the thinkers who see the situation of the world as so severe that 'sustainability' is an outdated concept.

My approach is interdisciplinary and I discuss especially the connections between EE and eco-psychology. Based on psychological research, I argue that the wide-scale unconscious anxiety, which people experience, should be taken very seriously in EE. My discussion thus contributes in a new kind of way to a long-standing key issue in EE, the gap between people's values and the perceived action.

Scholars of eco-anxiety have argued that instead of not caring, many people in fact care too much, and have to resort to psychological defenses of denial and disavowal. Thus, the question in EE is not anymore whether EE should deal with anxiety, for anxiety is already there. The prevailing attitude in EE writing is right in emphasizing positive matters and empowerment, but the relation between hope and optimism must be carefully thought about and a certain sense of tragedy must be included. Therefore, my article participates in the discussion about the role of 'fear appeals' in EE.

My discussion is directed to anyone who wants to understand the reasons for inaction and the ways in which these may be overcome.

Introduction

People have different understandings of what environmental education (EE) is. Like the concept 'education' itself, EE is often seen to refer to children and youth in particular. These age groups are in a major role in EE, but a wider view includes all age groups. A classic definition was made already in the late 1970s: 'Environmental education should cater to all ages and socio-professional groups in the population' (Tbilisi Declaration 1977).

Thus defined, it is clear that EE is pursued in many areas and disciplines where the actual term is not used. A title of a recent book suggests this wider vision: *Environmental Education and Advocacy* (Johnson and Mappin 2009). All activities which aim at shaping people's nature relationships can be seen to have a dimension of EE. Even more widely, other activities can be analyzed for their implicit views on EE in the sense of asking what kind of views of human–nature relationships they convey. Naturally there is a need for a focused and explicit EE, both as an academic discipline and a practice, but it is crucial to understand the wide nature of the issue.

During the last decades, when terminology related to sustainability has been popular, the term EE has often been replaced by 'education for sustainable development' and related terms, such as 'sustainability education' and 'education for sustainability' (Gough 2013, 13; cf. Berryman and Sauvé 2013; Sterling 2001). The use of terms has been related to differing views of education, environmental action and the balance between the needs of human communities and ecosystems, and also to more accidental factors such as the prevalence of a certain term and discipline in the institution where a certain scholar is educated or working. Similarities are found from the thoughts of people working under different terms for their fields.

In this article, I discuss the challenge posed to EE by those thinkers who claim that we should stop using the term sustainability, because the global situation is so severe. This is one of the reasons that I use the term EE as a general concept, but I want to emphasize that my discussion is closely related to what many people call sustainable education. Other relevant terms include 'climate change education' and 'futures educa-tion'. My main point is that EE (as widely understood) needs a realistic sense of tragedy. A major reason for this is the wide unconscious anxiety that people have. Hope and empowerment are still the responses to the situation, but the relation between hope and optimism must be clarified.

I will provide ideas and even outlines for practical activities, but the main point is to engage in thinking (and feeling) about the requirements and aims of EE in the current situation. My approach is interdisciplinary and I discuss especially the connections between EE and 'psychologies of the environment', which I later call ecopsychology for brevity (for the various related terms, see Paidas 2011; Scott et al. 2016; Clayton and Myers 2015). This means that I discuss heavy themes such as anxiety and mortality, but also hope and joy.

As a result, some may think that my discussion is quite far from EE as it is often understood on a popular level: as practical activities where people learn how ecosys-tems function, care together for local environments, and so on. However, there has always been a wider dimension in thinking about EE, and in addition many of these deep themes have been implicitly present. I argue that in the current situation, we need more explicit and carefully thought-out treatment of them.

My discussion contributes in a rather new kind of way to a long-standing key issue in research on EE, the gap between people's values and the perceived action. While related psychological and to some extent existential factors have been somewhat discussed by scholars in EE (f.ex. Brownlee, Powell, and Hallo 2013; Selby 2011; Jickling and Wals 2008; Kollmuss and Agyeman 2002; cf. Stevenson et al. 2013, 514–515), I draw more exten-sively on the latest ecopsychological research on the scale and seriousness of uncon-scious anxiety as a factor which prevents positive action. This explains also the phenomenon that many people seem to be indifferent about climate change and related issues: the reason may be that instead of not caring, people in fact care too much, and resort to psychological defenses or paralyzing anxiety, apathy and help-lessness. Thus, my article is related also to the discussion of 'fear appeals' in EE.

Drawing from my own field of expertise, religious studies and theology, I discuss the role of existential and spiritual factors in the phenomenon. Some of the EE activities that I discuss have a general spiritual tone in the sense that they deal with the deep dimensions of existence and meaning. I argue that these kinds of activities can be conducted either within or without a certain spiritual or religious tradition. However, I do believe, as some other scholars that I discuss here, that there are some 'best practices' by spiritual and religious communities that can be very helpful in addressing the deep dimensions of EE in an age of crisis.

Among scholars working in the field of EE, I emphasize the importance of the work of David Hicks. It is fascinating that we have ended up in many similar views and recom-mendations: I knew Hicks' earlier work, but only after I had completed the first draft of this article did I read his *Educating for Hope in Troubled Times* (2014), which includes many similarities with my work. In the history of Hicks' work, there is a movement toward more caution as regards optimism and this is most evident in this latest book of his. Drawing from some of the similar sources that I do and from the famous EE thinker David Orr (2009), Hicks includes more pessimism about the future and argues for the need to deal with this situation in (environmental) education. I will refer to Hicks' work in many places in my article, but may it be said already here that a certain difference between our views is that I discuss tragedy and anxiety more, and I make a stronger difference between hope and optimism. The closest approach to mine is the one taken by Kelsey and Armstrong (2012).

My article, like Hicks' work, includes a strong dimension of futures education. As Hicks and Bord (2001), I emphasize the need for the performer of EE, the 'environmental educator' or who I call a 'leader', to engage in a personal process of dealing with visions of future (cf. Kelsey and Armstrong 2012, 197). In practice, this means wrestling with anxiety and the relation of despair and hope. By the term 'leader' I do not wish to overemphasize that role, for I believe in much of what theorists of constructive learning have argued, but I join those who argue that in times of crisis, including the climate crisis, the importance of good leadership turns crucial (Välimäki and Lehtonen 2009; Randall 2009, 126).

The psychoanalysts have pointed out that their possible insight into socio-environmental situations will most probably generate resistance, since that is the usual reaction when unconscious processes are called into daylight (Rustin 2013, 171). Hicks has discussed a similar kind of resistance that has arisen in connection with the ideas that he has been discussing (2014, 66). I expect that my deeper plunge into troubling issues, such as mortality, will probably meet resistance also, perhaps for various reasons. However, I hope that the challenge posed by the thinkers who I'm discussing would be carefully considered, perhaps over time if necessary.

Thus, my discussion is linked to several of the recognized needs for further research in EE (Stevenson et al. 2013), such as the role of emotions, hope and worldviews. I hope that my article will spark further discussion between various disciplines. For example, ecopsychologists rarely cite works in EE, even when they in practice discuss same themes.

Anxiety, denial and disavowal

> Even beyond the threat of nuclear warfare, I think, the ecological crisis is the greatest threat mankind collectively has ever faced .... My hypothesis is that man [sic] is hampered in his meeting of this environmental crisis by a severe and pervasive apathy which is based largely upon feelings and attitudes of which he is unconscious. (Searles 1972)

EE has always tried to balance between two things: a realistic account of the threats that the world is facing and an *ethos* which would motivate and empower people. Like many other environmental disciplines, EE has existed in essence for a long time, but it has been greatly strengthened since the late 1960s and the birth of the wider environmental movement (Gough 2013). In that movement, a major tenet has been consciousness about the severity of environmental problems and the possibility of a major crisis, even an apocalyptic one. It has remained a contested issue (a) whether a major crisis is coming and (b) how should information and fears about such a crisis be discussed (f. ex. Buell 1995, Chapter 9; cf. Skrimshire 2010; Eckersley 2008).

Some have thought that it is only realistic to be serious about the threats and that the gravity of the situation will spark action. Others have pointed out that there is psychological evidence that 'fear appeals' do not in general generate positive action, but may instead be counterproductive (see Dickinson et al. 2013; Marshall 2015, 138–144). In environmentalism, there has been much discussion and debate about this issue. As a result, many, indeed most, of those who wish to advance environmental matters (later: environmentalists[1]) have stressed that anxiety and guilt should not be generated (Lertzman 2015, 4; Weintrobe 2013a, 33).

Thus, this is a key issue in EE, both in the specific field of EE and in the EE dimensions in all environmentalism. There are various major theories of EE, but practically all of them emphasize the need for a positive vision, where the individual is able to see that her actions can contribute to the state of things and thus can experience empowerment (Gough 2013; cf. Palmer 1998; Hungerford and Volk 1990). Educator David Sobel (1996) warns about generating 'eco-phobia' by discussing too many negative things related to environmental conditions (cf. Kelsey and Armstrong 2012, 187–188). Many scholars in both EE and psychology emphasize 'optimism' as a key issue, in varying measure (Stevenson et al. 2013, 514; Clayton, Manning and Hodge 2014, 41; Fritze et al. 2008; Chang 2014, 107). Some have believed in technological solutions (cf. Huckle as quoted in Hicks 2002, 69).

However, two major and intertwined issues partly challenge this traditional understanding. First, if Clive Hamilton, John Foster and many others are right, the socio-environmental situation of the world is so severe that a major crisis is truly coming and indeed has already started. Second, these authors also point out that there is widespread denial and disavowal, because the crisis is so difficult to bear, and because it stands in opposition to a major traditional belief system, belief in progress (Hamilton [2011] 2015; Foster 2015; cf. Jamieson 2014). How should and could this situation be dealt with in EE? In Susan Koger's (2015, 246) words: 'Somehow, we need to convey the urgency of the situation and engage and empower our audiences without overwhelming them or sending them into despair or retail therapy'.

A starting point is to recognize and admit that it is difficult to think about these issues for leaders in EE also. Two recent popular but well-researched books introduce the wide variety of factors which make it difficult for us deal with these questions. The titles are telling: *What are we Thinking When we are not Thinking about Climate Change* (Stoknes 2015) and *Don't Even Think about it: Why Our Brains are Wired to Ignore Climate Change* (Marshall 2015). There are biological, social, psychological and political reasons for denial and disavowal. These two books make for excellent reading for both educators and educational activities (for youth and adults).

David Orr (2009, 184) tells that he has not met many educators who would be willing to consider the seriousness of the situation. This has direct links with the absence of activities related to emotions and existential themes in EE (Zeyer and Kelsey 2013; Kagawa and Selby 2010; Kool and Kelsey 2006). Indeed, an emphasis on the importance of emotional preparation for teachers in climate change education is absent from many books, which usually stress the cognitive dimensions (cf. Chang 2014). A telling example is mentioned by Hicks (2014, 66): when he proposed that the emotional dimension should be dealt with, an educator replied that 'I don't expect to have to be a therapist in my work'. However, as Macy and Johnstone (2012, 2) argue: 'How can we even begin to tackle the mess we're in if we consider it too depressing to think about?'

Care must be taken in thinking about how to present troubling information (cf. Hicks and Bord 2001), but it is important to realize that the beginning of the conversation can also be relieving. One can start simply by asking himself and the audience: how do we feel about the socio-environmental situation of the world and about climate change? (To keep the text flowing, I shall often use the terms 'climate change' or 'crisis' to describe the wide socio-environmental crisis.) Questions and guidelines for both personal and group reflection are offered by Hicks (2014, 75–76, 88–89), as well as Macy and Johnstone (2012, 72, 76–78).

In other words, the EE leader should wrestle with the 'difficult problem of anxiety' (term used by Weintrobe 2013a). I use the term anxiety both for a specific emotion and more widely: anxiety is linked to many other emotions, such as fear, helplessness, hatred, despair and depression (cf. Miceli and Castelfranchi 2010, 264–265). In psychological and psychoanalytical literature, there is now enlightening research and discussion about this phenomena (Clayton et al. 2015; Weintrobe 2013; Nicholsen 2002), and I will discuss several aspects of it below. For its part, this research explains the inaction that is experienced in relation to climate change (cf. Brownlee, Powell, and Hallo 2013; Gifford 2011). There is a grave need to help people to understand the scale and hiddenness of this anxiety, which is often called eco-anxiety. Philosopher Joanna Macy, who has developed many EE activities, has been a pioneer in discussing this 'environmental despair' (1983, 1995).

The environmental crisis and climate change have both direct and indirect, gradual effects (Doherty and Clayton 2011; Clayton, Manning and Hodge 2014; cf. Weissbecker 2011). The indirect effects are often difficult to notice for several reasons. First, they may happen gradually and avoid attention. Second, they are often unconscious. There is an increasing scholarly discussion about these indirect effects and I can only refer to some major tenets here. An illuminating comparison can be made to the threat of nuclear devastation and the research that has been conducted of people's reactions to it. Because these kinds of problems are very difficult to solve and because they cause constant threat, people feel disempowered. Depression rates increase and especially the people who are, for various reasons, in a vulnerable position are prone to serious health effects, such as disorders and severe depression (Kidner 2007; Fritze et al. 2008; Doherty and Clayton 2011; Clayton, Manning and Hodge 2014).

There are various methods that people use to survive the anxiety. The best ways of adaptation are linked to positive action (cf. Randall 2009, 122–124; Reser and Swim 2011), but often the anxiety results in various forms of denial and disavowal as psychological defenses. Outright denialism is only one form of these (Stoknes 2015, 9–84; Foster 2015, Chapter 1). Psychoanalysts have warned that denial as disavowal may be more dangerous, because it builds a situation where reality both is and is not accepted. People find a way to live on their lives, ignoring the grave dangers even while information about them grows. Sally Weintrobe summaries the phenomenon:

- The reality has become too obvious to be simply denied with negation.

- There is anxiety that the damage is already too great to repair.

- There is felt to be not enough support and help to bear the anxiety and suffering that knowledge of reality brings. (Weintrobe 2013a, 44)

Avoiding the subject of anxiety does not make people's anxieties about climate change go away. The defenses used to minimize anxieties drive them underground, where they are not worked through and can escalate. People need genuine emotional support to bear their anxieties … .(46)

EE thinkers Hicks and Bord (2001) have warned that leaders can make only things worse if they are not careful about the ways in which global problems are dealt with. There must be enough time and resources to engage the matters with the audience, and the audience must have opportunities for self-reflection and peer group work. Emotional support from the leaders is required (cf. Hicks 2014, Chapter 4, 173–176; Lehtonen, Cantell, and Salonen, forthcoming; Næss 2002). Otherwise, there is the danger that anxiety or the 'wall of denial' only grows stronger (Stoknes 2015, 78).

A factor which proves the importance of such activities, and helps in them, is the fact that people do have a certain resonance with the situation. Weintrobe (2013a) points out that 'Deep down … most people know this, at least unconsciously' (similarly Stoknes 2015, 7–8). Norgaard's study (2011) on the cultural forms on denial supports this: sometimes, the anxiety behind all the 'acting' shows itself, for example, late at night. My own experiences of discussing with people in Europe and North America confirm this, although I have collected no scientific data of these talks (cf. Moe-Lobeda 2013, 95–96). Roy Scranton argues strikingly:

The problem with our response to climate change isn't a problem with passing the right laws or finding the right place for carbon or changing people's minds or raising awareness. *Everybody already knows.* The problem is that the problem is too big. The problem is that different people want different things. The problem is that nobody has real answers. The problem is that the problem is us. (2015, 68, italics in original)

Thus, the question in EE is not anymore whether EE should deal with anxiety, for anxiety is already there (similar views in EE literature have been taken by Hicks 2014; Zeyer and Kelsey 2013; Kelsey and Armstrong 2012, 188–193; Selby 2011; Lehtonen 2015; cf. Forrest and Feder 2011). The question is *how* anxiety is dealt with; how unconscious anxiety is lured into daylight and processed in such a way as to generate positive action and resilience. Despair and 'doom and gloom' must not have the final word, but still the problems have to be faced. The prevailing attitude in EE writing is right in emphasizing positive matters and empowerment, but the relation between hope and optimism must be carefully thought about and a certain sense of tragedy must be included. I will return to this theme of hope after I have discussed several major facets related to this anxiety and the ways in which EE can function in relation to them.

Mortality, finitude and fear

A major source of eco-anxiety is fear related to the future: what will happen to us, our loved ones and nature? Some thinkers believe that fear is the key: people want to avoid it and those who want to use power use fear to control the masses (Wuthnow 2010; Pyszczynski 2004; cf. Klein 2007, 2014). Many thinkers have stressed that these fears are closely linked with mortality and finitude. Regarding climate change, people realize that it posits a danger of causing loss and even death. This is almost unbearable. As a result, people resort into denial and disavowal related to climate change. However, because anxiety is not dealt with, but instead it is repressed, it only gets worse (Foster 2015; Marshall 2015, 205–210; Scranton 2015; Weintrobe 2013a, 42–43; Dickinson 2009; Nicholsen 2002, esp. 108–112, 137–141; Pyszczynski, Greenberg, and Solomon 1999).

The denial of death is an ancient issue and its role in technological societies has been deemed great (Becker 1973). Overly optimistic belief in the possibilities of science and technology can be seen as an effort to find a means to overcome mortality. The most extreme forms of transhumanism are current examples of this, and it should be kept in mind that several transhumanists are positive about climate engineering (and related notions, of which see Jamieson 2014, Chapter 7) as a means to deal with the mounting climate crisis (cf. Bonneuil 2015, 23–26). Foster (2015) links this with faith in progress: because people are too anxious about finitude, they resort to belief in progressivism.

Nicholsen (2002, 130–131) has raised up the important notion of 'symbolic immortality' in relation to human–environment relations and eco-anxiety. Drawing on Robert J. Lifton's classic research, she discusses how people search for meaning by desiring that their life would continue to have significance after they have died. People wish that their lives would continue symbolically, which means a combination of actual continuation and metaphorical continuation, in various ways: either in their close ones (especially children), in the legacy of their work efforts, in the legacy of their artistic or creative efforts, in some kind of eternal life offered by religious faith, or, notably, in nature. I draw special attention to the last point: many people are comforted, often half-consciously, by the thought that nature, the ecosystems will go on, life will continue, and their bodies and actions will be transformed into particles in the lasting process of nature (cf. Weintrobe 2013b).

Now in the time of environmental crisis and the threat of atomic warfare, Nicholsen emphasizes, all these forms of symbolic immortality are threatened. Many people in industrialized countries do not find solace in the faiths of traditional religions (cf. Jamieson 2014, 200; Foster 2015, 111), and the environmental catastrophe threatens to take away all other aspects of symbolic immortality. This is why the situation is so traumatic and causes so much anxiety, Nicholsen argues (similarly, with different concepts, Weintrobe 2013b, 42–43; Steiner 2013, 81–82; Kidner 2007, 138).

If these thinkers are right, as I believe they are, if our fear of mortality causes anxiety which results in denial, disavowal and wrong types of environment-related behavior, then EE must in some way deal with this problem. Some may think that this goes beyond what EE is, but, given the situation, these deep issues have to be wrestled with, if anxiety is to be realized and burdens relieved. The two challenges for EE are:

- Helping people realize how mortality is related to our fears, anxieties and denial of climate change, and
- Helping people to come to grips with mortality, which is a source of empowerment and resilience.

However, the challenge is that when this issue of mortality is evoked, it can generate very strong emotions in audiences and even result in counterproductive action. Janis Dickinson, who has given deep thought to this issue, writes:

> While climate change is a dire problem, one that is threatening to people's lifestyle, health, and survival, there is evidence that framing it within the context of threats, a strategy known as 'fear appeals,' can have the opposite of the intended effect. One suspected reason for this is that **when asked to think about mortality people have a set of anxiety-buffering defenses that they subconsciously evoke** … (Dickinson et al. 2013, 147, emphasis mine)

Others have noticed the same phenomenon: when confronted, people desperately cling on to the path that they have earlier chosen. It would be too painful to confront reality. Sometimes, it seems, this results in concentrating on work in a manner which suggests that implicitly work is for that person a major hope for symbolic immortality (cf. Hamilton, Bonneuil, and Gemenne 2015, 215–216).

Thus, dealing with mortality requires care, but it is of utmost importance. Explicitly death has been dealt with very little in EE, but implicitly it has been related to numerous facets of it. Some beginnings have been made by Joshua Russell's recent article (2016), which focuses on children's experiences of deaths of companion animals. Russell explores 'the cognitive, affective, and moral potential of an environmentally-centered death education' (13). I share Russell's interest on the theme and emphasize its relevance to eco-anxiety. Dealing with the mortality of animals is linked with dealing with our own mortality. It can also strengthen our understanding of interconnections between humans and other nature.

Mortality is an undercurrent in all futures education, although usually unconsciously. In addition, I think that EE has also implicitly helped people to deal with their mortality by strengthening their connections with natural environments, which people find therapeutic. What is needed now is more explicit integration of 'education in mortality' with EE. Insights for this can be gained by reading Roy Scranton's *Learning to Die in the Anthropocene* (2015), which is an enlarged version of his much discussed writing in *The New York Times*. Drawing from his experiences as a soldier in the American–Iraq war, Scranton argues that we must retrieve the ancient task of philosophy (and, I would add, religion): dealing with mortality, accepting that we will die. In the line of Hamilton, Foster and others, Scranton discusses the severity of the environmental crisis and argues that in order to be able to live, we must first learn to die (cf. Foster 2015, 191–192).

There are some studies in EE which admit that a careful use of 'fear appeals' can provide positive results (Li 2014; cf. Dickinson et al. 2013; De Young 2013, 239). Harrison and Mallett (2013) argue that 'mortality salience' can positively influence environmental behavior, if there is already some concern for it. Further research is evidently needed. However, what I am arguing here is that education in mortality can and should include gentle aspects, which makes it quite different from fear appeals as apocalyptic warnings.

What would such an EE be like? There is a need to develop it collectively, by listening to different voices and developing contextual methods. Along with fear and mortality, things that should be discussed and processed include grief, loss, guilt and shame; however, a deeper treatment of these themes must be left to another article. Some of the rudiments include:

- The important role of natural environments, even parks or riversides in cities, as places where there is solace enough to engage oneself and others in encountering our mortality

- The crucial role of wrestling with classics in arts and literature. As examples, I mention Shakespeare's *The Tempest*, Harry Martinson's *Aniara*, Albert Camus' *The Plague* (cf. the discussion about it in Hamilton 2013; Stoknes 2015, 225–226; Gibbons 2013a, 2013b), and the movie *The Dead Poets' Society*. The literature on ecocriticism offers insights for this (see Buell 2005; cf. Orr 2009, 192).

- The use of drama and art-based EE (see van Boeckel 2013). For example, Finnish art educators have conducted an activity for children in which they seek three items from nature: one related to birth, one to living and one to death (van Boeckel 2009, 147).

- The possibilities offered by spiritual (generally defined) activities and experiences (cf. Koger 2015; Selby 2011, 8; Christie 2013), such as: experiencing deeper connection with nature; burials of animals; and other ritual-type activities where mortality is encountered. Cooperation with various organizations, for example, in the line of action research (see Stevenson and Robottom 2013), provides help in these kind of activities. One option is collaboration with various local spiritual communities and leaders (Ramsay and Manderson 2011; Hitzhusen 2012, 2011, 2007, 2006; Hitzhusen and Tucker 2013; Toh and Cavagas 2010).

Tragedy

Many environmentalists and environmental educators warn about using tragedy to describe the situation in the world. Philip Smith and Nicholas Howe argue in their insightful book, *Climate Change as Social Drama* (2015) that the narrative of tragedy tends to give a message that things are beyond the control of people. Like many other environmental thinkers, they see this as counterproductive.

On the other hand, many thinkers emphasize the gravity of the situation and either explicitly or implicitly discuss tragedy in its various forms. Among these thinkers, John Foster has given special attention to defining tragedy. In his view, events are made tragic not only because of the evil in them but also because of the ways in which even good intentions often have tragic consequences. Tragedy reveals troubling aspects of the structure of being itself and is thus closely linked to finitude. 'Tragedy in the full sense arises when disaster ensues from and expresses destructive weaknesses which are *inherent in the key life-strengths* of an agent, whether an individual, an institution or, as in the present case, a mode of civilisation' (Foster 2015, 93, italics in original).

I think that Foster is right: we should stop and see the tragic elements of reality (cf. Eagleton 2015; McIntosh 2008). In addition, perhaps surprisingly for many, a sense of tragedy can help us to remain resilient. If we are honest, we see that massive forces in the human world contribute to the current crisis. Social structures can be made better, but it is very difficult, especially in the long run. Currently, the situation is that people are offered as a standard relatively small options for 'greening' their lifestyles and making an impact (cf. Marshall 2015, 192–197; Stoknes 2015; Brulle and Dunlap 2015, 8–12). This can lead to what Sapiains, Beeton, and Walker (2015) call 'dissociative experience'. Many people feel social and personal (conscience-related) pressure to do something to alleviate the crisis. Even if they resort to the minor options that are available, they end up experiencing anxiety, because deep down they know that this is not enough. As a psychological defense, they then tend to dissociate their own behavior and the actual demands of global situation (cf. Ojala 2012), ending up in a kind of neurotic behavior (cf. Lehtonen and Välimäki 2013). Another option is that they become depressed because they carry the whole world on their shoulders, which is a symptom many environmentalists have (Stoknes 2015, 88; Randall 2013).

A sense of tragedy, together with various means for strengthening resilience, can allow us to face the reality: our actions, both personal and social, are inadequate. We are caught in a plight. We are both guilty and victims, which makes the situation both tricky (Nicholsen 2002, 142) and potentially relieving. This kind of tragic realism can alleviate anxiety, but further work is needed to address the question of hope, so that we do not end up in inaction or despair. The critics of the use of tragedy are right in saying that without hope, anxiety grows. This is closely related to the question of inevitability.

Some thinkers relate inevitability and necessity closely with tragedy and I think that the critique of the use of tragedy in EE is linked with this kind of view (cf. Smith and Howe 2015; MacLellan 2015, 52–53). However, there is a difference here between tragic drama and life. A tragic drama is a play, a setting of boundaries, an aspect of reality. Observing a tragic drama is a kind of a vaccination: it can provide health by injecting a suitable amount of the sickness in us and indeed reminding us that we have the potential for the sickness. At the same time, its role is to remind us of the good things that still remain, especially in contrast to the scenario that the tragic drama creates.

If tragedy is the only and all-comprehensive narrative as related to climate change and the future of the world, then the critics of its use in EE are right: such a narrative is to be avoided. But tragedy has its important place as a reminder and exploration of key aspects of reality. It is the setting for 'deep hope' (Hicks 2014, 106) or 'realistic hope' (Orr 2009, 185). After all, one of the historical aims of tragedy has been to generate compassion (Wallace 2007, 5–6; Bushnell 2008).

Hope, meaning and joy

What is needed is hope in the midst of tragedy. It is important to note that the concepts 'hope' and 'optimism' are used in various ways, as is the adjective 'hopeful' (Alarcon, Bowling, and Khazon 2013; Scioli and Biller 2009; Webb 2007; McGeer 2004; Miceli and Castelfranchi 2010). I join those thinkers who argue that it is useful to separate hope and optimism in relation to the different views of future inherent in them. Optimism is linked with belief in a better future, often in 'progress' (Foster 2015; Nicholsen 2002, 183; cf.

Eagleton 2015). As David Orr (2009, 181–186) notes, optimism often generates good results, but it can sometimes be dangerous (cf. Scott et al. 2016, 190–191).

Hamilton ([2011] 2015, 129–133) discusses 'illusions' and 'delusions' as related to hope and optimism. 'Positive illusions', referring to a famous book with the same title by Shelley Taylor, can be empowering and important for the psyche. However, there is a danger that they turn into harmful delusions, which enable people to avoid making necessary changes and choices. Even Martin Seligman, a guru of Positive Psychology, admits that when positive thinking is not able to change the future, people 'must have the courage to endure pessimism' (131).

Hamilton himself (2013) suggests that the required attitude is 'pessimism of strength' or 'active nihilism' (28, borrowing the last concept from Nietzsche). Personally, I join those who see that the concept of hope has much possibility for EE. Hope is a powerful word, it has a long history and it has an implicit relation to tragedy and finitude, even when this has to be discussed and brought into daylight (Scioli and Biller 2009). Webb's (2007) discussion of five different 'modes of hoping' is important reading for environmental educators: in the proposals about hope made by various thinkers, there is manifested a certain variety of views of hope, such as patient hope and utopian hope.

The crucial point is that hope can be strongly related to a process of creating meaning and positive action, not so much to a certain goal or state of the future (cf. Clayton and Myers 2009, 204–205; Jamieson 2014, 237–238). Naturally a vision is needed, but the difference between hope and optimism is that hope can prevail even when there is no certainty at all about the future. This is the 'radical hope' that philosopher Jonathan Lear and educators Orr and Hicks champion: 'it is directed toward a future goodness that transcends the current ability to understand what it is. Radical hope anticipates a good for which those who have the hope as yet lack the appropriate concepts with which to understand it' (Lear as quoted in Orr 2009, 173 and; Hicks 2014, 109; cf. Williston 2012).

Foster (2015, 17) takes a very similar view and argues that: 'the opposite of despair is not optimism … but hope'. Hope is a conviction that there is still something worthwhile; contrary to despair, which believes that there is nothing left. There is a possibility for something more honest, more resilient; it may not be 'better' in the modern sense of 'progress', but still a step forward in another sense. As Orr notes (2009, 181–185), there is sometimes a tenet in optimism that achieving a better future is relatively easy; he and the other advocates of 'deep hope' point out that it will be very difficult. One could say that for them (and me) hope is a virtue, a habit of finding meaning and resilience, not giving up. Hope 'can mean the clear-eyed determination to live anyway' (Foster 2015, 92).

Several other thinkers agree. Macy and Johnstone (2012, 3) champion 'active hope', which does not require optimism and can be practiced even when we feel hopeless. Stoknes (2015, 220–222) emphasizes 'active pessimism' and 'grounded hope': 'It's hope-less and I'll give it my all', he summarizes.

However, it takes courage to encounter reality and to be able to hope (Orr 2009, 173, 184–185; van; Boeckel 2009, 158; in theology, see Tillich 1965, 1952). This is a tough challenge for leaders in education and advocacy. The leaders must have the courage to engage in working with the 'affective and existential' dimensions of the situation (cf. Hicks and Bord 2001, 424).

Even despair can contain seeds of hope, as James Hillman and several others have pointed out (Stoknes 2015, 188–189, 219; Nicholsen 2002, 183–185; Hicks 2014, 106–109). Separation of hope from a certain clearly defined state of the future helps also to avoid what McGeer (2004, 110–111) calls 'willful hope', which often results in using others only as tools to advance one's goals, and in depression if the result is not achieved. Orr (2009, 189–190) compares the certain heart-breaking situation that realism brings with a situation of a doctor who knows how serious a perceived illness is: the patient must be told, and as a result, surprising courage and determination often occurs. As pointed out above, this requires that the teacher, the environmental educator, must first process these things herself.

In research on EE, the studies by Ojala (2016, 2012, 2007) confirm the crucial importance of hope for people living in our times. Ojala's studies focus on young people, who are an excellent source, because many of them have not yet resorted to forms of denial. Many studies have revealed that youth experience much anxiety about the global situation. As a needed response to the situation, Ojala (2012) defines three main themes for what she calls 'constructive hope', as differentiated from 'hope' as denial, which means wishful thinking (cf. McGeer 2004). Based on the analysis of interviews, people needed 'positive reappraisal', the ability to see something meaningful and promising after encountering the situation of the world. This was often related to 'trust in sources outside oneself': people wanted and often needed to believe that there are forces and institutions which are working toward good. And finally, people needed 'trust in one's own ability to influence environmental problems in a positive direction'.

Ojala does not discuss tragedy per se, but a discussion with her results provides an example about the ways in which hope and tragedy can be combined. She notes that hope gives 'energy to act even in the absence of certainties' (Ojala 2012, 627). This absence and its tragic character can be strengthened in relation to the three main themes she describes. Positive reappraisal can be linked with creating meaning, stressing hope and not optimism. Ojala herself notes that trust in others is not necessarily well founded or beneficial for environmental responsibility, for it can be a form of externalizing action to others (628). Thirdly, the trust in one's own ability to influence environmental problems in a positive direction can be interpreted as development of resilience: the positive direction need not be 'progress' in the traditional sense, but a more honest, meaningful and resilient situation (cf. Hicks 2002, 76–77).

Many people, deep down, resonate with the need for a realistic hope. They are aware that there are no easy solutions to the vast problems (cf. Marshall 2015, 145–149; Smith and Howe 2015, 199–200). Realistic hope has its discomforting elements, but it can also be deeply relieving for teachers, for example. Many teachers who have the task of dealing with climate education have struggled with the problem of anxiety, despair and hope (cf. Kelsey and Armstrong 2012, 189). They have the idea that they must not express their anxieties to children and youth, for that would generate despair (Hamilton, Bonneuil, and Gemenne 2015, 129). These warnings, which are often found in climate education materials, are relevant in the sense that the teacher must be careful not to project her anxieties to children (Österlind 2012, 46); and it should be kept in mind that the relations between the generations are a tricky issue psychologically (cf. Nicholsen 2002, 11, 135).

However, realistic discussion, where both tragedy and hope are dealt with, can be empowering for both the teacher and the audience. As discussed above, there is already anxiety that should be dealt with. Dickinson et al. (2013, 156) argue: 'If psychological resilience in the face of dire problems is a matter of tolerating increased anxiety, rather than suppressing it, then a combination of empowerment (collective efficacy) with compassion for other organisms may be a favorable emotional outcome of climate change education'. As Kelsey and Armstrong (2012), I argue that EE must build on hope as resilience.

Hicks provides many practical recommendations for educators in relation to discussing realistic hope (2014, 70–77, 85–90, 100–104, 144–146). His research of the 'sources of hope' for people has provided an important list of things to be grateful for (110–120; cf. Macy and Johnstone 2012, Chapter 3; Kelsey 2014). This points to a crucial dimension of joy and play, which may sound somewhat absurd after all the discussion above about anxiety, grief and other heavy matters. However, some of the most profound joy is found from places and people who have a strong sense of the tragic: that has helped them to appreciate daily life and ordinary things, and realistic hope can bring empowerment (cf. Stoknes 2015, 188–189).

Basically, there are two possibilities to respond to mortality and all that it contains: one can despair of the brevity of time (cf. Sigmund Freud on transience, quoted in Lertzman 2013, 124–126) or one can practice the art of *carpe diem*, living in the present. Writers such as Annie Dillard (1974) and Rachel Carson (1965) have written eloquently of the joy that a sense of wonder and a capacity to remain open to the world, despite the pain involved, can bring (cf. Foster 2015, 97–98, 109–110). As Carson's example shows, such an attitude can be strongly linked with positive action. A third writer, Vaclav Havel condensed some elementary aspects of such an attitude in his discussion of hope:

> Hope ... is not prognostication. It is an orientation of the spirit, an orientation of the heart; it transcends the world that is immediately experienced, and is anchored somewhere beyond its horizons .... Hope, in this deep and powerful sense, is not the same as joy that things are going well, ... but, rather, an ability to work for something because it is good. (quoted in Orr 2009, 182)

Others have described this kind of attitude by emphasizing the importance of retaining an ability to play well (cf. Clayton and Myers 2015, 295–296). Theologian Hugo Rahner goes so far as to say that only a *homo ludens*, the human at play, is able to take in both the tragedy and the joy. He seeks to describe 'that attitude that is poised between gaiety and gravity, between mirth and tragedy, and which the Greeks designated by the inimitable expression ... the 'grave-merry' man. Such a man [sic] is capable of making his life into a game, and a very lovely one at that, because he knows that this life is either a comedy or tragedy' (Rahner 1972, 9).

Thus, there is a link to 'well-being' and 'happiness' (cf. Weissbecker 2011; Kelsey and Armstrong 2012) in my argument, but I emphasize the need to encounter the tragic situation realistically. The way in which I would frame the narrative for our socio-environmental situation (cf. Smith and Howe 2015) is not melodrama and neither a simple tragedy, but a combination of tragedy and hope. It should be noted here that some thinkers use the concept of optimism in ways which come close to what I have discussed as hope. Examples include the application of Victor Frankl's 'tragic optimism' as meaning-creating activity which builds resilience (Ramsay and Manderson 2011, 168–171), Hicks's 'cautious optimism' (2014, 175) and the 'dark optimism' discussed by Hoggett (2013).

A somewhat similar stance is taken by one of the most influential environmental thinkers of the twentieth century, Aldo Leopold (1886–1948), who provided pioneering reflections on EE also. He believed that 'fear and indignation' are not the ways in which children and youth should be educated. Manifesting what has been called above 'realistic hope', Leopold ([1955] 1993) stated that: 'we shall not achieve harmony with land, any more than we shall achieve justice or liberty for people. In these higher aspirations, the important point is not to achieve, but to strive' (155–157).

It's a tough task. But an honest one, and one much needed.

Note

1. There is a problem in labeling people who wish to advance environmental matters as 'environmentalists', because the use of the term is often related to identity politics. However, I use the term here for brevity.

Acknowledgments

I express gratitude for comments on the draft of this article by EE scholars Anna Lehtonen and Essi Aarnio-Linnanvuori.

Disclosure statement

No potential conflict of interest was reported by the author.

References

Alarcon, G. M., N. A. Bowling, and S. Khazon. 2013. "Great Expectations: A Meta-Analytic Examination of Optimism and Hope." *Personality and Individual Differences* 54 (7): 821–827. doi:10.1016/j.paid.2012.12.004.

Becker, E. 1973. *The Denial of Death*. New York, NY: Free Press.

Berryman, T., and S. Lucie. 2013. "Languages and Discources of Education, Environment, and Sustainable Development." In *International Handbook of Research on Environmental Education*, edited by R. B. Stevenson, M. Brody, J. Dillon, and A. E. J. Wals, 133–146. New York, NY: Routledge.

Boeckel, J. V. 2013. "At the Heart of Art and Earth: An Exploration of Practices in Arts-Based Environmental Education." Diss., Aalto University, School of Arts, Design and Architecture, Helsinki.

Boeckel, J. V. 2009. "Arts-Based Environmental Education and the Ecological Crisis: Between Opening the Senses and Coping with Psychic Numbing." In *Metamorphoses in Children's Literature and Culture*, edited by B. Drillsma-Milgrom and L. Kirstinä, 145–164. Turku: Enostone.

Bonneuil, C. 2015. "The Geological Turn: Narratives of the Anthropocene." In *The Anthropocene and the Global Environmental Crisis: Rethinking Modernity in a New Epoch*, edited by C. Hamilton, C. Bonneuil, and F. Gemenne, 17–31. London: Routledge.

Brownlee, M. T. J., R. B. Powell, and J. C. Hallo. 2013. "A Review of the Foundational Processes that Influence Beliefs in Climate Change: Opportunities for Environmental Education Research." *Environmental Education Research* 19 (1): 1–20. doi:10.1080/13504622.2012.683389.

Brulle, R. J., and R. E. Dunlap. 2015. "Sociology and Global Climate Change." In *Climate Change and Society: Sociological Perspectives*, edited by R. E. Dunlap and R. J. Brulle, 1–30. New York, NY: Oxford University Press.

Buell, L. 1995. *The Environmental Imagination: Thoreau, Nature Writing, and the Formation of American Culture*. Cambridge: Belknap.

Buell, L. 2005. *The Future of Environmental Criticism: Environmental Crisis and Literary Imagination*. Blackwell Manifestos. Malden: Blackwell.

Bushnell, R. 2008. *Tragedy: A Short Introduction. Blackwell Introductions to Literature 18*. Malden: Blackwell.

Carson, R. 1965. *The Sense of Wonder*. New York, NY: Harper & Row.

Chang, C. H. 2014. *Climate Change Education: Knowing, Doing and Being*. Oxfordshire: Routledge.

Christie, D. E. 2013. *The Blue Sapphire of the Mind: Notes for a Contemplative Ecology*. New York, NY: Oxford University Press.

Clayton, S., P. Devine-Wright, P. Stern, L. Whitmarsh, A. Carrico, L. Steg, J. Swim, and M. Bonnes. 2015. "Psychological Research and Global Climate Change." *Nature Climate Change* 5 (7): 640–646. doi:10.1038/nclimate2622.

Clayton, S., and G. Myers. 2009. *Conservation Psychology: Understanding and Promoting Human Care for Nature*. 1st ed. Chichester: Wiley-Blackwell.

Clayton, S., and G. Myers. 2015. *Conservation Psychology Understanding and Promoting Human Care for Nature*. 2nd ed. West Sussex: John Wiley & Sons Ltd.

Clayton, S., C. Manning, and C. Hodge. 2014. *Beyond Storms & Droughts: The Psychological Impacts of Climate Change*. Washington, DC: APA and ecoAmerica.

De Young, R. 2013. "Transitioning to a New Normal: How Ecopsychology can Help Society Prepare for the Harder Times Ahead." *Ecopsychology* 5 (4): 237–239. doi: 10.1089/eco.2013.0065.

Dickinson, J. L. 2009. "The People Paradox: Self-Esteem Striving, Immortality Ideologies, and Human Response to Climate Change." *Ecology & Society* 14 (1): 1–17. doi:10.5751/ES-02849-140134.

Dickinson, J. L., R. Crain, S. Yalowitz, and T. M. Cherry. 2013. "How Framing Climate Change Influences Citizen Scientists' Intentions to Do Something about it." *The Journal of Environmental Education* 44 (3): 145–158. doi:10.1080/00958964.2012.742032.

Dillard, A. 1974. *Pilgrim at Tinker Creek*. New York, NY: Harper's Magazine Press.

Doherty, T. J., and S. Clayton. 2011. "The Psychological Impacts of Global Climate Change." *American Psychologist* 66 (4): 265–276. doi:10.1037/a0023141.

Eagleton, T. 2015. *Hope without Optimism*. Charlottesville: University of Virginia Press.

Eckersley, R. 2008. "Nihilism, Fundamentalism, or Activism: Three Responses to Fears of the Apocalypse." *Futurist* 42 (1): 35–39.

Forest, S., and M. A. Feder. 2011. *Climate Change Education: Goals, Audiences, and Strategies: A Workshop Summary*. Board on Science Education. Washington, DC: National Academies Press.

Foster, J. 2015. *After Sustainability: Denial, Hope, Retrieval*. London: Routledge.

Fritze, J., G. A. Blashki, S. Burke, and J. Wiseman. 2008. "Hope, Despair and Transformation: Climate Change and the Promotion of Mental Health and Wellbeing." *International Journal of Mental Health Systems* 2 (1): 13. doi:10.1186/1752-4458-2-13.

Gibbons, A. 2013a. "The Teaching of Tragedy: Narrative and Education." *Educational Philosophy & Theory* 45 (11): 1150–1161. doi:10.1080/00131857.2013.772707.

Gibbons, A. 2013b. "Tragedy and Teaching: The Education of Narrative." *Educational Philosophy & Theory* 45 (11): 1162–1174. doi:10.1080/00131857.2013.774516.

Gifford, R. 2011. "The Dragons of Inaction: Psychological Barriers that Limit Climate Change Mitigation and Adaptation." *American Psychologist* 66 (4): 290–302. doi: 10.1037/a0023566

Gough, A. 2013. "The Emergence of Environmental Education Research." In *International Handbook of Research on Environmental Education*, edited by R. B. Stevenson, M. Brody, J. Dillon, and A. E. J. Wals, 13–22. New York, NY: Routledge.

Hamilton, C. 2015. *Requiem for a Species: Why We Resist the Truth about Climate Change*, 2011. New York, NY: Earthscan.

Hamilton, C., C. Bonneuil, and F. Gemenne, eds. 2015. *The Anthropocene and the Global Environmental Crisis*. London: Routledge.

Hamilton, C. 2013. "What History can Teach us about Climate Change Denial." In *Engaging with Climate Change: Psychoanalytic and Interdisciplinary Perspectives*, edited by S. Weintrobe, 16–32. London: Routledge.

Harrison, P. R., and R. K. Mallett. 2013. "Mortality Salience Motivates the Defense of Environmental Values and Increases Collective Ecoguilt." *Ecopsychology* 5 (1): 36–43. doi:10.1089/eco.2012.0070.

Hicks, D. 2002. *Lessons for the Future: The Missing Dimension in Education. Futures and Education Series*. London: Routledge.

Hicks, D. 2014. *Educating for Hope in Troubled Times: Climate Change and the Transition to a Post-Carbon Future*. London: Institute of Education Press.

Hicks, D., and A. Bord. 2001. "Learning about Global Issues: Why Most Educators Only Make Things Worse." *Environmental Education Research* 7 (4): 413–425. doi:10.1080/13504620120081287.

Hitzhusen, G. E. 2006. "Religion and Environmental Education: Building on Common Ground." *Canadian Journal of Environmental Education* 11 (1): 9–25.

Hitzhusen, G. E. 2007. "Judeo-Christian Theology and the Environment: Moving beyond Scepticism to New Sources for Environmental Education in the United States." *Environmental Education Research* 13 (1): 55–74. doi:10.1080/13504620601122699.

Hitzhusen, G. E. 2011. "Climate Change Education for Faith Based Groups." Unpublished Manuscript. Available at http://sites.nationalacademies.org/cs/groups/dbassesite/documents/webpage/dbasse_072575.pdf (accessed 11 February 2017).

Hitzhusen, G. E. 2012. "Going Green and Renewing Life: Environmental Education in Faith Communities." *New Directions for Adult and Continuing Education* 133 (Spring): 35–44. doi:10.1002/ace.20005.

Hitzhusen, G. E., and M. E. Tucker. 2013. "The Potential of Religion for Earth Stewardship." *Frontiers in Ecology and the Environment* 11 (7): 368–376. doi:10.1890/120322.

Hoggett, P. 2013. "Discussion: Climate Change in a Perverse Culture." In *Engaging with Climate Change: Psychoanalytic and Interdisciplinary Perspectives*, edited by S. Weintrobe, 84–86. London: Routledge.

Hungerford, H. R., and T. L. Volk. 1990. "Changing Learner Behavior through Environmental Education." *The Journal of Environmental Education* 21 (3): 8–21. doi:10.1080/00958964.1990.10753743.

Jamieson, D. 2014. *Reason in a Dark Time: Why the Struggle against Climate Change Failed – And What It Means for Our Future*. Oxford: Oxford University Press.

Jickling, B., and A. E. J. Wals. 2008. "Globalization and Environmental Education: Looking beyond Sustainable Development." *Journal of Curriculum Studies* 40 (1): 1–21. doi:10.1080/00220270701684667.

Johnson, E. A., and M. J. Mappin. 2009. *Environmental Education and Advocacy: Changing Perspectives of Ecology and Education*. Cambridge: Cambridge University Press.

Kagawa, F., and D. Selby. 2010. *Education and Climate Change: Living and Learning in Interesting Times*. London: Routledge.

Kelsey, E., ed. 2014. *Beyond Doom and Gloom: An Exploration through Letters*. Munich: RCC.

Kelsey, E., and C. Armstrong. 2012. "Finding Hope in a World of Environmental Catastrophe." In *Learning for Sustainability in Times of Accelerating Change*, edited by A. E. J. Wals and P. B. Corcoran, 187–200. Netherlands: Wageningen Academic Pub.

Kidner, D. W. 2007. "Depression and the Natural World: Towards a Critical Ecology of Psychological Distress." *Critical Psychology* 19: 123.

Klein, N. 2007. *The Shock Doctrine: The Rise of Disaster Capitalism*. New York, NY: Metropolitan Books/Henry Holt.

Klein, N. 2014. *This Changes Everything: Capitalism Vs. the Climate*. London: Penguin.

Koger, S. M. 2015. "A Burgeoning Ecopsychological Recovery Movement." *Ecopsychology* 7 (4): 245–250. doi:10.1089/eco.2015.0021.

Kollmuss, A., and J. Agyeman. 2002. "Mind the Gap: Why do People Act Environmentally and What are the Barriers to Pro-Environmental Behavior?" *Environmental Education Research* 8 (3): 239–260. doi:10.1080/13504620220145401.

Kool, R., and E. Kelsey. 2006. "Dealing with Despair: The Psychological Implications of Environmental Issues." In *Innovative Approaches to Education for Sustainable Development*, edited by W. L. Filho and M. Salomone, 193–202. Frankfurt: Peter Lang.

Lehtonen, A. 2015. "Calls for Creative Collaboration: How Can Drama Provide Creative and Collaborative Learning Methods for Climate Change Education?" *Nordisk Dramapedagogisk Tidskrift* 52 (3): 34–37.

Lehtonen, A., H. Cantell, and A. Salonen. Forthcoming. "Climate Change Education in the Era of Anthropocene." In *Learning at the Edge of History*, edited by J. Lähdemäki and J. Cook. London: Palgrave Macmillan.

Lehtonen, J., and V. Jukka. 2013. "The Environmental Neurosis of Modern Man: The Illusion of Autonomy and the Real Dependence Denied." In *Engaging with Climate Change: Psychoanalytic and Interdisciplinary Perspectives*, edited by S. Weintrobe, 48–51. London: Routledge.

Leopold, A. 1993. *Round River: From the Journals of Aldo Leopold*, 1955. Oxford: Oxford University Press.

Lertzman, R. A. 2015. *Environmental Melancholia: Psychoanalytic Dimensions of Engagement*. Hove: Routledge.

Lertzman, R. A. 2013. "The Myth of Apathy: Psychoanalytic Explorations of Environmental Subjectivity." In *Engaging with Climate Change: Psychoanalytic and Interdisciplinary Perspectives*, edited by S. Weintrobe, 117–133. London: Routledge.

Li, S-C. S. 2014. "Fear Appeals and College Students' Attitudes and Behavioral Intentions Toward Global Warming." *the Journal Of Environmental Education* 45 (4): 243–257. doi: 10.1080/00958964.2014.930399.

MacLellan, M. 2015. "The Tragedy of Limitless Growth: Re-Interpreting the Tragedy of the Commons for a Century of Climate Change." *Environmental Humanities* 7 (1): 41–58. doi:10.1215/22011919-3616326.

Macy, J. 1983. *Despair and Personal Power in the Nuclear Age*. Philadelphia, PA: New Society Publishers.

Macy, J., and C. Johnstone. 2012. *Active Hope: How to Face the Mess We're in without Going Crazy*. Novato: New World Library.

Macy, J. 1995. "Working through Environmental Despair." In *Ecopsychology: Restoring the Earth, Healing the Mind*, edited by T. Roszak, M. E. Gomes, and A. D. Kanner, 240–269. San Francisco, CA: Sierra Club.

Marshall, G. 2015. *Don't Even Think about It: Why Our Brains are Wired to Ignore Climate Change*. New York, NY: Bloomsbury Publishing USA.

McGeer, V. 2004. "The Art of Good Hope." *The Annals of the American Academy of Political and Social Science* 592: 100–127. doi:10.1177/0002716203261781.

McIntosh, A. 2008. *Hell and High Water: Climate Change, Hope and the Human Condition*. Edinburgh: Birlinn.

Miceli, M., and C. Castelfranchi. 2010. "Hope: The Power of Wish and Possibility." *Theory & Psychology* 20 (2): 251–276. doi:10.1177/0959354309354393.

Moe-Lobeda, C. D. 2013. *Resisting Structural Evil: Love as Ecological-Economic Vocation*. Minneapolis, MN: Fortress Press.

Næss, A. 2002. *Life's Philosophy: Reason and Feeling in a Deeper World*. Athens: University of Georgia Press.

Nicholsen, S. W. 2002. *The Love of Nature and the End of the World: The Unspoken Dimensions of Environmental Concern*. Cambridge: MIT Press.

Norgaard, K. M. 2011. *Living in Denial: Climate Change, Emotions, and Everyday Life*. Cambridge: MIT Press.

Ojala, M. 2007. *Hope and Worry: Exploring Young People's Values, Emotions, and Behavior regarding Global Environmental Problems*. Örebro: Örebro University Universitetsbiblioteket.

Ojala, M. 2012. "Hope and Climate Change: The Importance of Hope for Environmental Engagement among Young People." *Environmental Education Research* 18 (5): 625–642. doi:10.1080/13504622.2011.637157.

Ojala, M. 2016. "Young People and Global Climate Change: Emotions, Coping, and Engagement in Everyday Life." In *Geographies of Global Issues: Change and Threat*, edited by N. Ansell, N. Klocker, and T. Skelton, 1–19. Singapore: Springer.

Orr, D. W. 2009. *Down to the Wire: Confronting Climate Collapse*. Oxford: Oxford University Press.

Österlind, E. 2012. "Emotions - Aesthetics - Education: Dilemmas Related to Students' Commitment in Education for Sustainable Development." *Journal of Artistic and Creative Education* 6 (1): 32–50.

Paidas, S. M. 2011. "Psychologies of the Environment: Searching for Themes in the Literature." *Ecopsychology* 3 (2): 125–138. doi:10.1089/eco.2011.0007.

Palmer, J. A. 1998. *Theory of Environmental Education*. Florence, KY: Routledge.

Pyszczynski, T. 2004. "What are We so Afraid of? A Terror Management Theory Perspective on the Politics of Fear." *Social Research* 71 (4): 827–848.

Pyszczynski, T., J. Greenberg, and S. Solomon. 1999. "A Dual-Process Model of Defense against Conscious and Unconscious Death-Related Thoughts: An Extension of Terror Management Theory." *Psychological Review* 106 (4): 835–845. doi:10.1037/0033-295X.106.4.835.

Rahner, H. 1972. *Man at Play*. New York, NY: Herder and Herder.

Ramsay, T., and L. Manderson. 2011. "Resilience, Spirituality and Posttraumatic Growth: Reshaping the Effects of Climate Change." In *Climate Change and Human Well-Being: Global Challenges and Opportunities*, edited by I. Weissbecker, 165–184. New York, NY: Springer.

Randall, R. 2009. "Loss and Climate Change: The Cost of Parallel Narratives." *Ecopsychology* 1 (3): 118–129. doi:10.1089/eco.2009.0034.

Randall, R. 2013. "Great Expectations: The Psychodynamics of Ecological Debt." In *Engaging with Climate Change: Psychoanalytic and Interdisciplinary Perspectives*, edited by S. Weintrobe, 87–102. London: Routledge.

Reser, J. P., and J. K. Swim. 2011. "Adapting to and Coping with the Threat and Impacts of Climate Change." *American Psychologist* 66 (4): 277–289. doi:10.1037/a0023412.

Russell, J. 2016. "'Everything has to Die One Day': Children's Explorations of the Meanings of Death in Human-Animal-Nature Relationships." *Environmental Education Research* 4 February 2016: 1–16 doi:10.1080/13504622.2016.1144175.

Rustin, M. 2013. "How is Climate Change an Issue for Psychoanalysis?" In *Engaging with Climate Change: Psychoanalytic and Interdisciplinary Perspectives*, edited by S. Weintrobe, 170–185. London: Routledge.

Sapiains, R., R. J. S. Beeton, and I. A. Walker. 2015. "The Dissociative Experience: Mediating the Tension between People's Awareness of Environmental Problems and their Inadequate Behavioral Responses." *Ecopsychology* 7 (1): 38–47. doi:10.1089/eco.2014.0048.

Scioli, A., and H. B. Biller. 2009. *Hope in the Age of Anxiety*. Oxford: Oxford University Press.

Scott, B. A., E. L. Amel, S. M. Koger, and C. M. Manning. 2016. *Psychology for Sustainability*. New York, NY: Routledge.

Scranton, R. 2015. *Learning to Die in the Anthropocene: Reflections on the End of a Civilization*. San Francisco, CA: City Lights Publishers.

Searles, H. 1972. "Unconscious Processes in Relation to the Environmental Crisis." *Psychoanalytic Review* 59 (3): 361–374.

Selby, D. E. 2011. "Education for Sustainable Contraction as Appropriate Response to Global Heating." *Journal for Activist Science and Technology Education* 3 (1): 1–14.

Skrimshire, S., ed. 2010. *Future Ethics: Climate Change and Apocalyptic Imagination*. London: Bloomsbury Publishing.

Smith, P., and N. Howe. 2015. *Climate Change as Social Drama: Global Warming in the Public Sphere*. Cambridge: Cambridge University Press.

Sobel, D. 1996. *Beyond Ecophobia: Reclaiming the Heart in Nature Education*. Great Barrington: Orion Society.

Steiner, J. 2013. "Discussion: Climate Change in a Perverse Culture." In *Engaging with Climate Change: Psychoanalytic and Interdisciplinary Perspectives*, edited by S. Weintrobe, 80–84. London: Routledge.

Sterling, S. R. 2001. *Sustainable Education: Re-Visioning Learning and Change.* Totnes: Green Books for the Schumacher Society.

Stevenson, R. B., A. E. Justin Dillon, J. Wals, and M. Brody. 2013. "The Evolving Characteristics of Environmental Education Research." In *International Handbook of Research on Environmental Education*, edited by R. B. Stevenson, M. Brody, J. Dillon, and A. E. J. Wals, 512–517. New York, NY: Routledge.

Stevenson, R. B., and I. Robottom. 2013. "Critical Action Research and Environmental Education: Conceptual Congruencies and Imperatives in Practice." In *International Handbook of Research on Environmental Education*, edited by R. B. Stevenson, M. Brody, J. Dillon, and A. E. J. Wals, 469–479. New York, NY: Routledge.

Stoknes, P. E. 2015. *What We Think about When We Try Not to Think about Global Warming: Toward a New Psychology of Climate Action.* White River Junction: Chelsea Green Publishing.

The Tbilisi Declaration. 1977. *The World's First Intergovernmental Conference on Environmental Education.* Paris: UNESCO and UNEP. Available at https://www.gdrc.org/uem/ee/EE-Tbilisi_1977.pdf (accessed 15 February 2017).

Tillich, P. 1952. *The Courage to Be.* New Haven, CT: Yale University Press.

Tillich, P. 1965. "Right to Hope." *Neue Zeitschrift Für Systematische Theologie Und Religionsphilosophie* 7 (3): 371–377.

Toh, S.-H., and V. F. Cawagas. 2010. "Transforming the Ecological Crisis: Challenges for Faith and Interfaith Education in Interesting Times." In *Education and Climate Change. Living and Learning in Interesting Times*, edited by F. Kagawa and D. Selby, 175–196. London: Routledge.

Välimäki, J., and J. Lehtonen. 2009. "Ilmastonmuutoksen torjuntaan tarvitaan johtajuutta." *Kanava* 6: 341–344.

Wallace, J. 2007. *The Cambridge Introduction to Tragedy.* Cambridge: Cambridge University Press.

Webb, D. 2007. "Modes of Hoping." *History of the Human Sciences* 20 (3): 65–83. doi:10.1177/0952695107079335.

Weintrobe, S., ed. 2013. *Engaging with Climate Change: Psychoanalytic and Interdisciplinary Perspectives.* London: Routledge.

Weintrobe, S. 2013a. "The Difficult Problem of Anxiety in Thinking about Climate Change." In *Engaging with Climate Change: Psychoanalytic and Interdisciplinary Perspectives*, edited by S. Weintrobe, 33–47. London: Routledge.

Weintrobe, S. 2013b. "On the Love of Nature and on Human Nature: Restoring Split Internal Landscapes." In *Engaging with Climate Change: Psychoanalytic and Interdisciplinary Perspectives*, edited by S. Weintrobe, 199–213. London: Routledge.

Weissbecker, I., ed. 2011. *Climate Change and Human Well-Being: Global Challenges and Opportunities.* New York, NY: Springer.

Williston, B. 2012. "Climate Change and Radical Hope." *Ethics & the Environment* 17 (2): 165–186. doi:10.2979/ethicsenviro.17.2.165.

Wuthnow, R. 2010. *Be Very Afraid: The Cultural Response to Terror, Pandemics, Environmental Devastation, Nuclear Annihilation, and Other Threats.* Oxford: Oxford University Press.

Zeyer, A., and E. Kelsey. 2013. "Environmental Education in a Cultural Context." In *International Handbook of Research on Environmental Education*, edited by R. B. Stevenson, M. Brody, J. Dillon, and A. E. J. Wals, 206–212. New York, NY: Routledge.

REPLY

Response to 'Environmental education after sustainability: hope in the midst of tragedy'

Katie Carr

This is a reply to:

Pihkala, Panu. 2017. "Environmental education after sustainability: hope in the midst of tragedy." *Global Discourse*. 7 (1): 109–127. http://dx.doi.org/10.1080/23269995.2017.1300412.

This article (Pihkala 2017) is a challenging one for a number of reasons. The themes it addresses (denial, mortality, grief, guilt, shame) are heavy, and even as a reader for whom these ideas are not novel, one must acknowledge the emotional response they evoke. But what is most challenging, from a practice perspective, is the seeming gulf between the author's recommendations, and the current tacit assumptions and aims within environmental education, and even more so within the formal education system more widely. The potential within this article, and what the author describes as an interdisciplinary approach, lies in the fact that it is positioned on the boundaries of a number of different discourses, attempting to bring the language and knowledge of psychology and philosophy into the field of environmental education, and in so doing bring fresh perspectives and ways of understanding – and consequently, solutions to – the challenge of environmental education in a post-sustainability world.

It is important to situate this response, in order to provide some context for the aforementioned challenges. I work in the field of education for sustainable development and global citizenship (ESDGC) in the UK, supporting educators – mainly primary school teachers – to develop and embed global citizenship and sustainability education into their teaching and learning. ESDGC can itself be conceptualised as a 'boundary practice' (Wenger 1998), that is, a practice whose purpose is to span the discourses of other practices in order to shed new light, address tensions and problems, and expand perspectives. In this case, there are influences from formal education, international development studies, critical theory and activism. Sustainability does not appear at all in the national curriculum in England, and climate change only in key stages 3 and above (from age 11). The organisation recently took part in a piece of international research which explored the policy enablers and barriers to embedding global citizenship education into the curriculum in over 10 different countries in Europe, and whilst it was found that the English context is particularly unconducive, generally formal education systems make it difficult for teachers – even very engaged and concerned individuals – to prioritise pedagogies and practices which put sustainability at centre-stage (Tarrozi and Inguaggiato 2016). Based on our extensive experience working with teachers in this field, many of the challenges they face, even prior to the difficulties that the author sets out in this paper around the personal psychological difficulties and sensitivities associated with grief, denial, guilt and mortality, are directly correlated with the fact that the education system, as is, functions as an institution for replicating and reinforcing the current Western worldview. There is a prescriptive curriculum which delivers discrete subject areas; children are constantly reminded that there are right and wrong answers to any problem, rather than being given 'the ability to encounter two various, even opposite notions at the same time'; and educators find themselves operating within a surveillance system of performance and standards management, which frames the purpose of education as being to prepare children for effective participation in a growth-oriented economy. Within these co-entangled factors, the spaces available in which teachers can realistically engage with complex global issues such as climate change, let alone participate in the kind of transformational personal journey that the author suggests, are strictly limited.

The article astutely illuminates another challenge that is borne out in our work with teachers in the UK, which is reluctance, in some cases, to address emotionally sensitive and difficult issues in their teaching, a view which could be summed up by a statement I heard recently from a teacher discussing whether and how to bring global news stories into the classroom (paraphrased here): 'It's part of our duty to protect children from some of the darker realities of the real world, they'll have to learn about those soon enough.' This view could be described not as denial as the author presents it, but *denial on others' behalf*. Traditional forms of ESDGC are based on assumptions of empowerment, of foregrounding children's agency and sense of self-efficacy through providing opportunities for them to imagine the kind of world they would like to live in, and then take action and make choices towards creating that world. Even this mental model is based on one of the underpinning archetypal *stories* of the Western world view, rooted in Enlightenment thinking, that, through application of reason, humans are able to coordinate their effort and *manage* the natural world.

If most national curricula and education systems are not conducive to even a traditional form of environmental education, at least many practitioners now look to the Sustainable Development Goals (SDGs) as an opportunity for justifying the inclusion of climate change on sustainability in their day to day work with children. Of particular relevance here is indicator 4.7, which states that 'by 2030, ensure that all learners acquire the knowledge and skills needed to promote sustainable development, including, among others, through education for sustainable development and sustainable lifestyles …'. Many schools in the UK are beginning to incorporate this indicator into their learning activities and outcomes, but, whilst it may offer space for exploration of some issues relevant to this article, the SDG framework itself could be seen as a global systematic denial, as they are defiantly growth-oriented. Even through reinforcing the ubiquity of the phrase *sustainable development*, the framework serves to obfuscate the inherent problematic nature of both of these individual concepts. Rather than unquestioningly taking on the SDGs in classrooms, children need to be given opportunity through education to develop criticality, to feel confident to challenge these concepts, and comfortable to exist in a world where certainty doesn't exist.

This piece provides a useful new perspective for environmental education, bringing together, as it does, the diverse realms of philosophy and psychotherapy. The challenge is that the discourses it brings together are so far removed from the lived experiences of educators, especially those in the formal sector, that nothing short of a paradigm shift is likely to create conditions in which some of the recommendations made become possible. If formal educators currently balk at the idea of involving their children in critical dialogue around the human causes, and likely global effects, of climate change, then I doubt that they would be enthused by the idea of 'environmentally-centered [sic] death education'. So as a step towards bridging the aforementioned gulf between the author's proposals, it may be useful to look for existing but less mainstream education practices which could afford opportunities for exploring at least some of the recommendations. Firstly, Philosophy for Children (P4C) is a dialogic, enquiry-based learning methodology, in which a skilled facilitator helps to create a safe space for relaxed, collaborative, co-constructive learning which encourages critical thinking amongst children, enables them to understand experientially the fact that multiple perspectives can and do exist, and can be used effectively for exploring sensitive complex real-life issues. The use of stories and storytelling, whilst not mentioned by the author explicitly as one of the arts or drama-based possibilities for exploring many of the issues raised, can be a powerful learning activity, both to explore issues such as death and finitude, but also – and I believe, with more potential for transformation – through drawing on non-Western and indigenous sources, stories which may provide alternative archetypes for understanding, for example, humanity's role and status in the world, or different spiritualities. And finally, school farms and the Forest Schools movement could be a useful site for further investigation into possible exploration of death and nature-related guilt. All of these practical approaches would give opportunities for practitioners to provide an educational affordances for bringing hope through 'a process of creating meaning and positive action' rather than through focusing on 'a certain goal or state of the future'

Disclosure statement

No potential conflict of interest was reported by the author.

References

Pihkala, P. 2017. "Environmental Education after Sustainability: Hope in the Midst of Tragedy." *Global Discourse* 7 (1). http://dx.doi.org/10.1080/23269995.2017.1300412

Tarrozi, M., and C. Inguaggiato. 2016. *Global Citizenship Education in Europe: A Comparative Study on Education Policies across 10 EU Countries*, available at http://www.globalschools.education/ Activities/GCE-in-Europe, accessed 18/01/2017.

Wenger, E. 1998. *Communities of Practice – Learning, Meaning, and Identity.* Cambridge: Cambridge University Press.

Education after sustainability

Steve Gough

ABSTRACT

There is nothing at all new about societies collapsing as a result of environmental crises caused by poor choices made under uncertainty. Indeed, such instances have been very well documented by, in particular, Jared Diamond; and some have been further explored from an educational perspective. However, and as Diamond himself points out, it can very well be argued that, because of the globalised nature of contemporary societies, a situation now arises in which it is the human species as a whole, rather than any particular and relatively isolated community, that faces possible collapse. It would seem, therefore, that the scale of the problem has increased; but we still might ask whether its underlying nature has changed all that much and, if not, whether in fact human societies have ever or even, ultimately, could ever be sustainable. The environmental extinction of societies has usually occurred when long, slow and powerful trends in nature have coincided with inappropriate social preoccupations that either ignore or are ignorant of them. The paper identifies education as a common denominator; itself both a long-term characteristic of evolved social behaviour and a short-term social preoccupation.

Introduction

Nature is made better by no mean
But nature makes that mean: so, o'er that art,
Which you say adds to nature, is an art
That nature makes.
The Winter's Tale, Act 4, Scene 4

There is a growing body of literature that suggests that the ideas of sustainability and sustainable development, which have been highly influential in academic and policy discourse for nearly 30 years, are now not only irrelevant to the achievement of global environmental security but actually also obstruct it. Further, it is proposed that even if sustainability was ever an achievable goal it isn't now. Human impact on the environment has gone too far, and we must prepare ourselves for the difficulties that will inevitably ensue. In this paper I accept this pessimistic prospectus. However, I would like to note in passing that it would not be fair, in my view, to suggest that nothing (which is not the same thing as 'not enough') has been achieved through the conceptual vehicle of sustainability. On the contrary, and for all its internal contradictions, the idea of being sustainable has a ready accessibility that explains its longevity and that any proposed alternative would do well to emulate. Against this it may well be argued, and with some justification, that 'ready accessibility' is part of the problem. However, that does not make it any more likely that abstruse and/or arcane alternatives will succeed where sustainability has failed.

This paper focuses on the educational implications of post-sustainability discourse. The literature of post-sustainability, much like the wider literature of environmental policy, tends to say little about education beyond a typically unelaborated claim that it is important, or even crucial. A further assumption is often implicit: that education is both capable of transmitting, and available to transmit, whatever knowledge, beliefs, skills, sensitivities, attitudes and dispositions policy is currently held to require. However, John Foster's (2001, 2008, 2015) work is exceptionally well-considered in relation to such matters, and I have focused upon it for that reason. Foster also takes a broadly Darwinian perspective, as do I. We might well note at this point that there exists a long-established and deeply rooted tradition within education that has a Darwinian foundation; even though, in contemporary writings, that foundation often goes unacknowledged. It is primarily derived from and through the work of John Dewey, who provides a further link to work in economic philosophy on which I draw below.

Also at this point, methodological rigour requires that I declare that John Foster and I are friends and long-time collaborators. As will be seen, this does not mean that we share the same views about everything.

It will not be possible, within this short paper, to develop from scratch all the conceptual, empirical and discursive scaffolding upon which my educational engagement with wider post-sustainability thinking rests. Nor would it be reasonable to expect readers with no background (or particular ongoing interest) in education to be patient while I did so. I therefore begin by setting out 10 initial premises that I am prepared to defend, and that I subsequently develop and/or justify as and when it seems necessary and appropriate. They are as follows:

(1) Whatever the post-sustainability educational message is to be, learners will not simply abandon everything they have previously believed the minute they hear it, and then transform their lives accordingly. Damascene conversions of this kind are not unknown perhaps, but they are rare. Education is not a quick fix. Further, environmentalists face a problem (to be quite clear, I am saying only that *they do* face it, not necessarily that *they deserve to face it*, in this instance) about the basis of belief. The situation is analogous to the case of stock markets: one can try to forecast their future movements using *fundamental analysis* – that is, by examining in detail the latest economic and corporate data – or by *technical analysis* that extrapolates past and present trends into the future. Both are, roughly speaking, equally (un)reliable. Environmentalists typically draw on the latest scientific data in shaping their prognoses and prescriptions; a fundamental approach in this sense. Members of the public, on the other hand, may prefer a 'technical' approach, noting that environmentalists have been predicting catastrophe for a very long time now and that it has invariably (as they see it, at least) failed to materialise. Hence, they may conclude, there is probably really

nothing much to worry about this time either. Educationally speaking, this presents a genuine problem. To put it another way, being right isn't the same as being convincing.

(2) Though it is almost impossible to avoid entirely, one should be most cautious about appearing to speak for the whole of humanity. Statements of the kind 'what we need is this' or 'people should be like that' are almost certain to be oversimplifications based on an (unavoidably) inadequate grasp of the rich variety of human experience and aspiration. Learners may not respond well if their experiences and aspirations are discounted, taken for granted or assumed out of existence.

(3) There is a useful distinction to be made between 'the environment' and 'nature'. The environment is rich with human meaning, and may be considered good or bad, better or worse, at a point in time. It is, we may say, socially constructed. It changes. It can be changed. If all this were not true there would be nothing to worry about, or to be done. Nature, by contrast, is what it is, and includes all persons and all time, as well as much (we can reasonably surmise) of which we humans remain entirely ignorant. Of course, 'environment' and 'nature' are in the end both just words, and they can mean whatever one wants them to mean: the point, however, is that the view from the summit of Ben Nevis (should one be visible) is not the same sort of thing as gravity or cell division, either pedagogically or in any other sense.

(4) What a person learns is not the same as what they are taught.

(5) There is widespread confusion about whom or what the beneficiaries of education should be. Even if we set aside claims that it should be 'the economy' or (actually rather differently) 'business' that is served, there is clearly no guarantee that teaching considered to be beneficial for society over a particular timescale will correspond to any given individual learner's perceived, or actual, best interests over that, or other, time periods. Any claim that people should be educated in the interests of 'the environment' is so vague and ill-formed as to face apparently insuperable difficulties of both content and justification.

(6) Education may be formal, non-formal or informal. For present purposes we might say that all these varieties have in common an instructional and purposive aspect. 'Learning' occurs: through education; independently of education and, quite often, in spite of education.

(7) In an environmental context, education must confront uncertainty about the future. Uncertainty may persist in the public mind even in the face of an apparently conclusive convergence of scientific evidence. It may also, in relation to particular issues and at particular times and places, be quite expunged from public discourse by all sorts of non-scientific, unscientific and even anti-scientific nonsense. People try to make sense of, and so resolve, uncertainties that they experience in a number of different ways, including through appeals to sets of rules, to substantive outcomes or to justice. For example, imagine a deep and attractive pool in the heart of the jungles of Northern Borneo (some do still exist, and I have one in particular in mind). It contains fish that are now considered rare because of the impacts of logging and siltation at a regional scale. National park legislation might impose a fishing ban, justified by biological data, as a

means to wildlife conservation. Social justice might require the restoration of traditional fishing rights for local people – who are not, after all, the ones responsible for the pressure on the environment that led to the decline of fish numbers or the setting up of the park. Substantively, the most effective practically available course of action at the point of decision might turn out to be to license further logging elsewhere the better to subsidise protection of this particular space, or even simply to sell the land to a private owner. Each option – and there may be others – will certainly be controversial. At this point some readers will note my debt here to, in particular, Michael Thompson (see, for example, 1997). However, I am here using these different sense-making perspectives as an heuristic only, and do not intend to enquire further into their empirical foundations or conceptual completeness.

(8) A thing can be necessary but not possible.

(9) There was never a 'golden age'. If there had been, we would not be able to go back to it. Time only goes forward.

(10) There are no social 'end-states', perfect or otherwise, to which societies may be brought in perpetuity. To suggest otherwise is ahistorical, anti-Darwinian and unscientific.

Precedents

There are plenty of historical examples of societies that have contributed to their own demise through, ultimately, catastrophic environmental change. Some have been famously catalogued and examined by Jared Diamond (see, in particular, 2005). Elsewhere, I have drawn on Diamond's work to consider the possible educational implications of two of these cases – the Greenland Norse, and the Easter Islanders (see, for example, Gough 2015). A number a salient points arise for the present discussion.

Firstly, the detail of catastrophe in both cases was consequent on a convergence of powerful, long-term, slow-moving factors with a series of shorter term events, decisions and actions. The Greenland Norse died out completely as a consequence, ultimately, of a long period of global cooling. The specific manifestations of this process in individual lives at particular times were mediated through contemporary religious and cultural practice. In their case, interestingly and from a retrospective view, a viable alternative was available since the Inuit (whom they preferred, rather, to kill) were perfectly comfortable with the climate and, in principle at least, might profitably have been imitated. It appears, however, this was not something that ever struck the Norse themselves as an 'alternative'. The Easter Islanders were also subject to long-term natural factors beyond their comprehension (for example, lack of airborne soil replenishment), but contributed spectacularly to their own eventual crash into destitution and cannibalism through prioritisation of the religious and cultural over sound resources management. The situation is somewhat analogous to a shipwreck; the slow actions of deep currents and ocean-spanning winds combine, at a particular point in time, with this wave or that, and with urgent human decision-making based on the apparent exigencies of the moment, to rupture the hull on a particular rock, causing particular damage with specific consequences.

This brings us to a second point: subsequent, post-disaster accounts or investigations (if anyone survives to carry them out) are likely to focus more on the 'exigencies of the moment' and less on long-term factors, even if (most improbably) the latter are known and understood in their entirety. To combine two insights from the work of Robert Nozick (2001, 1993; respectively), we human beings are evolutionarily equipped to develop a view of things that is *useful* rather than necessarily true; and, a powerful time preference – a disposition to discount the future in favour of the present – has proved, evolutionarily, very useful. We should note that, firstly, our view of things (whatever it may be) will often be found even more useful if we can convince others (and, indeed, ourselves) that it is true, and, secondly, the fact that an evolved characteristic may have proved useful in the past says nothing about its consequences in the future.

All of the foregoing means that, thirdly, when the day of post-sustainability reckoning arrives it seems naive to imagine that it will be widely acclaimed as a vindication of the environmentalist case. Rather, as things go from bad to worse, it is very much more likely that popular explanation will focus on proximate difficulties and solutions – the prevention of mass migration, perhaps; or, local flood and storm mitigation, disease control, the securing of food supplies or preparations for war. For these things there is precedent. Anyone wishing to assert that there is an alternative, equal, and more attractive precedent for the emergence of traditional, small-scale, harmonious and democratic social structures should challenge themselves by examining Diamond's (2012) detailed discussion. This includes, *inter alia*, compelling evidence that, if we compare modern and traditional societies in terms of war-related death rates (that is, the *percentage* of the population dying as a result of warfare averaged over significant periods), we find that even in the cases of twentieth-century Russia and Germany the rate is only one-third of the average for traditional, pre-industrial societies. This is indeed an astonishing result, but the data are there to review.

What might be an outline of an educational response to all of this? Trying to teach the Greenland Vikings that they should abandon their Christian religion, their Norse culture and their agricultural economy, and instead live like Inuit, sounds like a potentially very unpromising and short-lived project. But one thing that they might have said, before, no doubt, unsheathing their axes, would have been that religion, culture and agricultural practices handed down since the dawn of their society were *more important* than sustainability, or even survival. Similarly, an attempt to teach the Easter Islanders that they should stop wasting their time and resources quarrying and erecting statues would have surely seemed to them to be the alien peddling of a nonsensical recipe for disaster; or, perhaps, a temptation sent by the Gods to test their resolve. The point is that telling others that they should simply be like you (or, more usually, like you think you would be in a perfect world) is, at a minimum, poor pedagogy.

Diamond (2005) makes the point that, because of globalisation in all its many aspects, we may now regard the whole of human society as being in the same relation to its resource base as the Greenland Norse and the Easter Islanders were to theirs in their day. Though this raises the stakes hugely, it doesn't alter educational dynamics much. At the same time, education seems attractive as a solution because it offers the hope that people might come to make better choices for themselves, rather than be in any way compelled. To see whether this is possible, we need to look more deeply at what education actually is.

Being human

It is most usual to locate the origins of our environmental difficulties in the industrial and scientific revolutions, and the enlightenment thinking that underpinned them. For most purposes this may be entirely appropriate. For present purposes I would like to stress the importance of another, much earlier event, known in ancient times as 'the lowering of kingship from Heaven to Earth'. It happened at a place called Eridu in Mesopotamia (Kriwaczek 2010) not less than 6,000 years ago. The changes that occurred at that time were immense. Top of my own personal ranking is the invention of writing. Others might prefer to emphasise the creation of the first cities, the division of labour, mathematics, law, monuments, wheeled vehicles or civil engineering. The list goes on. At this point the creation of surplus made possible new conditions in which further surpluses were not only possible but also necessary to meet expanding obligations. A seed had germinated. The future became pregnant with possibilities, and perhaps some certainties. This was the moment when, to borrow the words of the poet Sylvia Plath, humanity found it had …:

> … eaten a bag of green apples
> Boarded the train there's no getting off.
> ('Metaphors'; The Colossus, 1960)

Or, to persist with apple metaphors, it was where the Snake tempted Eve, Eve tempted Adam and humans were expelled from Paradise, or at least from Neolithic agriculture. After this, perhaps, the industrial revolution, or something essentially like it, was almost bound to happen, somewhere, sooner or later. Also after this, perhaps, human society was doomed to *ultimate* unsustainability. More importantly for present purposes education, in some form and for some people, became both possible and necessary. Knowledge was cumulative, specialised and could be stored; even maintenance of the status quo required its transmission between generations. We might even ask, therefore, whether education is itself a *product* of unsustainability?

Whatever the truth of this disturbing suggestion, we should note that taking a longer term, post-Eridu view has two main advantages. Firstly, it enables one to see education as a long-standing, fundamental aspect of human social life, rather than as merely, for example, a policy tool or source of 'human capital'. Secondly, it invites consideration of topics that include very long-term elements (such as climatic change, for example, or the role of instinct) without *necessary* or *exclusive* reference to an essentially recent, post-industrial set of sociopolitical concepts (including 'socialism', for example, or 'neo-liberalism'). In saying this I do not seek to pick a fight with colleagues for whom challenging neo-liberalism is the main goal, and the environmental threat an opportunity to pursue it. Indeed, a longer term perspective exposes more sharply those instances where particular interests are served by presenting problems that are clearly of a contemporary and political nature as being, rather, the unintended consequences of natural processes. This happens, for example, when an unjust distribution of scarce water is recast as an unavoidable consequence of low rainfall (Loftus 2015). But this is not my focus. Rather, I want to explore, in a particular way, the proposition that: 'attending to nature in its actual workings – embracing the object prior to abstractions of any kind' (Philo 2015, 324) can be liberating and, ultimately, educational.

Time

'Not even the weather belongs to the moment. It is a product of past emissions' (Malm 2016, 7). This statement, to which one might add that weather is also the product of a range of wholly natural and sometimes very slow-moving variables, forms part of a recent refutation of a specific claim of contemporary Marxist geography. This claim is that we should now seek the source of social change across the dimension of space rather than through the dimension of time, because globalisation means that everything happens simultaneously everywhere.

I may well be missing something of the detail here, but at the most general level any such change of focus would seem to me tantamount to a final abandonment, rather than an adjustment, of a Marxist frame of reference. As Geoffrey Hodgson (2006) has pointed out, the perspectives taken by Marx and Darwin had much in common. One such common element is a focus on the material world and, specifically, on change over time. So, insights from Marx are helpful in thinking about human activities in a context of underlying Darwinian assumptions; for example, the former's observation that all production entails an 'appropriation of nature' (Marx 1858/1973).

However, Hodgson also makes the point that Marx focused on the essence of entities, holding that one could most usefully think, for example, in terms of collectivities such as 'the proletariat' or 'the bourgeoisie' that embodied the essential characteristics of their component individuals. For Darwin, by complete contrast, the crucial property of a collectivity such as, particularly, a species, was its ability to generate internal variety. From an educational perspective these fundamental positions appear to point in totally different directions, particularly, perhaps, in a time of environmental crisis.

If a class of geographers (or other social scientists) have abandoned Darwinism, or even time itself, as a parameter of their enquiries, it will not result in their becoming professional outcasts. Historically, social scientists have tended to exclude Darwinism from their thinking anyway (see Hodgson 2002, 2004, 2006; for a full discussion). Indeed, the topic can be a sensitive one. It is not that educationalists (for example) do not believe in Darwinism, but rather that they wish to insist that it is no longer of relevance to their enquiries. Their view, as expressed for example by historian of education David Hamilton (1990), is that at the point where humans began to appropriate nature (whenever that actually was) they also took control of unfolding history, rendering evolutionary processes irrelevant.

And indeed, most of the time, they *are* irrelevant to the job at hand. If one is critiquing assessment protocols (say), or developing pedagogies for e-learning, one can take the evolutionary context as pretty much given. Further, past attempts to extrapolate Darwinian (or what have been supposed to be Darwinian) principles into the social realm at a policy level have been at best misguided, and at worst an excuse for doing evil things to other people. Given that this is so, the impulse to have nothing to do with such principles is quite understandable. On the other hand, the objection to Darwin looks odd when one considers the almost universal rejection, by contemporary educational theorists, of any form of theoretical mind–body dualism. In this difficult context, before attempting to move on, we should note the following – really very necessary – clarifications:

- As Wilson (2012) shows, there is no reason to suppose that evolution has stopped happening. It does, however, occur at a pace that humans find hard to think – or care – about. We should note in passing that in this work Wilson radically and controversially revises his earlier deterministic (and probably even more controversial) view of the relationship between the biological and the social.
- Darwinism has nothing to say about 'progress'. It *can have nothing* to say. The concept of progress is an artefact of human thought and discourse. It exists nowhere else. Natural selection is a blind process in nature, not a form of qualitative judgement.
- Darwinism requires that there can be no such thing as an uncaused cause. Hodgson (2004, 96) refers to this as the 'principle of determinacy'. It creates problems for the idea of human agency, to which I return below.
- We can ask – very cautiously indeed, and at a high level of abstraction – whether the core Darwinian concepts of variation, selection and replication provide a potentially useful means of better understanding social phenomena (Hodgson and Knudsen 2010). Of course, one *could* ask this question using the term 'social evolution'. I have deliberately avoided doing so, not only because that phrase brings with it far too much unwanted and inappropriate baggage but also because it is theoretically clumsy. I am not suggesting, even slightly, that social processes are an extension of biological ones; nor, since E.O. Wilson had the change of heart mentioned above, is anyone else of whom I am aware doing so. What I am asking, however, is whether, in the abstract, a degree of conceptual continuity across the separate realms of physical and social phenomena might be useful; whether, in particular, it might enable us to better understand the immediate, short-term pressures that bear on our decisions and actions by illuminating the context of slow-moving, powerful, long-term forces in which they are embedded.

This way of thinking, which is being discussed at a most sophisticated and scholarly level in the present by, in particular, Hodgson and Knudsen, is not, of course, new. On the contrary, it has been developed over many years. It finds early expression in the works of, for example, Thorstein Veblen and John Dewey. Dewey, in turn, was a major influence on the work of Richard Rorty, who makes the following observation:

> There is no way in which tools can take one out of touch with reality. No matter whether the tool is a hammer or a gun or a belief or a statement, tool-using is part of the interaction of the organism with its environment. To see the employment of words as the use of tools to deal with the environment, rather than as an attempt to represent the intrinsic nature of that environment, is to repudiate the question of whether human minds are in touch with reality .... The very idea of being 'out of touch with reality' presupposes the un-Darwinian, Cartesian picture of a mind which somehow swings free of the causal forces exerted on the body. (Rorty 1999, xxiii)

I want to suggest that, firstly, this statement is of the utmost significance to any proper understanding of human action in relation to the environment and, secondly, that two caveats should attach to it. The importance of Rorty's insight lies in the fact that it tells us that there simply is no place outside of nature from which nature (including human beings) can be observed. Even astronauts observing earthrise over the moon are tool using, evolved creatures who are, by nature, embedded in their environment. This environment includes not only foundational phenomena such as (in that case) the mass of the Earth, light, gravity and so on but also socially constructed elements such as the need to uphold national pride, loyalty to one's comrades, personal career aspirations, good wishes from friends and family and Earth-bound campaigners who argue that space flight is an expensive insult to the poor and so should be abandoned. There is no way at all of smuggling oneself out of this naturally embedded condition. However, the attempt is frequently, almost routinely, made. Success is often claimed, by all sorts of people, on all sorts of spurious grounds. After all, if others believe you to have a key to understanding the weft and warp of human life in all its complexity, then, whether you yourself really believe in it or not, your 'key' will have proved a most effective tool for you in dealing with your own environment.

The first caveat here is that Rorty's view should not be taken as a dismissal of the enlightenment. On the contrary, he refers to its ideals as 'our most precious cultural heritage' (Rorty 1979, 333). It has given rise to many very useful ways of 'dealing with the environment'. His comprehensive discussion is to be found in *Philosophy and the Mirror of Nature*, and I will not attempt to summarise it in a few words here.

Secondly, though it takes nothing away from Rorty's point to say it, if the words 'out of touch with nature' have the meaning he gives to them, then we need another form of words to describe the condition of the Greenland Norse back in the fourteenth century, as they struggled with increasingly long and fierce winters brought on by climatic processes they knew nothing about. We might say that the worsening weather and the need for Christian observance were both real to them, but that, in the end, the former enjoyed an ontological precedence over the latter.

According to Rorty (1979, 1999) what we should hope for, over time, is not 'truth' but 'edification'. Such a formulation would seem to confer on education both a starring role and a mighty burden of responsibility. Further, it suggests that it is at least as much the case that 'society matters because it educates', as it is that 'education matters because it does things for society'.

Dark self? Or, what you see is what you get?

I turn now to a discussion of post-sustainability ideas as presented by Foster (2015). I do so because I consider the approach he takes to be a particularly powerful and suggestive one, and I apologise because whatever highlights I pick out in the course of the following short, highly selective discussion, which is explicitly guided by my desire to progress my own arguments, will not do it justice. However, I do also wish to suggest that, beyond a certain point, Foster's argument might better be developed in a different direction.

One of four themes that lie at the heart of Foster's prospectus for hope out of despair is that of 'wildness not well-being'. He defines wildness as: 'our ability to live and act as whole, natural beings, undisintegrated and unalienated' (12). Broadly speaking (we shall consider the matter more narrowly later) this seems not inconsistent with both the formulation of Philo (2015, quoted above), and the overall case I have made myself to this point. Foster's argument develops by pointing out that the future is not given but under construction, and by suggesting that contemporary *progressivism*, that is, the belief that only constant material improvements can give meaning to life, has its root in an inability to make sense of the inescapability of our own mortality. This claim has considerable advantages from the perspective of the present discussion. It focuses attention on the human individual, that is, at the intersection of collectivism and reductionism, and so makes possible an integrated discussion. The alternative can only be that social and natural scientists continue to have largely separate conversations. It is also (as Foster himself subsequently shows) fully consistent with a Darwinian view. Finally, it leads to conclusions that are, at least initially, educationally suggestive of variety and adaptiveness:

> Hope ... Can mean the clear-eyed determination to live anyway, the life-courage of trusting oneself to the chance, thus kept open beyond anything that either optimism or pessimism could anticipate, that the unforeseen may yet reward us. (Foster 2015, 92)

The problem remains, however, that given the Darwinian natural selection and the principle of determinacy it is difficult to see how the conscious individual can think about her/his own consciousness in a way that permits personal agency; but it is even harder to believe – let alone live as if – such agency is unachievable. I am an evolved, determinate being, but I believe I am free to choose and to act.

Foster addresses this problem by means of a sustained piece of virtuoso reasoning which, given its own premise, I certainly would not think of contradicting. However, I want to suggest that there is a false premise at work, and that, in consequence, all the previous good work done by the arguments of the book is steered, finally, towards an unfortunate conclusion. The premise in question is that: 'to remain free to choose on the very cusp of action .... I have to think of my willing self as something beyond the domain of sufficient reason' (127), that is, as non-determinate. From this starting point, the argument leads to the conclusion that individuals possess consciously unknowable 'dark selves', that is: 'our real selves (organism and consciousness in combination)' (135). Foster then goes on to argue that: 'what we encounter as external wildness is *our own dark-selfhood externalised*' (155, original emphasis).

Philosophically elegant though they are, these last moves land us in a place that is at best disturbing. The key problem is that having shown that the dark self is inherently unknowable, Foster has now talked himself into believing that he himself knows what it is like – not only in his own case but for everyone else as well. Hence, we find ourselves confronting a version of the catch-all of all positive freedom discourses (see Berlin 2002, for the classical exposition of this term): people should be free to choose, and we will know that they have made truly free choices when what they choose is what we initiates have already perceived to be right for them. Fears on this score are in no way allayed when Foster suggests a passage from the Communist Manifesto as a model or, come to that, engages in a rather grumpy-old-man style tirade against, among other things, the London Olympics, reality TV and tourism.

I shall not dwell on this. Suffice it to say that the best response to radical uncertainty is never to convince yourself that you know the one right answer, however tempting that may be; and education ceases to be educational when it becomes the vehicle for any such 'right answer'.

My main purpose is to suggest there is a better way of concluding Foster's initial argument. Its approach resembles Foster's own in one respect, in that it draws on the concept of resilience. However, it also dispenses with the need for a dark self, arguing rather that our compulsion to think of ourselves as being separate from the rest of nature, and as possessing agency in relation to it, is itself simply an evolved characteristic. It therefore requires no more special explanation than do the facts that we have two legs and give birth to live young. To make this case, I draw on the concept of emergent properties as presented within the Institutionalist tradition.

Resilience, institutions and habits

As Welsh (2014) has pointed out, the concept of resilience has developed in two different forms from two quite distinct disciplinary genres. One of these is primarily associated with psychology, the other with ecology. It is the second of these traditions that most concerns us here. Walsh also makes the point that the concept has become rather overworked in recent years. It has been deployed, as metaphor or analytical tool, to address a wide range of complex problems and has in the process, perhaps, lost some or most of its cutting edge. Whatever the truth of this may be, the present discussion begins from the foundational work on resilience theory associated with the ecologist C.S. Holling and his associates. We might note in parentheses that Holling's work has also been an important influence on the anthropological studies of human environmental sense-making under uncertainty associated with Michael Thompson and his collaborators and mentioned above.

Holling (2010a, 2010b) distinguishes two forms of resilience in natural systems. 'Engineering resilience' focuses on securing a return to an equilibrium state following disturbance. It is enhanced if the speed of such a return can be increased, and/or if the range of tolerable disturbance from the equilibrium can be increased. Engineering resilience is exhibited by many human-made physical structures, such as bridges and flood defences, and also by reptiles which can tolerate wide variation around their internal body temperature. However, if the limits of the tolerable range are exceeded, the bridge will collapse, the water will breach the defences, or the creature will die. Applied as a metaphor to human social systems, we might say that engineering resilience was characteristic of Neolithic agriculture and, indeed, of Greenland Norse society (it is, perhaps, questionable whether the Easter Islanders exhibited much resilience of any kind). There is also an implicit appeal to engineering resilience in all environmentalist discourse that either; harks back to an imagined 'golden age' or 'true state of human nature', or, urges us all on towards some future, sustainable or post-sustainable, Shangri-La. The emergence of such equilibrium-focused projects is not surprising, nor is it evidence of silliness. In times of trouble one wants to go home, get back to normal, expiate ones sins or start a new and better life. The question, however, is whether such responses are of any use – in a post-sustainability context, or, actually, any other. They tell us what is (alleged to be) necessary, but make unsupported, and often unsupportable claims about what is possible.

By contrast with engineering resilience, ecological resilience is concerned with constant adaptability at the limits of being. Learning is central to it. It is exhibited by, for example, human beings, all other mammals, predator drones and advanced chess-playing software. As you read this your internal body temperature lies within a view degrees of the fatal level. Your tolerance to variations around the optimum temperature is tiny. Every moment of every day your body's systems adapt to keep within tolerable limits. Toleration of variability in the external environment is thus hugely increased. In consequence, mammals in general, and humans in particular, have spread to every corner of the Earth. Also exhibiting ecological resilience, a tornado jet fighter cannot glide, but it can fly close to the ground across rough terrain at almost unimaginable speed, adjusting the interrelation-ships of vital, complex variables, moment by moment, as it does so.

I would like to be clear at this point that I do not wish automatically to rubbish all appeals to engineering resilience. It has served snakes and crocodiles very well. In addition, stability has a human value that should not be ignored or trivialised; and, ecological resilience is enhanced by variety so, at the level of life on the planet, the existence of forms of engineering resilience of itself makes a contribution to ecological resilience. However, all that being said, snakes and crocodiles haven't changed much over the millennia, determined stability doesn't offer the best educational opportunities and, of course, the whole point about accepting the post-sustainability premise is that, anyway, stability just isn't on offer any more, even if it ever was. Post-Eridu, and certainly since the industrial revolution, ecological resilience of some sort is our species' only genuine option.

On the face of it, this conclusion would appear to accord with Foster's view (though it is true that he also discusses psychological resilience). We have already noted his references to 'life-courage' and 'trusting oneself to the chance'. He further comments (2015, 194): 'this whole book is really about … *existential* resilience … a way of resiliently decentred *being*, unsubverted as far as is humanly possible by the ego-self' (Foster 2015, 194, original emphasis). And yet, at the same time, we find him, *inter alia*:

- Asserting what kinds of experience everyone must have (for example, 170: 'We must be genuinely exposed, beyond any game and without safeguards …').
- Equating modern democracy with *'mass-mediated sound bite populism'* (202).
- Launching an assault on contemporary educational practice that seems, at best, to have been informed by an overview of political policy statements rather than any engagement with what actually goes on between real teachers and real students in contemporary classrooms (200).
- After a great deal of intellectual hand-wringing, concluding that: 'Authority legiti-mated by self-appointment … makes sense if it is from the dark self' (206), on which latter subject, of course, the 'self-appointed authority' is also the self-appointed authority.

Well, thanks, but no thanks. To take these points in order:

- Isn't the fact that we actually are exposed to danger from nature supposed to be the whole problem in the first place? And does it really count for nothing that very many people don't like/want to be exposed and without safeguards?
- Modern democracy may not be perfect. That doesn't mean that any other plan is automatically better.
- Much good teaching in relation to the environment takes place. It does so under ethical constraints that include a proper prohibition on making children feel guilty or frightened.
- The essence of resilience is variety. It is one thing to point out that climate science is simply not taken seriously enough, and another to pretend that any self-selecting group knows, or could ever know, enough to plan the future successfully.

I, for one, would rather 'trust myself to the chance', in Foster's own phrase. But all of this is a great shame, because what we have here is a most promising baby that unfortunately finds itself sitting in a few teaspoons full of rather unappealing bath water.

It seems to me that the heart of the problem is that the device of 'the dark self' has allowed Foster imagine he has escaped his (actually inescapable) embeddedness in nature, and crossed the border, so to speak, to reach a vantage point from which all may be seen and understood. It is a clever, bold and provocative attempt to solve the problem of determinacy versus agency, and in criticising, as I have, it's final moves, I incur a responsibility to propose an alternative. This I now do, though unlike Foster's arguments, mine are not original.

Modern Institutionalism (Hodgson 2002, 2004, 2006; Hodgson and Knudsen 2010) proposes a fully Darwinian account of human interrelations with the rest of nature that depends on a conception of layered ontologies. This is to say that we might think about the world at a molecular level, for example, or at a cellular level. We might also think of a person as an individual, or as a member of a family or of a productive organisation. The person, clearly, is made of cells, and these in turn are made up of molecules. The Institutionalist suggestion is that, at each successive level, emergent properties may arise. Thus, a cell has properties that cannot be fully predicted from the study of molecules, and an individual person has properties that cannot be fully predicted from the study of cells. An institution, in turn, may behave in ways not fully explicable from the characteristics of the individuals who comprise it.

It is important to note that in these exemplar cases, and in all others, the higher ontological level cannot behave in ways that contradict the laws governing lower levels; for example, cell division cannot happen in ways that flout the laws of physics, even as it cannot be fully explained by them.

This formulation enables Hodgson (2007, 7) to propose the possibility of 'endogenous and situation-dependent preference formation'. Learning, understood through the Deweyan lens of habit formation (Dewey, 1922), is central to such preference development and so, therefore, are education and educational institutions. Hodgson (2007, 8) writes:

> People do not develop new preferences, wants or purposes simply because 'values' or 'social forces' control them. Instead, the framing, shifting and constraining capacities of social institutions give rise to new perceptions and dispositions within individuals. Upon new habits of thought and behaviour, new preferences and intentions emerge.

Institutions operate upon habits. As habits are operationalised under complex and changing circumstances, new individual inclinations and practices develop, leading, in turn, to institutional changes. Individual agency is retained in this way, as is the agency of institutions. Variety is acknowledged and respected. Both methodological reductionism and methodological collectivism are rejected. There is a point to what we do, think and learn, but at the same time the sense of our embeddedness in both physical and social worlds is retained. As I write these words, I am doing what the words themselves say: I am bringing my own institutionally-mediated habits of thought and practice to bear on a new situation of a familiar type. It is all I can do, but only I can do it in this particular way.

In fact, there exist numerous examples of the power of education to change habits of thought and action, under radically unsustainable circumstances, theorised in terms of resilience and recovery and focusing on engagement with the natural world (see, in particular, Tidball and Krasny 2014, and also the educational work of the UK Wiltshire Wildlife Trust). Some of these projects do indeed focus on 'wildness', as Foster would have us do. The work of the US Sierra Club with wounded and/or traumatised military veterans is, in fact, quite a bit wilder than most of us could cope with. However, other projects concentrate on husbandry of nature, which is, I would argue, every bit as natural, every bit as concerned with the 'actual workings' of nature 'prior to abstractions' as anything can ever be, including 'wildness'. Therapeutic benefits, improvements in human relationships and positive changes of attitude to the natural world are consistently reported.

The great educationalist Eric Hoyle once remarked that his life's work had been devoted to securing steady improvements, but that: *'What do we want? Steady improvement! When do we want it? In due course!!'* was a chant certain never to be heard on the streets. Radicals will object that working educationally to change habits and reshape institutions is something we don't have time for. It simply doesn't meet the requirements of what is *necessary*, they will say. There may even be those who conclude that education really is a product of unsustainability, and so should be curtailed or abolished. Views of this latter kind are (sadly) already far from unknown in our modern world. But, before insisting on what we think is necessary, we should reflect closely on what we think is important.

Disclosure statement

No potential conflict of interest was reported by the author.

References

Berlin, I. 2002. *Liberty*. Oxford: Oxford University Press.
Dewey, J. 1922. *Human Nature and Conduct: An Introduction to Social Psychology*. 1st ed. New York: Holt.
Diamond, J. 2005. *Collapse: How Societies Choose to Fail or Survive*. London: Allen Lane.
Diamond, J. 2012. *The World until Yesterday: What Can We Learn from Traditional Societies?* London: Allen Lane.
Foster, J. 2001. "Education as Sustainability." *Environmental Education Research* 7 (2): 153–165. doi:10.1080/13504620120043162.
Foster, J. 2008. *The Sustainability Mirage*. London: Earthscan.
Foster, J. 2015. *After Sustainability: Denial, Hope, Retrieval*. London: Earthscan from Routledge.
Gough, S. 2015. *Education, Nature and Society*. New York: Routledge.
Hamilton, D. 1990. *Curriculum History*. Geelong: Deakin University Press.
Hodgson, G. M., ed. 2002. *A Modern Reader in Institutional and Evolutionary Economics*. Cheltenham: Edward Elgar.
Hodgson, G. M. 2004. *The Evolution of Institutional Economics: Agency, Structure and Darwinism in American Institutionalism*. London: Routledge.
Hodgson, G. M. 2006. *Economics in the Shadows of Darwin and Marx: Essays on Institutional and Evolutionary Themes*. Cheltenham: Edward Elgar.
Hodgson, G. M. 2007. "Introduction." In *The Evolution of Economic Institutions: A Critical Reader*, edited by G. M. Hodgson, 1–15. Cheltenham: Edward Elgar.
Hodgson, G. M., and T. Knudsen. 2010. *Darwin's Conjecture: The Search for General Principles of Social and Economic Evolution*. Chicago: University of Chicago Press.

Holling, C. S. 2010a. "Engineering Resilience versus Ecological Resilience." In *Foundations of Ecological Resilience*, edited by L. H. Gunderson, C. R. Allen, and C. S. Holling, 51–66. Washington, DC: Island Press.

Holling, C. S. 2010b. "The Resilience of Terrestrial Ecosystems." In *Foundations of Ecological Resilience*, edited by L. H. Gunderson, C. R. Allen, and C. S. Holling, 67–114. Washington, DC: Island Press.

Kriwaczek, P. 2010. *Babylon: Mesopotamia and the Birth of Civilisation*. London: Atlantic Books.

Loftus, A. 2015. "Water (In)Security: Securing the Right to Water." *The Geographical Journal* 181 (4): 350–356. doi:10.1111/geoj.2015.181.issue-4.

Malm, A. 2016. *Fossil Capital: The Rise of Steam Power and the Roots of Global Warming*. London: Verso.

Marx, K. 1858/1973. *Grundisse: Foundations of the Critique of Political Economy*. London: Penguin.

Nozick, R. 1993. *The Nature of Rationality*. Princeton, NJ: Princeton University Press.

Nozick, R. 2001. *Invariances: The Structure of the Objective World*. Cambridge, MA: Belknap/Harvard University Press.

Philo, C. 2015. "(In)Secure Environments and the Domination of Nature: Introduction to Themed Section." *The Geographical Journal* 181 (4): 322–327. doi:10.1111/geoj.2015.181.issue-4.

Rorty, R. 1979. *Philosophy and the Mirror of Nature*. Princeton, NJ: Princeton University Press.

Rorty, R. 1999. *Philosophy and Social Hope*. London: Penguin.

Thompson, M. 1997. "Security and Solidarity: An Anti-Reductionist Framework for Thinking about the Relationship between Us and the Rest of Nature." *The Geographical Journal* 163 (2): 141–149. doi:10.2307/3060177.

Tidball, K. G., and M. E. Krasny. 2014. *Greening in the Red Zone: Disaster, Resilience and Community Greening*. New York: Springer.

Welsh, M. 2014. "Resilience and Responsibility: Governing Uncertainty in a Complex World." *The Geographical Journal* 180 (1): 15–26. doi:10.1111/geoj.2014.180.issue-1.

Wilson, E. O. 2012. *The Social Conquest of the Earth*. New York: W.W. Norton.

Learning and education after sustainability

William Scott

This is a reply to:

Gough, Steve. 2017."Education after sustainability." *Global Discourse*. 7 (1): 131–145. http://dx. doi.org/10.1080/23269995.2017.1300435.

I liked this paper (Gough 2017). It is written with style and wit (some of it biting), and I found it refreshingly clear in its arguments. Quite a lot, although not all, of the paper's themes and foci will be familiar to anyone who has followed Stephen Gough's work over the last 15 years, but the way that these have been brought together here is novel, and a valuable contribution to our understanding and thinking about these important matters. In particular, I have in mind his writings about catastrophic environmental change (e.g. the Greenland Norse), Darwinism and Resilience, and his critical appreciation of the work of Rorty, Foster, Dewey, Thompson, Berlin and others. The paper's stance is also novel in the sense that it offers a scholarly critique from a particular perspective of a major book.

The paper has new things to say about how we might think about education itself and about its interrelationship with the environment. Not everyone will like these, but that's all to the good. I found Gough's taking us back to Eridu to be particularly instructive. He writes,

> ... perhaps, the industrial revolution, or something essentially like it, was almost bound to happen, somewhere, sooner or later. Also after this, perhaps, human society was doomed to *ultimate* unsustainability. More importantly for present purposes education, in some form and for some people, became both possible and necessary. Knowledge was cumulative, specialised and could be stored; even maintenance of the status quo required its transmission between generations. (Gough 2017, 6)

Gough also asks, 'We might even ask, therefore, whether education is itself a product of unsustainability'. Well, we might, but this isn't the sort of sustainability that the rest of the paper is mostly concerned with. Rather, it seems to be about social continuity (and maybe even that slippery idea, progress) rather than being environmental in character. I say this as, back in Eridu, there wasn't a specific threat from nature, other than the quotidian one of combatting danger, finding food and shelter, and staying alive. What the Greenland Norse experienced, or what we may be faced with, having given nature a significant shove by the way we have chosen to live, are very different in nature.

Gough's point that education, in some form, and for some people, became both possible and necessary because, 'as knowledge was cumulative, specialised and could be stored, even maintenance of the status quo required its transmission between generations', is self-evidently the case once you think about it. I came to much the same view in early 2016 as I listened to the outcomes of research (Wilson 2017) into the lives of the young people who lived around the Stonehenge landscape in the Mesolithic period. There obviously were children in Mesolithic times, and Pauline Wilson asked: *How can we shed light on what they got up to?* Maybe they were out there learning, she suggested; that is, preparing for their economic and social roles in later life: acquiring skills and competencies, as we might put it today. Wilson was speculating, of course, as the archaeological record does not really speak about the youth of yesterday, but she established a plausible case that there must have been a formalisation of learning to some degree, as the induction of the young into the evolving skills necessary to stay alive and thrive at that time needed to happen. She suggested that there might have been a sort of monitorial system where those children who knew more instructed the others; to go farther, perhaps there was even learning through play. In some ways, the picture Wilson painted seemed very like today's experiences and maybe what we see today in forest schools in particular, and in the outdoor classroom more generally, are but faint echoes of those far-off times.

If there were valuable skills and dispositions to be learned, then that might suggest, one way or another, an organisational conceptual frame, outline schemes of work, and favoured pedagogies; and a curriculum; although to write it down like this seems like over-egging the pudding. But if there were a curriculum or sorts, would there also inevitably have been disputation about it, even if it were not quite what Benjamin (1939) suggested in his magisterial satire, the *Sabre-tooth curriculum*. That said, Mesolithic arguments about timeless qualities versus practical skills for the future, that lie at the heart of Benjamin's work, are plausible.

Gough goes on to say that

> … we should note that taking a longer term, post-Eridu view has two main advantages. Firstly, it enables one to see education as a long-standing, fundamental aspect of human social life, rather than as merely, for example, a policy tool or source of 'human capital'. Secondly, it invites consideration of topics that include very long-term elements (such as climatic change, for example, or the role of instinct) without *necessary* or *exclusive* reference to an essentially recent, post-industrial set of sociopolitical concepts …. (Gough 2017, 6)

Whilst I think that this is both right, and helpful, I wonder whether the word *learning* fits the first part of this argument better than does the word *education*. After all, as Gough points out in his 10 premises, a lot of the learning we do (and, plausibly, have always done) goes on out of the sight of educators. However, it is *education* not learning that is the policy tool, so all this can be rather difficult to formulate.

I wonder what others will make of the 10 initial premises. In a broad general sense, they seem fine to me, even though I don't go along with all of them in quite the way they are constructed. However, as I have premises of my own, that's hardly surprising. I found some rather telegraphic, especially #4: 'What a person learns is not the same as what they are taught', and I find that when I say that to people (usually in its even pithier variant: 'learners don't learn what teachers teach'), they can be very puzzled indeed as not everyone spends too much time teasing out the canonical differences between education and learning. I certainly wondered whether #9: 'There was never a "golden age". If there had been, we would not be able to go back to it. Time only goes forwards' might be usefully combined with #10: 'There are no social "end-states", perfect or otherwise, to which societies may be brought in perpetuity. To suggest otherwise is ahistorical, anti-Darwinian and unscientific', as they seem to be addressing the same point from different perspectives. That, of course, would mean that there were now only nine premises, which would seem unfinished, and so I'll suggest a 10th: 'Schools cannot change the nature and purpose of society as fast as society can change the purpose and nature of schools'. It seems to me that this truth (which governments of all stripes validate all the time) has huge implications for an education that takes environment and sustainability (of whatever sort) seriously. This is particularly the case if you are intent that the education you provide should change society's approach to the environment/sustainability, as so many environmental and sustainability programmes (and educators) so confidently and hubristically are.

My final point is to note that I read the paper with the Abstract in mind because the last part of this holds out a particular promise for the paper. It says

> The paper … identifies education as a common denominator; itself both a long term character- istic of evolved social behaviour and a short term social preoccupation. (Gough 2017, 1)

At the end of the paper, I asked myself whether it had done justice to that idea, and to that *potential*. And I don't think it quite does as much as it might have. I thought about this as I read the last part of the paper, starting from 'Modern Institutionalism …'. I think that the way that Gough deals with Hodgson's work (particularly through the 2007 quote) is valuable here. It seems to me that the 'people' that Hodgson was writing about must include the young, but I wonder if young people are sufficiently a special case to warrant a separate comment. They are, after all, subject to two forms of influence that most other people are not, both of which involve a moral guardianship: the home and family, and the school. Both these institutions are intent on inculcating good habits, often under the general heading of *educating*, and some- times are in sharp opposition to each other. Think, for example, of Jamie Oliver's school food trials and the Yorkshire mothers who thrust burgers through school railings to ensure that their children got, what was in their view, proper food. Inevitably, they got little thanks for taking an active interest in their children's welfare.

In the end, the most important of Gough's points might just be this:

> Education seems attractive as a solution because it offers the hope that people might come to make better choices for themselves, rather than be in any way compelled. (Gough 2017, 5)

Oh, if only all environmental educators saw things so clearly.

Disclosure statement

No potential conflict of interest was reported by the author.

References

Benjamin, H. R. W. 1939. *The Saber-Tooth Curriculum, Including Other Lectures in the History of Paleolithic Education*. New York: McGraw-Hill.

Gough, S. 2017. "Education after Sustainability." *Global Discourse* 7 (1). http://dx.doi.org/10.1080/23269995.2017.1300435

Wilson, P. 2017. "Towards a Methodological Framework for Identifying the Presence of and Analysing the Child in the Archaeological Record, Using the Case of Mesolithic Children in Post-Glacial Northern Europe." In *Studies in the British Mesolithic and Neolithic*. 2. Oxford: Peter Lang.

On preparing for the great gift of community that climate disasters can give us

Rupert Read

ABSTRACT

There is a widespread (if rarely voiced) assumption, among those who dare to understand the future which climate chaos is likely to yield, that civility will give way and a Hobbesian war of all against all will be unleashed. Thankfully, this assumption is highly questionable. The field of 'Disaster Studies', as shown in Rebecca Solnit's *A Paradise Built in Hell*, makes clear that it is at least as likely that, tested in the crucible of back-to-back disasters, humanity will rise to the challenge, and we will find ourselves manifesting a truer humanity than we currently think ourselves to have. Thus the post-sustainability world will offer us a tremendous gift amidst the carnage. But how well we realise this gift depends on our preparing the way for it. In order to prepare, the fantasy of sustainable development needs to be jettisoned, along with the bargain-making mentality underpinning it. Instead, the inter-personal virtues of generosity, fraternity and care-taking need fostering. One role a philosophically informed deep reframing can play in this process of virtuous preparation for disaster is in helping people to understand that, in order to care for their children, they need to care for their children in turn, and so on, ad infinitum.

'That we carry on like this *is* the catastrophe.' – Walter Benjamin.

'The recovery of [a sense of] purpose and closeness without crisis or pressure is the great contemporary task of being human. Or perhaps the dawning era of economic and environmental disasters will solve the conundrum for us more harshly.' (Solnit 2009)

The greenhouse gases we've already unleashed commit us to grave new natural (*sic*) disasters.

There is a widespread (if rarely spoken about) assumption, among those who dare (as few do) to understand – to see with open eyes – the character of the future which climate chaos is likely to yield, the world of escalating 'natural' (*sic*) disasters which we are bequeathing to our children and to their children. That assumption is that civility will give way and a Hobbesian war of all against all will be unleashed. (Think *The Road*, or at best *The Hunger Games*.)

Thankfully, the assumption is highly *questionable*.

In this article, I set out why, by appealing to too-little-known results that have been found in the interdisciplinary academic field of 'Disaster Studies' (Section 2). I then outline that we nevertheless need to find a deliberate and proactive way of *answering* the question (of whether civility will be diminished or perhaps instead in truth even significantly *improved*, by climate disasters) in the right way (Section 3); we most certainly cannot just leave it to 'history' to sort things out, without our own agency. I then emphasise a dimension of the agency that we have as philosophers/intellectuals/ communicators: a practicable way of getting us to think/feel/care for others, locally *and* globally, *and* across time. Namely, by starting from the recognition of the importance to us of our own children (Section 4). I round things out with a few conclusions – mainly through bringing together the insights of Sections 3 and 4 – and some thoughts of further directions for research (Section 5).

Before any of that, however, I need briefly to address the worry that my title may already have raised, for some readers, perhaps putting them off. How dare one speak of disaster as potentially the bringer of a *gift* (Section 1)?

1.

We know now that dangerous anthropogenic climate change is not merely a matter of a glacially slow steady increase in world temperature. Such global overheat (aka 'global warming') is real and may well be the worst single element of anthropogenic climate change. But the more immediately noticeable effect, for most people, for a long time to come is likely to be climate *chaos*. And the weather chaos that is the most immediate manifestation thereof. We are talking an increased incidence of ultra-powerful storms, floods, droughts; and more striking or surprising phenomena such as the possibility of the Gulf Stream temporarily or permanently 'switching off', or of a permanent El Nino.

In other words, for a long time to come, the most noticeable and perhaps the most damaging impact of the heating that we have unleashed will be events that will manifest as disasters. We are going to see 'biblical' (*sic*) floods, hurricanes of unprecedented scale and much more.

These will *be* disasters. I am not quarrelling with that verdict, that nomenclature. We can foresee right now the deaths of millions, perhaps of tens or even hundreds of millions, from these disasters. That is a terrible thing. It is a terrible thing even to have to foresee, to contemplate it; let alone for it to be experienced, suffered, as it almost certainly will be.

In the current piece, I explain why these disasters, though terrible, will nevertheless not be *unmitigated*. In fact, they will provide us with an opportunity for something wonderful and necessary.

When disaster occurs, one can simply be defeated by it. Or indeed one can use it to make things even worse for others, as in 'The Shock Doctrine', named by Naomi Klein (2007). *Or* one can quite literally make the best of it. *I think that we should make absolutely no apology for choosing, if ever possible, the third of these three options.*

The argument that I make in the following section is that making the best of disaster is in simple fact (though the fact is remarkable and gives great hope) *what comes naturally* to human beings. In particular, I shall suggest that human beings today – particularly in those parts of the world (more and more of it) where terrible strain has been put on any and all traditional embedding of life in communities that can be relied upon – are even yearning for such an opportunity. I don't, of course, mean that people are yearning for disaster to strike. I mean that very many of us are living lives of quiet desperation, more or less inchoately awaiting *something* that can enable such communities to be *recreated*.

Disaster, when it comes, is of course unwelcome, terrible. It would be a twisted theodicy which would try to make of such disasters nothing but a good thing. It is not the best of all possible times, if one has to endure disaster (still less, obviously, if that disaster wipes one and/or one's loved ones out). *But yet*, disaster can yield an astonishing, direly needed gift, as I shall now describe.

2.

Let me begin the body of this essay by speaking personally. In doing so, I will try to break further through a wall of 'stealth denial' that I think we virtually all tend to build around us, today, even those of us who are well aware of the likelihood (on a business-as-usual pathway) of a potentially irrecoverable civilisational collapse within the next generation or three.

For well over a decade now, I have been afraid of the nightmare that (I thought) would unfold, if true disaster, likely as a result of climate-chaos, for example, through food shortage, comes to a place like England, where I live. I have engaged in some fragments of serious through seemingly hopeless 'prepping': that is the term used by those (of us) who are actively preparing for the contingency of such future disasters through trying to equip ourselves and our loved ones with some means to survive them. I have not infrequently been in a state of some anxiety about such possible futures. I believe, incidentally, that one of the main reasons why disaster movies and (especially) apocalypse movies (and it is notable that the latter have been increasing in number in recent years) are popular is that they provide a 'safe' environment for the mass public to explore their (our) conscious or unconscious fears about the feasible coming of such disasters.[1]

It is by coming to understand something of the field of *Disaster Studies* that I have finally reached a state of some peace and indeed optimism, in relation to all this.

And how did I become open to the ideas of this field, in the first place? 'Disaster Studies', as I understand it, yields conclusions that fly wildly in the face of 'conventional wisdom' about disasters and chaos and that meet and answer many of my (and perhaps your) anxieties about how quickly things could collapse and how dire they could get in our fragile, long-supply-lined, overly complex 'globalised' world. How does one even get to the point where one can contemplate an alternative to frantic 'prepping' and to anxiety, or indeed to the more usual response, of denial?

For me, what is in retrospect the key moment came early in 2002. I couldn't process it at the time – it pretty much 'bounced off' the frame through which I saw the world. But it came back to me and motivated me, when, much more recently, I happened across Rebecca Solnit's work.

It consisted in this: I was conversing, in January 2002, in New York, with an American friend, a New Yorker, about his having been present in the city during the

11 September 2001 attacks. I had recently wandered around the 'Ground Zero' ex-World -Trade-Centre site and been concerned and downhearted by the often-violent graffiti and messages left there expressing a desire for vengeance on those who had carried out the attack (and sometimes on anyone who looked like them or shared ancestry with them). I said to my friend, whose politics were close to mine: 'It must have been just awful, being in New York in those days after the attacks. I mean: with all the death, the terrible smell, the deadly pollution, the chaos and worst of all the ferocious yells for vengeance.' His reply completely flummoxed me. He said:

> 'Actually, it was the one time in my life that I ever felt part of a community. It sounds strange to say it, but it was actually a happy time. People spoke to each other. Strangers helped each other – and this is New York, remember! Distinctions fell away.'

And, after a pause, he said, again, 'It was truly the one time in my life when I have *ever* felt like I was really: part of a *community*.'

Years later, when I came into contact with Rebecca Solnit's *A Paradise Built in Hell: The Extraordinary Communities that Arise in Disaster* (2009), that memory suddenly came powerfully back to me. And instantly I saw how maybe this very surprising, very encouraging thing could be true. Perhaps, contrary to what, in our 'liberal' individualist culture we assume, people don't become degraded and reduced to nasty brutish selfish types, when they are put under extreme pressure: perhaps that isn't our actual 'state of nature'. Perhaps, more often, the reverse.

I am no scholar of Disaster Studies. So I will use here as my guides to the field two main sources: Solnit's recent book, and Charles Fritz's (1996) classic of the field, tragically unpublished for 35 years after it was written, *Disasters and Mental Health: Therapeutic Principles Drawn from Disaster Studies*.

What does their work show?

Drawing in detail on many examples, from the 1906 San Francisco earthquake to 11 September 2001, from the devastating explosion in Halifax Nova Scotia to Hiroshima, from the Blitz to Hurricane Katrina, Fritz and Solnit suggest to us that disaster tends to enable new communities to be born. Instantly and often lastingly.

They relate how, against our expectations of chaos and panic, people in the immediate aftermath of a disaster are often remarkably calm. How they tend rapidly to develop mutual networks of support, based on need rather than on prior distinctions whether of wealth of ethnicity or what-have-you. How looting, though often assumed to be inevitable, is actually rare (and how, in any case, some of what is described as looting would be much more reasonably described as the harnessing of supplies; for remember, we are talking here, often, about people suddenly desperately short of life's necessities).[2] How, remarkably, it is at least as common for people to 'converge' on the scene of a disaster, in order to help, as it is for people to flee.[3]

And how all of this – against a backdrop, remember, of fear, loss, injury, death, often affecting most of the survivors directly – happens relatively spontaneously, rapidly, and even *joyfully*. How this festival of altruism is not even experienced primarily under that star: people don't find themselves, as they help and care for others, in the aftermath of disaster, to be engaging in self-*sacrificial* behaviour. It comes naturally to them, rather, and is experienced by them as something they want to do, even something it actually helps *them* to engage in doing (Solnit 2009, 197).

Here is a contemporary account of the phenomenon from a survivor of the great San Francisco earthquake:

> 'Most of us since [the earthquake] have run the whole gamut of human emotions from glad to sad and back again, but underneath it all a new note is struck, a quiet bubbling joy is felt. It is that note that makes all our loss worth the while. It is the note of a millennial good fellowship... In all the grand exodus [from the most devastated areas of San Francisco] ... everybody was your friend and you in turn everybody's friend. *The individual, the isolated self was dead. The social self was regnant.* Never even when the four walls of one's own room in a new city shall close around us again shall we sense the old lonesomeness shutting us off from our neighbours... And that is the sweetness and the gladness of the earthquake and the fire. Not of bravery, nor of strength, nor of a new city, but of a new inclusiveness. // The joy is in the other fellow.' (Solnit 2009, 32, emphasis mine)

This, I believe, is a key to the meaning of what happens in disasters. A possibility of joy, because of community that was previously absent. (Note how we in the United Kingdom often remark, and are vaguely surprised by, the nostalgia that so many have for the Second World War. This is the explanation of it, I believe. The Blitz wasn't in the main experienced (only) as an awful, anxiety-making mortal threat. It was experienced (more) as the occasion for a new, genuine community.)

We are living, nowadays, in ways that involve us in a virtually permanent and (to coin a phrase) disastrous absence of community. Disasters enable this to be overcome.

It is important to note that, for this overcoming to take place, typically, there has to be a *disaster*. Not merely an accident or something bad. Fritz emphasises this point especially. He writes that disasters need to be big enough to *not* leave 'an undisturbed, intact social system' (1996, 21). Only if that system IS disrupted sufficiently can the new forms of community emerge. The *ground* has to change, so to speak. *Only then can a new figure emerge.*

'Disaster provides an unstructured social situation that enables persons and groups to perceive the possibility of introducing desired innovations into the social system', Fritz goes on to argue (Fritz 1996, 56). Moreover, in disaster (though not in lesser upheavals), 'Many pre-existing invidious social distinctions and constraints to social mobility are removed; there is a general democratization [sic] of the social structure' (Fritz 1996, 66).

This latter feature in particular can have really helpful 'knock-on' effects. Consider the way that, to almost everyone's surprise, the British electorate in 1945 ejected the 'war hero' Prime Minister Churchill from office and replaced him with the great reforming Labour Government that began that year and created the NHS and so much more. This amazing event I think starts to make more sense, under the aspect that I have sought to make prominent here.

Or consider a fascinating lesser-known example that Solnit sets out at some length in Chapter III: that of the 1985 Mexico City earthquake, that is widely credited by those who know with creating the conditions of possibility for the ejection from power (after three generations in constant control) of the basically corrupt PRI Party in that country.

We hear a lot today about post-traumatic stress. Fritz et al. seek to teach us about something less well known, but just as important. It is sometimes now called 'post-traumatic growth' (Cf. Solnit 2009, 220).

Solnit makes the most of this by means of offering some deft reminders of etymology, reminders worth quoting at length:

'The word *emergency* comes from *emerge*, to rise out of, the opposite of emerge, which comes from *mergere*, to be within or under a liquid, immersed, submerged. An emergency is a separation from the familiar, a sudden emergence into a new atmosphere, one that demands we ourselves rise to the occasion. *Catastrophe* comes from the Greek *kata*, or down, and *streiphen*, or turning over. It means an upset of what is expected and was originally used to mean a plot twist. To emerge into the unexpected is not always terrible, though these words have evolved to imply ill fortune. The word *disaster* comes from the Latin compound of *dis-* or away, without, and *astro*, star or planet: literally, without a star.

In some of the disasters of the twentieth century – the big northeastern blackouts in 1965 and 2003, the 1989 Loma Prieta earthquake in the San Francisco Bay Area, 2005's Hurricane Katrina on the Gulf Coast [and, in a different way, the blackout in the Blitz] – the loss of electrical power meant that the light pollution blotting out the night sky vanished. In these disaster-struck cities, people suddenly found themselves under the canopy of stars still visible in small and remote places. On the warm night of August 15 2003, the Milky Way could be seen in New York City, a heavenly realm long lost to view until the blackout that hit the NorthEast late that afternoon. You can think of the current social order as something akin to this artificial light: another kind of power that fails in disaster. In its place appears a reversion to improvised, collaborative, cooperative and local society. However beautiful the stars of a suddenly visible night sky, few nowadays could find their way by them. But the constellations of solidarity, altruism and improvisation are within most of us and reappear at these times... This is the paradise entered through hell. (Solnit 2009, 10)

Solnit's rather beautiful thoughts here rhyme with those of Thomas Homer-Dixon, who, in *The upside of down: Catastrophe, creativity, and the renewal of civilization* (2006) goes one further, coining (Homer-Dixon 2006 22) a new word, *catagenesis*. Meaning the birth of something original from out of something disastrous. Or, as he more bluntly characterises it: 'the creative renewal of our technologies, institutions, and societies in the aftermath of breakdown' (268).

Perhaps you have figured out where I am going with all this. My hypothesis is that the rising tide of disasters that climate chaos will bring could be the (re-)making of us. These two wonderful works, of Fritz's and Solnit's, make evident that, when actually tested in the crucible of back-to-back disasters, it is at *least* as likely that humanity will rise to the challenge, and be transformed for the better in the process, as it is that we will shun the victims. What Fritz et al. suggest, on my extrapolation of it, is that we will likely find ourselves manifesting a truer humanity than we currently think ourselves to have, in this climate-stressed future that we are now entering into. We do not have to be gripped by the doomy thought that we are about to prove Hobbes and his many contemporary followers right. Instead, we can be optimistic that we are about to prove them wrong, as they have in fact, if largely unnoticedly, been proven wrong so many times before.

Thus the post-normal, climate-stressed world offers us a tremendous gift amidst the carnage, a gift we may well, remarkably, even welcome and literally make the best of.

3.

I have argued that an escalating series of climate disasters will yet carry with them as an unexpected boon an opportunity for the development of community. A great chance for us to show our quality.

But how much and how well we actually realise this gift depends on our preparing the way for it, rather than probabilifying the other main realistic possibility – unrestrained destructive authoritarian elite panic in the face of disaster.

For just this is something else that Fritz and Solnit alike make clear: that often things *do* go wrong in the wake of disaster, and most often as a result of (a largely delusive, but nevertheless consequential) elite fear of selfish, 'Hobbesian' reactions on the part of ordinary people. A striking example is New Orleans after Katrina, when black people desperate for help were painted as selfish villains, when baseless stories of savagery among the 'natives' fuelled a violent and repressive response by government, police and army, as well as by 'vigilantes'.

Moreover, one needs to be wary even of well-intentioned accounts that dwell on such *elite* Hobbesianism and disempower ordinary people in the process. Such an account is Naomi Klein's in *The Shock Doctrine* (2007). Klein is absolutely right to point to the tendency of ruthless elite/rich elements in society to seek to exploit disasters and to reconstruct afterwards in a way that points in a very different direction to the democratic, quasi-revolutionary spirit unleashed by the people's collective self-help response to the Mexico City earthquake. This elite panic, I would say, is partly *about* stopping the upsurge of citizenship, fervour and hope that can arise in disaster. But where Klein goes wrong is in suggesting sometimes that this elite activity *succeeds* in disempowering the victims of disaster, stripping them of their agency. Here is Solnit on this:

> [Klein's book] is a trenchant investigation of how economic policies benefitting elites are thrust upon people in times of crisis. But it describes those people in all the old unexamined terms and sees the aftermath of disaster as an opportunity for conquest from above rather than a contest of power whose outcome is sometimes populist or even revolutionary… It's a surprisingly disempowering portrait from the Left and one that echoes the [unfounded, as the Blitz proved] fears of pre-war British authorities, the apparent product of assumptions rather than research…

She goes on to cite how Fritz himself shows a different path:

> Fritz's first radical premise is that everyday life is already a disaster of sorts, one from which actual disaster liberates us. He points out that people suffer and die daily, though in ordinary times, they do so privately, separately. And he writes, 'The traditional contrast between "normal" and "disaster" almost always ignores or minimises these recurrent stresses of everyday life and their personal and social effects. It also ignores a historically consistent and continually growing body of political and social analyses that points to the failure of modern societies to fulfil an individual's basic human needs for community identity'. (Solnit 2009, 107)

We should add to that last sentence, I believe, something implicit in my epigraph from Benjamin: that much of ordinary life under the rule of atomisatory neoliberalism is a kind of constant low-level disaster. Life is characterized as low-grade loneliness and despair. Thus, extraordinarily, disasters are felt as a *release*. What the love, frankly, that people have for disasters that they had to 'endure' shows us – including the actual love that was engendered in them and practiced by them – is the paucity of the 'normal' condition, in the contemporary world. How dehumanised 'normal' human life is. How our isolated, meaning-weak condition is thrown into stark relief by a situation that, though horrific, *is nevertheless preferable to that condition*. Because at last, for the first time perhaps, we experience real community.

What emerges in disaster is that real community, the very opposite of what the Hobbesian script told us would emerge.

The Hobbesian script is, we should note here, among other things quite literally that, a *script*. An alarming number of books and films and TV shows suppose that disaster necessarily unleashes the worst in human beings. Consider this, again from Solnit:

> One of the more amusing recent manifestations of Hobbes came as entertainment, starting with the 2000 American television series *Survivor*... The show seemed to reference *Lord of the flies* and other epics of savage regression and primordial competition, but merely dropping a bunch of people in a remote location and asking them to cope might have produced uneventful co-operation or unpredictable improvisation. Instead, the show's creators and directors divided the cast into teams. The teams competed with each other for rewards. Eliminating fellow members was one of the competitive games they were obliged to play to increase insecurity and drama within teams. The goal was to produce a single winner rather than a surviving society, a competitive pyramid rather than a party of cooperation. Toiling for food and shelter was overshadowed by the scramble to win out in a wholly gratuitous competition based on arbitrary rules. Capitalism is based on the idea that there is not enough to go around, and the rules for *Survivor* built scarcity and competition and winners and losers into the system. These people were not in the wilderness but living under an arbitrary autocratic regime that might as well have been Los Angeles or London. The producers pretended we were seeing raw human nature in crisis conditions but stacked the deck carefully to produce Hobbesian behaviour – or rather marketplace behaviour, which amounts to the same thing here. (Solnit 2009, 93)

There are many-too-many run-of-the-mill disaster movies, so on, that have basically the same format as this. Though, interestingly, there are also many that at least posit some kind of heroic team building as a means to community among the chaos. And then there are the standout cases, real art, where the whole faux-Hobbesian architecture gets *aufgehoben*.

I mentioned earlier *The Road* and *The Hunger Games* trilogy. These are, actually, clear cases of the latter.

The Road (McCarthy, 2006) is, on the surface, a remarkably, extremely bleak book/film, a vision of a post-apocalyptic world indeed peopled by Hobbesian monsters. The scenario in *The Road* is so grim because the author has manipulated the conditions in his fiction a little like those in charge of *Survivor* manipulated the 'reality' of the contestants: in the scenario of *The Road*, some kind of ecological catastrophe has occurred so extreme that it appears that the entire biosphere is dead, except for humans. Thus leading to the remaining few denizens of the world devouring each other, often literally. *And yet*, what is often missed is the stunningly moving, redemptive ending of the story, as the dying protagonist refuses to give up on the life of his son, refuses to take him out of the world with him, refuses to give up on the future; and as the son is found, after his father's death, by a family who want to take him in, and whose dog – the blessing, added to human fellowship, of a non-human other, loved even more in the absence of other life-forms for us to love – evidently persuades him to say yes.

The Hunger Games may well have put many off from watching/reading it by, once again, the extreme – in this case *explicitly* manipulative – horror of its premise. A climate-devastated, much-depleted future America is held together by a rabidly authoritarian regime of the 1%, lording it over the destitute rest in particular by means of subjecting them to ritual combat (as a 'reality TV' show) annually. The combat taking the form of randomly selected teen children from each of the poor districts having to seek to survive hunger and cold and fight it out to the death to the last survivor in an arena rigidly controlled for mass audience entertainment by their rulers. *And yet*, the actual story of the *Hunger Games* is of an emergent struggle *against* this utterly vicious system; a system that pretends to *reveal*, as Hobbes claimed to reveal, that only centrally administered violence and inequality can restrain the lower classes from tearing each other apart. (If one disliked the idea of (and perhaps avoided watching) *The Hunger Games* because one assumed that it was *essentially* a reality-show-style spectacle of mutual savagery, then there is a risk that one is in fact buying into the highly dubious elite assumption of what ordinary folk are 'really' like…) In the first part of the trilogy, that struggle begins, with the refusal of the two last survivors to kill each other, an extraordinary act of defiance. In the second part, that act of defiance, that spark, catches fire and in the end launches an outright rebellion, when many of the participants in the new hunger games, participants chosen by virtue of having been survivors of all the previous hunger games, tacitly refuse to kill one another and in particular strive to keep alive the girl who had initiated that defiant first act of refusal. The third part is the story of that rebellion as, with immense self-sacrifice, the districts rise up and finally overwhelm their oppressors. This story explores in gripping and moving detail how human beings can be transformed for the better 'even' by an imposed disaster. I would hypothesise that it is one of the most successful box-office films of all time *because* of this.

Given the possibility especially of elite responses to or uses of disaster that amount to a 'second arrow', a new disaster imposed upon the first occurrence of a disaster, the good news offered in Section 2 offers no *guarantees*. We need to sow the seeds for a healthy response to disaster. How then do we do this?

My first suggestion is a simple one: we need to interpret and celebrate stories like *The Hunger Games*.

And, more important still (for fact is harder to dismiss than fiction): we need to learn and disseminate the learning that Fritz et al. achieved,[4] overcoming deep-set Hobbesian prejudices about ourselves in the process. The remarkable stories of 1906, of 1940–45, of 1985, of 2001, so on, need to be told and re-told until we have started collectively to twig that we humans are not 'underneath it all' as rubbish as we are have been told we are. (The ideological claim that 'human nature' is Hobbesian is a false but dangerously self-fulfilling one.)

My next suggestion is that we heed the *recommendations* offered by Fritz. Consider in particular this remarkable culminatory portion of his text (Frtiz 1996, 79–80; emphases mine):

The situational therapeutic features of disaster and the natural spontaneous techniques of group therapy developed in the community of sufferers might be translated into the following therapeutic action directives [for society/politics]:

(1) *Utilize the device of shock for disrupting dysfunctional habit patterns and for demonstrating their inapplicability to present needs.*
(2) Objectify the nature of the crisis and the threat which it poses to the integrity of the personal and social system. *Convert anxiety into fear.*
(3) Clearly specify the remedial needs as ones that require *social,* as well as individual, *adaptation* and physical manipulation of the external environment, as well as symbolic manipulation of the intrapsychic processes.
(4) *Slough off dysfunctional pre-existing interactional norms* and values and permit norms and values to emerge in response to present situational imperatives.
(5) Establish transcendent goals, which continually challenge individual effort and provide people with a sense of mission in life. Provide people with work roles that clearly and meaningfully relate to societal goals.
(6) Democratize social relationships by eliminating invidious social distinctions and material blocks to social mobility and achievement.
(7) *Change the reward structure of the group so that social recognition and reward are based on crisis-induced need and the achievement of social goals, rather than on pre-existent ascriptive status.*
(8) Eliminate formalized role relationships, free the channels for intimate communication, and *provide positive social sanctions for spontaneous, direct, informal, sentimental communication and the emotional sharing of experiences.*
(9) *Utilize a few extreme sufferers as a social reference point for enabling others to assess their pain and privation within a relative context.*
(10) *Dramatize the crisis or stress as an event, utilize it as a socially recognized juncture in life experience, and provide social absolution for guilt-ridden actions that preceded the event.*

I think if we systematically worked through that list, and applied it in relation to actual climate-induced disasters, and were in readiness to apply it to the 'next generation' of worsening climate disasters, we would be in good shape. (Think for instance of how we could make a societal habit of numbers 9 and 10, here. Think, ultimately, how a healthy 'survivors' ethos[5] might be developed around moving beyond the narrative of blame for those (all of us, to a greater *or* lesser extent) whose actions have precipitated the crisis.) The climate crisis is going to provide us, for better and for worse, with a whole series of opportunities to work through 1–10 on Fritz's list. Let us help make it be for better: by being ready, and even hopeful.[6]

And my *next* suggestion is that we think deeply about how deeply things need to be overturned – including, about how only something like disaster will, it would seem, do the trick – if we are to turn our current path into something that will not nevertheless yield simply an ever-escalating sequence of disasters until there is no one left to tell any stories. In other words, what assumptions and paradigms do we need to lose and gain, if we are to be able not only to enter but to thrive in the paradises Solnit has suggested are potentially open to us? How do we make the most of disaster and even breakdown, ensuring that this does not become simply complete collapse?

As Foster argues in *The Sustainability Mirage* (2008), 'sustainable development' and more-or-less Rawlsian liberal conceptions of contract/justice/fairness do not produce a solid enough basis to resist temptations towards denial and short-termism (temptations that will only underscore the momentum towards outright collapse), under such pressure. They are part of the paradigm which needs overcoming. Preparing our societies for the onslaught they are very likely to face requires instead the development of some true selflessness *and* of the healthy enlightened selfishness of taking care of oneself, one's family, one's 'village', one's neighbours: of charity beginning at home.

In the next section, I suggest one way in which intellectuals might contribute to that process of preparation. Namely, by highlighting a happy, under-understood connection between our care for our children and a more general care for posterity. This connection can help generate a bridge between warm local care and even (enlightened) selfishness, on the one hand, and 'sacrifice' for the sake of the deep future, on the other.

4.

I would argue that, in response to the great peril that our species faces, one thing we must do is seek to *relocalise* our world.[7] To improve resilience; to achieve democracy where it can actually be achieved, in communities; and to ensure that there are at least 'islands' that survive the grave peril. We ought to take advantage of the growth of community spirit that, if we are prepared in the right way, we can grow from the pressure that we get put under by a rising tide of climate disasters. Community spirit normally begins locally (the word 'community' is, obviously, a clue here…).

So then, what if – in looking for tools with which to reimagine our world such that we are better prepared to find and grow this new (spirit of) community – we started *as locally as possible*? What if we started with our own families?

For, once more, I think that one thing that Foster has helpfully shown, in his books critiquing 'sustainability' (Foster 2008, 2015), is how implausible it is to think that nostrums such as 'global justice' and 'sustainable development' are going adequately to motivate the kinds of actions/thinking now needed. We *need* to start, quite literally, closer to home; we need to start with something adequately motivating. The claim that a survivor of disaster makes on us when they present themselves to us is a model here. Their *vulnerability* is what first moves us.[8]

Following Foster, I am sceptical of the claim that new 'global values' such as are embodied in the global justice paradigm, or in the Millennium Development Goals (or their contemporary heirs, the Sustainable Development Goals) would be adequate – *and* I am sceptical that they are *needed*. I think that what we ought to be doing is helping everyone to see that the values that they already have are enough, if only those values get thought through properly, and acted upon. This will be the remarkable, hopeful claim of this section.

What *do* people value? Well, isn't the one thing we still value above all others *our children* – even in our debased liberal society that, as well as delivering some real emancipation, has damaged the meaning of family, by raising commercial bonds to a far greater importance? This perhaps stems from their utter vulnerability, their profound dependence. Doesn't *everyone*, from the most idealistic to the most cynical, concur in profoundly valuing at the very least their own children?

What *is* it to value one's own children?

You might think that valuing only one's own children won't take things very far. That it would result in a selfish, short-termist, present-centric way of being. But if you *truly* value your own children, two important points follow that completely contradict such pessimism. Once they are understood, if they become widely *enough* understood, then the change of priorities needed in order to head off the vast threat that at present humankind poses to its own posterity (e.g. via our messing with the climate) might conceivably start at last to come about:

(1) If you value your children not just for your sake but for their own, it immediately follows that you must value what they most value. If you were to stomp on everything your children held most dear, you would be denying them their independence, their selves, their lives. What can we expect our own children to value above all other things? A reasonable expectation is that they will be *broadly* similar to us; for after all, they are not only animals, but mammals; not only mammals, but primates; not only primates, but human; and not only that, but – our very own children. In other words: the one thing they are likely to value above all others is their own children, and so on. It can quickly be seen that this point repeats endlessly. In other words: Merely valuing profoundly one's own children ramifies into valuing *just as profoundly* all one's descendants. If you truly care about your kids, then you care about their kids: and so on, ad infinitum. (It is important to be clear that the degree of care mustn't ebb a little with each generation: if you really care most of all for your kids, then, as I've said, you will care *just as profoundly* for what they care for – their kids – and so on, indefinitely into the future. If you weren't to care as much for your grandchildren as you do about your children, then that would just be a roundabout way of saying that you didn't care as much as you claimed to do about your children. So your care for your children directly motivates care for theirs, and so on, wonderfully, endlessly…).

(2) Who will one's descendants be? How can one determine who exactly to care for so profoundly? A reasonable expectation is that, just as one has more and more ancestors as one goes back in time (twice as many grandparents as parents, and so on), so one will probably have more and more descendants as one goes forward in time. With each successive generation, then, one's descendants become more and more widespread. Over time, they are likely to be spread wider and wider across the world. If you truly care about your kids, then, we have established (see (1), aforementioned) that you care about all your descendants just as much. Now we see that those descendants are legion, more numerous and almost certainly more geographically widespread with every generation. (Given that you cannot anticipate exactly where your descendants will end up, the only sensible, precautious course is to assume that there will be no geographical limits to their spread, given enough passage of time.) You can't take care of that worldwide legion across aeons by (e.g.) making them all rich, or building them a fort. The only way you can do it is by preventing them from being subject to catastrophic threats. Of which, in the present article, we have been dwelling as an exemplar on one in particular, the one pressing hardest on us: that of climate-catastrophe and its baggage of climate-induced 'natural' disasters.

We humans are not used to thinking this way because none of us can anticipate the *precise* details of our future family tree. But such precise knowledge is unnecessary: the earlier mentioned points (1) and (2) together add up to an incredibly powerful 'reminder' of what it is that our children really are to us.

What is the best way we can take care of what we most value? (And: What we most value, we can now see, is not only our own kids narrowly conceived, but the ongoing unfolding of the generations that will follow them.)

One doesn't need to be a tree hugger or a wildlife lover (or anything else that you, dear *Global Discourse* reader, probably are, but that you might despair that most of the populace are not), in order to become clear that we simply have to take care, together, of the future of our home. Our fragile Earth. For, without this home, what we most value is nothing.

One doesn't even need to care about 'future generations' in the abstract. *All one needs to do is to care about one's very own children, for themselves* (as opposed to: as playthings, for you). That is enough to unleash a care that encompasses the entire human future timewise, and the entire globe space-wise. If you truly care about your own kids, as surely you do, as pretty much *everybody* does, then, whether or not you have realised it before, you care about all your descendants just as much, and they will encompass all the future and (eventually) all the globe.

What are the practical implications of this? I'm asking you and all of us to *think* about – to imagine, to envision and to feel in your heart – the effects of our policy decisions (e.g. in relation to climate) on our children, and on their children, and on their children, and so on.

Take an example: fracking. If you care about your kids, as you surely do, you might think that, if you're only thinking of them, fracking will at least benefit them (and you) by providing them (and you) with power. But once you are thinking just as much, as you must if you are truly to care for your children, about your grandchildren, your great-grandchildren and your many scattered greatgreatgreatgreatgreatgreatgreatgreat-greatgreatgreatgreatgreat …grandchildren, then fracking – with its long-term shattered landscapes, its methane leakage, its hefty contribution to climate damage, its locking in on patterns of dependence on fossil fuels, its corporate capture – starts to look a rather less attractive option.

Take another example: Christmas. If you care only, narrowly, about your kids, you are perhaps already buying them big presents for next 25th December. After all, who wants to be a 'Scrooge'?! But, once you get clear that what it is to really care about your kids is to care about their descendants, *ad infinitum*, then the matter becomes different; and, in a way, simple. It is just wrong to give kids presents that come at the cost of the future, and so on. It is doing wrong to them, to do this. (Sure, when they are very young, they may struggle to understand this. But when they are just slightly older, you can explain it to them, and they'll be grateful, or at least intrigued. And one thing that follows from this article is: You must explain it to them. And even: to everyone. This idea, that true care for one's own kids must translate into care not just for the 7th but for the 777th generation, needs the widest possible dissemination…)

Before finishing this section, let me consider one important possible objection. Does my argument presume that people who are engaged in environmentally destructive activities (e.g. CEOs of oil companies) don't really care about (their own) kids? The answer is no. What I have done in this section, rather, is to seek to set out how caring for one's kids, *once one understands what really caring for one's kids entails*, already motivates any and all of us NO LONGER to engage in environmentally destructive behaviour. Because, once the CEO of Shell truly realises that to care for his own children *means* caring for future generations across the world, then he will instantaneously be motivated to at least look again at his practices. (So, if you get a chance, please show him this article, or at least relate to him the point of this section of it... That would be a really great way to show that you care for your kids....)

The argument that I've made in the present section should provide some hope. If we can only spread some deep awareness of these fundamental points that I have made here, then humankind might start to act with more serious long-term vision. This vision begins from and in a way ends with the care that we preternaturally have for our own children. Once we as parents realise that we cannot mean it when we say we love our own kids unless we think and act in a truly long-term and global fashion – and once this 'meme' starts itself to spread around the globe – then hope might at last start to undo threat. For, remarkably, it will be enough to save this world as a place for human beings to flourish far into the future if only we take seriously enough that we love our own kids.

What our values require of us is at minimum: decisive action, with determination, to do everything we can for our children, *and all that this means*. In order to serve our children adequately, we must do right by *their* children. Once we get enough folk to understand what I've argued here, the tide may at last start to turn in our favour. And what that *means*, given what our values are, is: in favour of our children, in favour of all our numberless descendants and in favour of what they need in order to flourish: flourishing restored ecosystems...

Don't do this just because it's 'green', nor even because it's 'rational'. *Do it for the children*. Do it from your heart. Take this idea seriously. For, way beyond the readership of this fine journal, it's an idea that can catch fire...

And it has the profound advantages over currently dominant 'sustainable development'-style thinking of (1) promising to motivate changes that will be *enough*, rather than superficial band-aids, *and* simultaneously of (2) not requiring excessive or over-ambitious generosity or values shifts. For it begins, literally, at home. It begins in care and in response to vulnerability (and there is nothing or no one more vulnerable to us and our power than our descendants). It begins in the same kind of 'place' that gets extended in the cases that Solnit et al. tell us of. Disasters yield community. The most elemental community of all, our own family/children, bids us, once we have thought matters through, do much more than we are doing to provide a basis for an ongoing human community that will not be shattered.

For we have never been isolated egos, even if that is what ad-men and too many philosophers alike tell us that we are.

And what the argument of this section does is to show how a care that *begins* at home cannot *remain* at home. The kind of immediate *pull* upon us that occurs with our own families, and that occurs in disaster, needs drawing out way across time and space if it is to be *realised*. You cannot *succeed* any more in caring for your kids by keeping your horizons narrow.

Foster, in his splendid, incendiary most recent book, *After Sustainability* (2015) emphasises rightly that our concern for a better future needs to take place now and needs to involve a rigorous and honest being in the moment. Typically, we are anxious about and ineffective at being honest/being in the moment, in part because we know deep down that we are sowing the seeds of the future's destruction.

Such being in the moment is actually one of the key things made possible by, unconcealed by, disaster. Disaster enables us to be *present*.

And this is a very good thing, a gift in time. For, just as Foster would suggest, the implications of taking the pulse of the future for how we feel, live and act *today* are of course critical. All our thinking about the impact of future disasters and, more generally, about the well-being (or otherwise) of future generations is in part, crucially, a way to think about how to do the right thing NOW. And what the ways of thinking about the future outlined in the present piece underline is what is in any case obvious: that today's (individual and especially collective) action WILL make a huge difference in the future. Changes now will not only make us be better prepared to deal with the coming disasters (including both the damage and the potential silver lining) but are also likely to help pre-empt disasters and reduce their scale. In other words, whether it is movies, scientific studies or philosophical articles, it is the thinking about future disasters which should wake us up RIGHT NOW.[9]

But I think it is clearly implicit in what I have said that we also – as well as a greater focus on the present, that Foster rightly urges – quite desperately need a greater focus on the deeper future. (Foster fails to distinguish between the *near*-future – 5/10 years – and *the deeper future* – 50, 500, even 50,000 years. That latter is what is ignored in our culture of chronic short-termism.) Properly understood, this emphasis on the deep future, on life splendidly going on in(de)finitely long beyond our horizons, goes hand in hand with a focus on ourselves now. We spend all our time running away from the present into the near-future (and into regret at the near-past, etc.). We distract ourselves, whether with plans for a new kitchen or for a new 'development' project. But such running away into the near-future is at the same time a running away FROM the deep future. For the sake of jam tomorrow, we are depriving our great-great-great, and so on, -grandchildren of life and love. In growing the pie, we are planting a depth charge under the ecosystems of the deeper future.

The argument of the present section has shown, at least from an engaged thoughtful and feelingful standpoint, the direction of a route to dissolving the depth charge. The focus on the deeper future, that we so badly need, can come, via the simple, powerful route of focussing our attention on our children,[10] and seeing them in their true sense: as themselves (not appendages of us) and as harbouring a permanent future.

Have I claimed here in Section 4, in a display of absurd idealism, that it would be *enough*, just to get everyone to think seriously about the argument I've made in this section? Yes and no! NO, in that I have been quite clear that there are many things that actually need to change, to be *done* and some of these changes will be a titanic struggle (one that we are likely, usually, to lose). And of course I've stressed upfront that there are *disasters* coming that we are already 'committed' to; that we cannot head off. But also Yes: in that if somehow one were able to get enough people to think through the argument of this section, that would be truly transformative; and yes, in that this is at least *something* that (suitably feeling-ful) intellectuals/

philosophers, can offer right now, that speaks to our condition; and yes finally, in that I believe, as I will conclude by suggesting more explicitly that the coming climate-induced disasters may well *concentrate the mind* such that we have more chance of reaching a tipping point *vis-a-vis* our care for our children and for each other than might, right now, seem likely to you.

5.

To conclude, William James famously suggested that we stand in need of a moral equivalent of war to give us meaning and bind us together, in times of (seeming) non-disaster, in times of peace. Without there being such a moral equivalent of war, James thought – rightly, in my view – that we would splinter into mutually indifferent pleasure centres. That scenario has, I fear, been realised much more than is prudent, in the modern North, under the rule of the political philosophy of liberalism. But it is on the point of being unrealised again.

And that may, for all its horrors, bring us a gift we badly need.

My hypothesis is that the moral equivalent of war is about to be forced upon us.

I have argued (Sections 1 and 2) that the sadly-likely litany of worsening climate-chaos-part-caused unnatural disasters that we will experience need not, as many fear (and as I too feared, till recently), simply sap our morale and resources, debase our culture and hasten a descent into a Hobbesian condition. Into collapse. What Rebecca Solnit et al. have helped show is that the Hobbesian assumption that people under severe strain become 'animals' is highly dubious. It is itself a piece of ideology that tends to be used to legitimate authoritarian, destructive behaviour by elites, behaviour that comes from fear (or sometimes venality) that is illicitly projected onto ordinary people.

What we need to do, therefore (Section 3), is to seek to *prepare* for these disasters, in a positive spirit. The word needs to be spread. People need to under-stand that they can expect others, and themselves, to be resolute, in the face of disaster. Disaster-preparedness plans should not emphasise repression and author-itarian control; they should emphasise empowering ordinary people to be amazing. As Disaster Studies appears to show people usually spontaneously are, unless elite-panic gets in the way.

We need to build for the resilience of immediate local practical action – and simulta-neously grow that into a new collectivistic ethic of long-term global *care* (Section 4). We need more than cool justice; something more immediate (though, remarkably, such care iterates, as I showed in (Section 4)). We need to foster the kind of care that is unleashed in disaster. In the disasters that are coming.

At the opening of Section 1, earlier, I spoke of the likelihood that our rupturing of the limits to growth (of which dangerous climate change is only the most developed example) may lead to an irrecoverable civilisation collapse, within the next generation or two. The remainder of this paper since then can naturally be read as an attempt to think through how yet to avert such an outcome.

But there is another way of reading it, too, both more pessimistic and more optimistic than that. For, if Fritz and Solnit are right – and I am confident that they are – then perhaps our worry about 'irrecoverable civilisational collapse' can be downgraded much further. Perhaps what we should assume instead is that, *even if* our rupturing of the limits to growth continues and humankind proceeds on the trajectory of collapse through rapidly rising mortality, so on, that we find in most of the Club of Rome scenarios, still human beings will rally, and will keep on and on turning the hells that we've created by so recklessly tampering with the conditions of our collective life-support system (the living planet) into mini-heavens.

And that is an encouraging thought.

The worry remains, even here, that the field of 'Disaster Studies' has focussed mostly on isolated disasters. The era of dangerous human-triggered climate change promises to some extent a new problem: a ratcheting up of connected, ramifying disasters (unless we manage to turn the supertanker of civilisation around, and start to reduce our exposure to the whirlwind, and (after a time-lag) to reduce the whirl-wind itself, rather than evermore reaping it). Will we be able to maintain the kind of admirable spirit and humanity that Disaster Studies seemingly shows us, under such long-term pressure?

Here is one reason for thinking that we will. I have suggested that what our atomised, individualised society desperately *needs* is: means and occasions to rebuild community.[11] The horror, death and squalor of climate-caused disasters will not be unmitigated, not by any means. I have suggested that it will likely, as a 'silver lining' to those unprecedented storm clouds, facilitate just such a rebuilding of community. Now, what if we were able to parlay that into something bigger? What if the spirit of community starts to reach more globally, and even across time? In Section 4, I suggested a concrete way in which one can start to imagine that happening. For I showed that one role that a philosophically informed deep reframing can play in the needful process of virtuous preparation for (and prevention of) disasters is in helping people to understand that, in order to care for their children, they need to care for *their* children in turn, and so on, ad infinitum. Philosophical thinking, global discourse, inter-temporal discourse could start, in other words, to *multiply* the renewed sense of community that I postulated and recounted in Section 2. We are willing, at times of crisis and disaster, to act in ways that astonish us and make us proud to be alive. Won't we show that same compassion to our own children? What doing so *means*, as I've laid out, is: planning now – starting now – to build down the terrible threat which we are currently hanging over them and theirs. As Homer-Dixon's work, drawing on the respected scholarly work of Joe Painter and Buzz Holling,[12] suggests, and as my work alongside Nassim Taleb (Taleb et al. 2015) on the precautionary principle also strongly suggests, we'll surely simplify and scale down our societies and reduce our impact on the natural world, at some point. The issue is whether the next run of climate disasters prompts this proactive catagenesis, or whether we have to wait for full-scale collapse to force it upon us, and so on.

Thus we can see clearly at last the outlines of the greatest gift that climate disasters can bring in their wake if we are ready to accept it. A gift that would stop us having to look for silver linings as we descend into collapse, and genuinely be able rather to head off that collapse, and so on. An *unleashing* of humanity, of decency, of care, that we can scale up.

Because: these disasters *show* the future on a business-as-usual scenario. They show it in its horror. *But* they *also* show us the riposte. Holderlin's great dictum holds true: Where the danger grows, so does the saving power.

For, if I am right in thinking that climate disasters can bring a massively enhanced community consciousness in their wake, that means that they do after all have the capacity that many of us have been hoping that they might: to *wake us up*. Thus, and here I think I differ from Foster, we really can still dare to hope that we may collectively wake up enough *before* we have committed our civilisation to breakdown, let alone to collapse.

Notes

1. I will return to this point in Section 3: by examining a couple of such movies that I have already mentioned.
2. Sometimes, sadly, the authorities and/or the media will describe a favoured group as gathering supplies, when the same activity engaged in by a non-favoured group is called looting. Solnit documents this as having happened in New Orleans, vis-à-vis whites and blacks, respectively (Solnit 2009, Ch.V)
3. This phenomenon of 'convergence' was particularly striking in the case of September 2001. See 'The need to help' (Solnit 2009, 195ff).
4. Not entirely incidentally, a side benefit of Fritz's work becoming widely read by those whose job it is to prepare for disasters, such as the military, would be that they would be less likely to engage in thoughtless aerial bombardment. For Fritz's work explains more clearly than I have ever seen it explained before why aerial bombardment alone, *even when enormously devastating*, usually fails to cow a population. For it is experienced as a *disaster* imposed deliberately upon the community – and the community pulls together remarkably against it. As Fritz documents (1996, 51–2), this phenomenon probably also goes a long way to helping explain the (phenomenal) success story, which has left many scratching their heads, of the Japanese and German economies after 1945.
5. My idea here is developed by loose analogy with what Mahmood Mamdani recommends as the kind of ethos ultimately needed in post-genocide situations, as opposed to an ethos of retributive justice.
6. Solnit herself speaks about what this hopeful readiness and community/citizen responsiveness actually means in powerful ways in this interview: http://www.truth-out.org/op-ed/item/14193-rebecca-solnit-on-how-disasters-can-move-us-from-a-sense-of-self-interest-to-a-sense-of-community (accessed 14.2.17). Cf. also Saci Lloyd's immensely hopeful brace of stories about collective response to incipient climate-chaos, *The carbon diaries* (2009).
7. Here, my thought is in concert with that of Helena Norberg-Hodge; see for instance her groundbreaking work, *Ancient futures* (2009).
8. Here, I am drawing on the argument of Christopher Groves's (2014) book, *Care, uncertainty and intergenerational ethics*.
9. Many thanks to Peter Kramer for formulations of his that I have borrowed to emphasise this point of mine. I return to emphasise this fundamental point at the close of my conclusion.
10. My idea here is close to that of Naomi Klein, in her *This Changes Everything* (2015) – see especially the closing chapters of that book. She sees the 'climate war' we are now starting to fight partly through the lens of her new motherhood. Anthropogenic climate change is hitting and will hit our kids hardest (of those who are alive today). And their kids, almost certainly, harder still, so on, If we really *attend* to our children, we have no option but to fight it.
11. Has our society already become too atomised even to be capable of a 'paradisical' response to disaster? I have already given my answer to this question: No. Let me put the point slightly humourously: if twenty-first century New Yorkers can manage it, then anyone can…
12. See especially Homer-Dixon (2006, 226–233) for his take on Painter and (especially) on Holling's 'panarchy' concept, giving us a clear upside of down: The chance to refresh and simplify our systems – much as ecosystems do, when they break down.

Acknowledgements

Thanks to Peter Kramer and Ian Christie for invaluable comments on earlier drafts. Thanks to Sam Earle for the concept of the 'imaginary', a concept that she is developing in her PhD thesis with me.

Disclosure statement

No potential conflict of interest was reported by the author.

References

Foster, J. 2008. *The Sustainability Mirage: Illusion and Reality in the Coming War on Climate Change*. London: Taylor & Francis Ltd.

Foster, J. 2015. *After Sustainability: Denial, Hope, Retrieval*. Routledge: Oxon.

Fritz, C. 1996. "Disasters and Mental Health: Therapeutic Principles Drawn from Disaster Studies". [Unpublished]. University of Delaware library: Available at http://udspace.udel.edu/handle/19716/1325

Groves, C. 2014. *Care, Uncertainty and Intergenerational Ethics*. Basingstoke: Palgrave Macmillan.

Homer-Dixon, T. 2006. *The Upside of Down: Catastrophe, Creativity, and the Renewal of Civilisation*. Washington: Island Press.

Klein, N. 2007. *The Shock Doctrine*. London: Penguin Books.

Klein, N. 2015. *This Changes Everything*. London: Penguin Books.

Lloyd, S. 2009. *The Carbon Diaries 2015*. New York: Holiday House.

McCarthy, C. 2006. *The Road*. New York: Random House.

Norberg-Hodge, H. 2009. *Ancient Futures: Lessons from Ladakh for a Globalizing World*. San Francisco: Sierra Club Books.

Solnit, R. 2009. *A Paradise Built in Hell: The Extraordinary Communities that Arise in Disaster*. London: Penguin Books.

Taleb N. N., R. Read, R. Douady, J. Norman, and Y. Bar-Yam. 2015. *The Precautionary Principle (With Application to the Genetic Modification of Organisms)*. NYU School of Engineering Working Paper Series. Available at: http://www.fooledbyrandomness.com/pp2.pdf

Caring for the future? – a response to Rupert Read

John Foster

This is a reply to:

Read, Rupert. 2017. "On preparing for the great gift of community that climate disasters can give us." *Global Discourse*. 7 (1): 149–167. http://dx.doi.org/10.1080/23269995.2017.1300440.

The first sentence of Rupert Read's challenging and original paper (Read 2017) acknowledges that the greenhouse gases we've already unleashed commit us to grave new natural disasters, while in the concluding sentence he hopes that we may collectively wake up *before* we have committed our civilisation to breakdown.

Between these positions there need be no contradiction, provided that the inescapable new disasters don't amount, just so far, to breakdown. But then, when he writes of climate *chaos*, and of the prospective deaths of tens or even hundreds of millions, this logically crucial gap seems to narrow; and when he accepts that, in order to re-empower a lost sense of community cohesion, such disasters 'need to be big enough to *not* leave an … intact social system', it is in danger of vanishing. So perhaps, and maybe without consciously intending to, Read is presenting us here with an argument which has certainly been made before – as, for instance, also unintentionally, by Clive Hamilton (2010) – to the effect that, if we can only admit anthropogenic climate chaos to be now inevitable, we may still at this eleventh hour spur ourselves into avoiding it. And that *is*, of course, (however temptingly) to contradict oneself.

I will return to this possibility, because it may account for things in the paper which otherwise I find inexplicable. Even if that were his underlying strategy, however, it wouldn't much detract from the power, passion and forthrightness with which Read actually confronts oncoming disaster. Rather than shirk it as unthinkable, the reaction of so many who offer to think about this, he tries to see beyond it to its deeper human meaning and to the anti-Hobbesian (as he hopes) values of altruism, mutual support and renewed social responsibility which it might help us retrieve.

This is admirable and vitally necessary work. I think he accepts too easily that the values which this transformative experience could reawaken in us would be familiar ones which we could readily recognise and welcome, and this goes, in my view, with his not fully admitting the genuinely tragic nature of our plight. (All the disasters for which he cites analyses from the intriguing field of Disaster Studies were, or were perceived by their sufferers as, inflicted from without, by accident or enemies; climate disaster, on the other hand, we shall have brought wholly on ourselves, through destructive flaws

inherent in great human strengths which Enlightenment rationality and technical creativity have deployed.) But I have engaged directly with Read on this matter in my own
paper for this Special Issue, so will say no more about it here. Whichever of us is right,
this part of his piece remains strong, cogent – and inspiring.

What I do want to address critically in this response is the argument in his Section 4,
where, accepting that retrieved community must mean a greatly intensified concentration on survival in our local and particular circumstances, he nevertheless tries to find in
this a new kind of impulse towards the universalism of protecting future generations for
their own sake. This move turns on the claim that, if we care profoundly for our (actual
or imaginary) children, as surely out of mere humanity we most of us do, then we must
care profoundly for what they will care profoundly about – that is, in turn, their own
children, for whom our transferred profound care will then again commit us to caring
profoundly for *their* children – and so the caring relation iterates transitively onwards
until we are caring, as profoundly as we care for our own children, for the nth generation
of our descendants multiplying incalculably across the Earth. Ordinary parental care is
thus 'enough to unleash a care that encompasses the entire human future time-wise and
the entire globe space-wise'.

Now I entirely agree, and have contended in my own work (which Read references in
generous terms) that our standardly-alleged liberal-contractual obligations of responsibility towards future generations amount only to a delusive shadow-stewardship; while
sounding impressive (from a distance), these pseudo-obligations will never effectively
constrain us from present actions grievously harmful to the interests of future people.
This alternative argument for stewardship, however, doesn't take us *ad infinitum*, as Read
explicitly claims, but – surely – *ad absurdum*. I do care, and profoundly, about my actual,
living children. I don't, though, give a hoot whether or not *Homo sapiens* as such, never
mind my own descendants, will be around on the planet in AD 21,000, nor, I very
strongly suspect, do most of my readers in respect of their descendants. So the conclusion that reason compels us all to give vastly more than a hoot must be a *reductio*.

Read (in conversation) has argued that my not giving a hoot is a case of unjustified
pure time preference, which should be overridden by ethical considerations. And for
sure, if I bury (say) an unmarked canister of plutonium in my garden, I ought to feel just
as worried about its potential effects on someone chancing to dig it up in twenty
thousand years, as in twenty – here, my clear responsibility for future harm does seem
to render the time-lapse irrelevant. But I could lead an ecologically blameless life, so that
no action of mine did anything except increase the chances of humans being still
around in AD 21,000, and still not give a hoot about whether or not they were. My
profound concern might be (as indeed it is) to avoid impoverishing biospheric life by my
actions in the single lifetime which I have available, and might bear no relation at all to
any envisaged distant-future state of the planet. For Read this would make me either
unethical (despite my ecological virtues) in not caring properly for my children, or
irrational. Since I take myself to be obviously (at least in this regard) neither, again
that conclusion must stand as a *reductio*.

As such, it must show something to be amiss with the argument as set out. The
problem seems to be with the hypothetical major premise. Where this goes wrong, I
take it, is in the supposed transitivity of 'profound caring'. If I care thus for my children, I
don't necessarily care profoundly for people or objects about which they care

profoundly, although I will (and perhaps by definition), in caring for my children, care profoundly *that* they care thus about whatever it is – so that I won't, for instance, mock or demean it nor as far as possible interfere with it, and if it is as near-future as a grandchild I will very probably also cherish it, for their and for its own sake. But over just one generation, my caring has already, as it were, taken a step back, and this seems wholly natural. Care, like concern and even interest, just fades as the generations flow on away from us. And well for us that it does – caring profoundly for one's own children, with all the joy, stress and anguish which go to fill the package, is quite exacting enough for one human life. Read's argument would require, by contrast, that we also feel the full intensity of parental concern for our grandchildren and great-grandchildren (to go no further), for whom actually and quite properly we feel only *grand*parental and (if we get there) *great*-grand-parental concern – and *n*th-great-grandparental concern, on that trajectory, will have long become wholly indistinguishable from complete indifference. That, luckily, is how we are.

How could so acute a philosopher as Read have come up with so strange an argument? I can only surmise him to have been drawn, perhaps subconsciously, to the strategy on which I remarked above – that of having the cake of honesty about inevitable climate chaos while nourishing oneself on the unextinguished option of last-minute avoidance. So we confront oncoming disaster by seeing through it to retrievable community, the renewed local focus of which *must* be made to unleash the kind of commitment to protecting the future by which disaster might even yet be forestalled. This is maybe impertinent speculation. But no small part of our inherently tragic human nature is our habitual yearning after such impossibilities.

For all that, Read's instinct about these issues and their human significance seems to me to point, compellingly, in the right direction. The values we already have, or some painfully-winnowed version of them, are indeed enough if we can come home again to acting on them. We shall not learn what may be learnable from this oncoming disaster unless we come to recognise in practice what we have all along deeply known, that deliberately trashing the ecological bases for continuing human and other life on Earth, however (way beyond our capacity to know or care) the consequences pan out, robs *our lives here in the present* of kinds of meaning which we can't do without, either for our own flourishing or for that of people for whom we do genuinely care profoundly. If climate tragedy teaches us that lesson, talking of it as a gift – as Read so bravely does – would then seem far from inappropriate.

Disclosure statement

No potential conflict of interest was reported by the author.

References

Hamilton, C. 2010. *Requiem for a Species*. London: Earthscan.
Read, R. 2017. "On Preparing for the Great Gift of Community that Climate Disasters Can Give Us." *Global Discourse* 7 (1). doi:10.1080/23269995.2017.1300440

On letting go

John Foster

ABSTRACT

Massively disruptive climate change, now inevitable, is the worst tragedy which human beings have yet brought on themselves. It is tragic in the full classical sense – a disaster entailed on the protagonist (here, humanity) by destructive weaknesses inherent in crucial strengths and virtues. There is thus no way of avoiding it by picking and choosing among our values, and its effects can neither be compensated for nor mitigated by prospective gains to offset against anticipated losses. But once we have discarded a strained and wilful last-ditch optimism, and recognised that we are not in control, we will still need to find genuine hope if we are to have any chance of coming through. This requires us to embrace the transformative power of tragic experience, letting go of values which we may hitherto have regarded as sacrosanct and welcoming the creative destruction of current assumptions and expectations as an affirmation of life.

> *Therefore the sage manages affairs without action*
> ....
> *Ten thousand things arise and he does not initiate them,*
> *They come to be and he claims no possession of them,*
> *He works without holding on....*
> Tao Te Ching[1]

I.

How do we approach the worst tragedy which human beings have ever brought on themselves, in the recognition that its coming to pass is now inevitable? How might we advance with eyes open into this ending of the world as we have known it, without taking it for the end of the world – letting go of what we must, without losing the hope which is essential to living? How can we give up pretending without giving up altogether?

The tragedy, of course, is anthropogenic climate change.[2] I assume here an audience which accepts without reservation, what the overwhelming majority of relevant scientific expertise has for a good while fully endorsed (see e.g. Oreskes 2004), that the global climate is being irreversibly altered and that human activity is responsible. But the further claims, that this entails a short-to-medium-term future both uniquely grievous and now inescapable, may well need defending even to people who accept the reality of the underlying process.

Inescapability is the simpler claim to demonstrate. The best way to enforce it is by appealing to what I have elsewhere called the Vicious Syllogism: if we had been going to avert the massively disruptive climate change and associated ecological degradation which will shortly start turning present global civilisation upside down, we'd have begun to put effective policies in place forty years ago when these concerns were first seriously mooted; we didn't; so we won't avoid it. This argument is valid and its premises are plainly true; in particular, the hypothetical major premise asserting that we are out of time is as well-grounded in the scientific evidence and in economic, sociological and geopolitical realism as any empirically-based counterfactual could hope to be. The prospect of our acting collectively to turn the lumbering super-tanker of the carbon-dependent global economy around on a sixpence in the few years we have left before levels of atmospheric carbon dioxide take us past the tipping point (if they haven't already) is simply incredible, on all those counts, to anyone seriously considering it. The conclusion of the syllogism follows by simple logic (the science of not being able to have things both ways at once) – which is not to say that refusal to accept it, indeed vehement denial of it, doesn't still prevail at all levels.

The deep roots of that denial are a separate issue – one which I tried to address in my recent book *After Sustainability* (Foster 2015), which starts from the above argument. These roots go down far beneath ordinary and understandable reluctance to face up to a frightening prospect. But such reluctance clearly plays a part and is by itself well justified. Underlying it is the tacit recognition that what now confronts us is not a problem, nor even the hyper-intensification of a clutch of problems – a so-called 'wicked problem' (see Hulme 2009, 334–40) – but a genuine tragedy. And while problems, even very challenging ones, can sometimes have solutions, genuine tragedy involves terrible loss, disastrous and uncompensated, for which nothing answering to the idea of a *solution* makes sense. This, for a modern mind accustomed to take material and social 'progress' as its unquestioned criterion for human affairs and the problem–solution mode as its default practical expectation, is simply not to be contemplated.

Nevertheless, and reluctance to recognise the facts notwithstanding: even if the worst-case scenario of runaway warming up to 6°C and beyond (Lynas 2007) is somehow avoided, the increasing climate instability to which we have already committed ourselves means that we face by around 2030, what a former UK government Chief Scientific Adviser (Beddington 2009) has described as a 'perfect storm' of food, water and energy shortages, entailing worldwide famine, disease and homelessness on an epic scale. This situation will certainly trigger enormous migrations and attempts at migration, and those currently temperate parts of the world where the immediate climatic effects of warming are likely to be comparatively less drastic will come under enormous pressure to admit refugees in numbers which would quickly overwhelm their resources and infrastructure, unless they take (as they mostly will) the hard decision to close their borders. This in turn will produce both intercommunal and international conflict, much of it inevitably armed. Gwynne Dyer's book *Climate Wars* (Dyer 2008) presents realistic possibilities here, under any of which it is clear that the world is set to become both a much less habitable and a much more divided, hostile and violent place.

II.

The genuinely tragic nature of this prospect shouldn't be much harder to appreciate. Tragedy is not just, in the crude journalistic solecism, any sufficiently drastic event involving death and mayhem. In the proper sense of the word, it arises when disaster ensues from and expresses destructive weaknesses which are *inherent in the key life-strengths* of an agent – whether that agent be an individual, an institution or, as in the present case, a mode of civilisation. This pattern is very apparent in the case of climate change. Deep-seated features of the secular and instrumentally-rational Enlightenment spirit which has produced so much worthwhile life- improvement across the world have also generated a pervasive inability to rein in the relevant activities before they do irreversible damage. What slogan-makers like to call 'the success of science' is visibly collapsing under the strain of its own contradictions. The trajectory launched by Baconian ambitions for technological mastery of nature is reaching the end it was always likely to reach, since humans remain part of nature whether or not they allow themselves to forget the fact, and setting themselves over against it in a spirit of attempted mastery has inevitably turned them dangerously destructive, both of their habitat and of their inner attunement to it. The biosphere has only been able to absorb so much of the consequences without damage, and the limits here have now been reached – indeed, if we are persuaded by the Vicious Syllogism, they have been decisively transgressed. Distinctive human strengths which Western civilisation in parti- cular has realised – the strengths to develop a sophisticated self-conception, to make rational deliberated choices, to base belief on evidence and empirical testing, to free ourselves from ignorance, superstition and dogma – are thus existentially rooted in aspirations to mastery and control which are responsible for this decisive eco-systemic damage. The epochal material successes hitherto consequent on our strengths have worked to blind us to what we are doing in exercising them and indeed to neutralise most strivings towards self-recognition. All the classic ingredients of tragedy are here.

Correspondingly, if we are to identify those whose fault this oncoming disaster is, they can only be *ourselves*, the worldwide human community, or at any rate its leading protagonists, the peoples of the West and North whom the rest strive increasingly to emulate. Attempting to blame everything on the institutional power and self-interest of corporations, for instance, while an understandable reaction in the face of much con- temporary corporate behaviour, is essentially an exercise in scapegoating. Corporations exercise vast irresponsible power, create damaging pseudo-needs (especially in children) through advertising and cause widespread ecological havoc in pursuit of their share- holders' short-term financial interests. But they could not do these things, indeed they would not exist in their current forms, had not aspiring billions across the globe (taking their cue from, but no longer confined to, the West) remained eager to buy their products and benefit materially from their innovations.

It is the equally classic *purity* of this pattern, as well as the extent and nature of the damage, which justifies the claim that climate change will constitute the worst tragedy which humankind has ever inflicted on itself. There have been many grievous episodes in history, some latterly producing chaos and suffering worldwide, though none, not even World War, has hitherto been systemically destructive enough to jeopardise the stability and integrity of large tracts of the biosphere on which human and all other life depends. But in every such episode to date, a driving role has been played by the traditional human vices of pride, greed and hatred, as appealed to by evil men (and women) in positions of power. This new disaster, however, we have brought upon ourselves by the headlong indulgence of what are in themselves perfectly creditable passions and desires – for equality, for recognition and respect, for general material betterment (that is, for the elimination of squalor, hunger and disease, as well as for lives smoothed and facilitated by 'consumer goods'). In the past, these progressivist goals have elicited much that was best in our collective activity. We have latterly (since the Industrial Revolution) tried to pursue them by trading on our unprecedented new powers to tap a massive store of fossilised energy in their service, and it is our having done this in careless ignorance – and more recently, in denial-driven disregard – of the associated ecological and climatic consequences, which has betrayed us.

At this point, some will ask: given that analysis, where is the tragic inevitability? Can we not retain the motives and aspirations, while redeploying our powers in ways which henceforth *do* respect the biospheric constraints under which we must work? – so that even if it is too late for avoidance, we may still hope to mitigate the damage done by neglect to date, and at least to minimise adverse impacts on future people.

This is of course the 'sustainability' model – and here it is necessary to recognise oncoming environmental and climate tragedy as in large measure a tragedy *of sustainability*, into which the related tragedies of *progress, growth* and (insofar as it differs) *sustainable development* are all now folded. This concept was meant to offer a paradigm for the way in which Enlightenment values could save us from their own consequences. It represented a progressivist solution to the problems of progressivism. Extending a universalist concern for human welfare rationally into the future, we were supposed to use our scientific knowledge to set 'planetary boundaries' (Rockstrom et al. 2009) guiding and limiting our pursuit of universal human welfare in the present. The twofold problem with this is (one might have thought) sufficiently glaring. In the first place, massively complex feedbacks and systemic sensitivities render human impacts on the biosphere into the medium-term future effectively indeterminable, so that the 'constraints' under which we are to operate have to be set by socially- and politically-driven *choices* rather than by the allegedly impersonal voice of science. And secondly, those choices can only be made by *us*, that is, by present people (worldwide) whose pursuit of their own material welfare is thus supposedly to be constrained.[3] This puts inter-generational humanity in essentially the situation of the well-intentioned alcoholic tasked with setting his own safe drinking levels (and really trying) – something which might seem to make for comedy, were the case not so evidently tragic. The sincerely universalist and scientifically-rational pursuit of real and urgent human good for the future undermines itself and defeats its own ends through just this pursuit of the same benefits for people presently alive.

It is crucial to underline again the genuinely tragic structure of what we face. Neither embedded gross vices nor malevolent intentions but its own collective well-meaning (while at the same time self-serving) activity, is now bringing humankind to grief. This tragic structure is typically obscured, for instance, in the recently burgeoning psychology literature which offers to analyse 'values' in relation to human environmental behaviour. This literature tends to classify groups of values in broadly opposed types, the favoured arrangement involving a four-quadrant diagram – Schwartz, for instance, a seminal voice here, sets self-transcendence against self-enhancement values, and those representing openness to change against those representing conservatism. By values he means, plausibly enough, broad conceptions of what is important in life, which serve as guiding principles in the life of a person or other social entity (Schwartz 1994). Universalism and benevolence are what he calls self-transcendence values, while achievement, power and hedonism are self-enhancement values. Characteristic sub-values falling under these various heads are then identified as

Universalism: equality, social justice, 'world at peace'
Benevolence: helpfulness, responsibility, forgiveness
Achievement: success, ambition, capability
Power: authority, wealth, recognition
Hedonism: pleasure, enjoyment of life

Schwartz claims that such sub-values are activated in packages, so that if one's behaviour is driven principally by self-transcendence values, one will be correspondingly less moved by those in the opposite quadrant (self-enhancement) and vice versa. Thus, someone concerned for equality and social justice is likely also to be concerned for helpfulness and responsibility towards others, and less likely to be motivated by wealth, recognition or the delights of consumerism.

There is certainly some cross-cultural empirical evidence for this clustering of values, and specifically in relation to environmental issues, with universalism values such as empathy for distant others and global equity being associated with ecologically-responsible and pro-environmental behaviour, whereas self-enhancement values like consumerism and competitiveness are associated with a lack of concern for the natural world, a disposition to doubt the reality of global warming and so on (see e.g. Schultz et al. 2005; also Andrews 2017; in this Special Issue). And if this rather Manichean picture of bi-polarity were the whole story, it would be easy enough to blame our present environmental plight on the dominance of self-enhancement values (those of consumerist materialism, fostered and embedded no doubt by neo-liberal capitalism) over those self-transcendence values which might have led us to recognise and respect biospheric limits.

But whatever the evidence from statistical surveys, which familiarly have their own problems of methodology and interpretation, bi-polarity is a potentially misleading guide where progressivism is concerned. If one considers the value-nexus involved, the above categorisations decisively break down. Values driving progressivism come from *every* segment of Schwartz's classification. It is about universalising, on terms of equality and social justice, the social power, family security, health, capability, autonomy and freedom of human beings, presupposing peace and (at least implicitly) environmental protection (the sustainability agenda has been about making this last requirement explicit). We have been able to put together an anthropocentrically-conceived combination of values from all these quarters, thanks to the availability of technologies for releasing and utilising fossil energy. This has certainly skewed our thinking away from wisdom and unity with nature, undermining effective environmental protection and diminishing our sense of responsibility so that it applies only to *human* betterment. The tragedy of progressivist value might then be identified as a tragedy of anthropocentric benevolence, given by technocratic means a false sense of impunity in respect of environmental constraints. But it *is* a tragedy in the full sense, rather than simply a black-and-white victory (temporary or permanent) of the environmentally damaging over the environmentally benign side of our nature, precisely because the damage which we are bringing on ourselves comes out of our full evaluative complexity as human beings. Tragedy is never black-and-white – values expressing all aspects of our nature are always involved, just as they have been here.

The unfolding of this disaster has thus displayed a Sophoclean remorselessness. What deters people from looking it in the face is as much what it implies for our self-understanding and our value commitments as for our material future. The values which it begins to look as if we shall have to give up, because not only have they been driving the damage but no imaginable state of human survival looks compatible with continuing to live by them, are the central Enlightenment values by which decent people have long defined themselves: the assertion of universal human rights to life, to equality of respect and political liberty and to the open-ended pursuit of material betterment. We can already, in fact, see breakdown of this value-consensus happening on a smaller scale in relation to the current Mediterranean refugee crisis. Escapees from intolerable conditions evidently have a basic right to pursue the good life elsewhere, and those in (still) comparatively comfortable Europe therefore an obligation to accommodate and help them. But equally, Europeans have a basic right to their established folk-ways, the inherited and deeply internalised structures of feeling and community which form an essential part of their own flourishing, and on which large influxes of culturally-different strangers are bound to inflict disruptive change. Oncoming climate chaos will write this kind of disabling conflict within our ruling value-schema very much larger, for all those currently temperate regions of the planet which will remain broadly habitable as global temperatures increase. It is because it threatens to prevent us from continuing to build our collective activity on the full range of these compelling evaluative attachments to which we have become so accustomed, but rather will set some of them more or less violently against others, that nothing as radically tragic as this has, indeed, ever happened to us before.

III.

To repeat, then: how *do* we approach a tragedy of this order and these dimensions?

I mean this in the first place not as the question: what plans and dispositions do we make in order to bring whatever we can of human civilisation through it (though very clearly that question must also be asked) – but rather: how do we *think* about it, in the present, as a now inevitable prospect?[4] This matters because our thinking must grapple with how we might now make room for *hope*, the absolutely necessary basis for any practical planning and preparing at all, without misconceiving such hope in a kind of last-ditch effort of denial and avoidance.

One thing which would clearly qualify as avoidance is the belief that if we can only bring ourselves to recognise that this is going to happen, that might spur us finally to exertions sufficient to prevent its happening…. That is just magic thinking. Less obviously muddled, but closely allied, is the belief that even if significant adverse climate change is now inevitable, we can at well past the eleventh hour divert its worst effects by scientific wizardry so that somehow it won't be so bad. That would just be to pursue a 'solution' in the technocratic top-down mode of would-be planetary management which has itself brought us to this pass. Both those reactions, in fact, would now only be exercises in willed optimism, not so much a basis for necessary forethought as a deliberate refusal to see our real situation for what it is. By contrast, the hope in pursuit of which we must now task our thinking can only be what we might call *tough hope*: something so difficult to achieve precisely because of its utter inconsistency with letting us off the hook which we have so vigorously prepared for ourselves.

That was the kind of hope to which I meant to refer in the subtitle of my book mentioned above. I wrote about it there in terms of the opportunity potentially afforded by prospective breakdown to repossess ways of understanding ourselves which current life-modes occlude from us, as means to developing the best forms of practical resilience that we can. But the approach required for its exposition at least a sketch of plausibly retrievable practical resilience on the ground, and the danger (perhaps not avoided in that book) is that aspiring to plausibility in any such sketch risks turning retrieval, however detached from the illusions of progress, into an offer to *palliate* the tragic, to offer some kind of compensation for it. Progress may be over, the thought then runs, but we can at least move to more satisfactorily human-scale communities, enabling fuller and more naturally responsible individual lives, in the process of building the resilience needed to cope with what is coming. At the very least, we shall develop stronger muscles and a more active community spirit when the smooth facility of mechanical civilisation starts to fail....

But this, I have since come to recognise, won't do either. It is an attempt to offset losses against gains, and profit-and-loss accounting of any kind is a conceptually as well as an emotionally inadequate response to tragedy. If we come to rest *there*, we have surely avoided or betrayed the tragic experience, shirking the reality of radical loss and damage which now actually confronts us. And such shirking, equally surely, offers no real hope for coming through.

We have rather to ask the much harder question: how can we see *the tragedy itself*, neither minimised nor shirked, and irrespective of whatever may ensue, as hopeful?

Here, we move onto terrain classically marked out by Friedrich Nietzsche. In *The Birth of Tragedy* he writes of 'the metaphysical solace which ... we derive from every true tragedy, the solace that in the ground of all things, and despite all changing appearances, life is indestructibly mighty and pleasurable....' (Nietzsche [1872] 1999, 39). And it is clear from the wider context that *solace* isn't meant to be even consolation, still less compensation: it is meant for a kind of exultation, both intellectual ('metaphysical') and more than intellectual, something which Yeats later called 'tragic joy',[5] that is implicit in our acknowledgement of the very forces which make the pain and destruction what they are.

But we cannot just take over Nietzsche's ideas unmodified in the present case. While we should, I believe, try to retain his perspective, which has the huge merit of taking tragedy with proper philosophical seriousness, there are two major difficulties with applying it to the tragedy of anthropogenic climate change.

The first is that Nietzsche is writing about (classical Greek) tragedy as *drama*, an art-form in relation to which our position is that of spectators, not protagonists. It requires a considerable effort of realignment to transfer this framework of understanding to tragedy which is going to happen *to us*, for real and not as symbolic representation. With tragedy on the stage, we contemplate a painful action involving the destruction of much that is admirable and good, and culminating very typically in the powerfully symbolic death of the person or persons at the centre of this action. From this we go away chastened but nevertheless with a sense of spirit somehow clarified, and a kind of enhanced vitality. But to experience this, we have to be *able* to walk away, back into our own continuing lives. In the tragedy now confronting us we do not have that option, and the climactic death looks destined for us, if not in every case as individuals, then as a civilisation and a way of life. The only way to take anything positive *from* that will be to take it *through* to the other side of it, and that requires us to imagine a further side that is plausibly habitable. We are thus apparently caught in a paradox of anticipation: if climate disaster is going to be terminal, its tragedy cannot yield us anything positive to take beyond it, since there will be no beyond – but to the extent that we don't see it as somehow terminal, its tragic significance will tend to be defused.

It is no surprise, accordingly, that in their interesting recent book *Climate Change as Social Drama*, sociologists Philip Smith and Nicolas Howe reject the classical Greek form of tragedy as an interpretive model for social action because, they claim, it 'keys to fatalism'. Since in these ancient dramas whatever the protagonist attempts is liable to be undone by the intervening gods or the power of destiny, seeing our current situation in that light 'does not encourage sacrifice for a cause and collective action but rather the kind of apathy that in the context of climate change leads to conventional carbon-hungry lifestyles' (2015, 38). This is a rather overdrawn picture of human abjectness even for Aeschylean tragedy, since after all the gods can only work on men and women through their natural aspirations and motivations. It does, however, flag up a constant worry for anyone advancing the kind of argument which I am making here. If one cannot find a convincing account of giving up pretending without giving up altogether, then exhorting people to recognise climate chaos as now tragically inevitable does indeed run a real risk of encouraging them to disengage from any kind of remedial action and cultivate their own technology-intensive gardens while there is still time.

Smith and Howe's enterprise is to deploy literary categories going back to Aristotle's *Poetics* – from heroic quest, through narrative to low comedy – for help in interpreting patterns of perception and action, or inaction, on climate change. Seeking to circumvent the dangers of fatalism and apathy, they prefer to invoke tragedy on the Renaissance model of the tragedy of character. The prospect of climate chaos is then to be approached as 'a *hypothetical* future outcome that can only arise *if* bad choices are made by complex sovereign decision-making agents … ranging from world leaders to ordinary citizens' (2015, 40). This, however, takes us straight back to climate change as no more than a very challenging or 'wicked' problem, to be solved by ensuring (surprise!) that we make *good* choices rather than bad. In effect, it reduces to the shroud-waving use of 'tragic' which talks up the inevitability of climate disaster in order to spur us into avoiding it. As we have already seen, that line of thought is an evasion. But then, recognising it as such, we are still left with the need to find positives to take from a tragedy in which we ourselves are protagonists, some of whom might conceivably come through.

The second major difficulty with invoking Nietzsche for help in confronting this prospect is represented by the kind of positive which he himself offers. His appeal is always to the 'Dionysian' life-energy which tragedy releases from the grip of Apollonian intellect (which must grasp the workings – out of Fate or circumstance in terms of their impacting on representative human character). We watch the tragic hero being inevitably defeated by the personified and stylised forces of nature and in the very same process are forcefully reminded that, as Schopenhauer had put it, we ourselves *are* nature (Schopenhauer [1819] 1958, 281–2). But such an invocation of the indestructible might of life takes on a peculiarly ironic note in a context where what is distinctive about the tragedy now in train is that it involves, precisely, the large-scale destruction of life, and not just of the non-human life beyond the human but of the underlying biospheric substrate which all life shares. Our being opened through tragedy to an influx of natural energy from this fundamental life-source was what for Nietzsche could put us back in touch with a power 'ineradicably behind and beyond civilisation' (Schopenhauer [1819] 1958), but the essence of our present tragedy is that, given the utterly unprecedented extent and colonising force of humanised life-space right across the biosphere, there is now in effect *nothing* 'beyond civilisation'. There remain, of course, even in the long-urbanised and over-populated British Isles, areas of wilderness and quasi-wilderness; but they subsist, while they still do, by permission or protection, and nothing genuinely wild does that. The result is that when, like safari tourists in a game reserve, we turn to the 'wild' for escape and renewal, we find only what lives within boundaries (however locally distant) which humans have set.

As I have suggested, we should hold onto a Nietzschean approach if we can – that is, the boldness to look *into* tragedy, rather than in various ways away from it or past it, for the possibility of hope. But what that means is that the 'metaphysical solace' of which he speaks must now be sought in the conditions of human action itself, rather than in any redemptive access of life-energy from the non-human. In our world now, only the necessary preconditions of human action lie 'beyond the reach of civilisation'. The only non-human domain that we haven't by now decisively humanised, because we can't ever 'humanise' it, lies in the conceptual grounds of all human activity. The only way we can reconnect with the *wild*, with life-energy form beyond humanity which might renew both hope and joy, is to embark as courageously as we can in a radical shake-up of *what we can't choose*, because it forms the conceptual framework for all our choices.

It will probably take the rest of the paper to make this claim intelligible (and the paper itself is only an exploratory first attempt on its subject-matter), but some initial clarification is obviously in order. By the grounds or necessary preconditions of human activity, I mean what is conceptually basic to that activity as such – what has to be there for it to be 'activity'. That means *personhood* – because without a person as the origin of action, there is no real activity, merely the causal involvement of a biological entity in species-appropriate initiations and reactions. Linked to personhood must be *value*, the fundamental form of motivation appertaining to persons as such (as opposed to instinct, appetite and aversion, all of which we share with other forms of animal life). Correspondingly, the third conceptually necessary element is *deliberate goal-directed engagement*, because our values call for realisation through our intentionally making some things happen in the real world rather than other things.

Now these fundamentals are, it would seem, conceptually inseparable – but within that nexus of implication perhaps they are capable of bearing more than one relation to one another. Standardly, we think of the capacity to identify goals in the light of our values, and to assess the outcomes of our actions towards these goals according to how far they have succeeded in implementing those values, as a centrally defining feature of the kind of personhood – conscious, agential, reflectively rational – which we take ourselves to have. This is 'Enlightenment man' in control of his own destiny – or at least, with the potential to be so, if he rises to Kant's demand that he 'dare to know'. But maybe neither value nor personhood need have these mutual bearings and implications, and maybe they can be differently understood in relation to our involvement in goal-directed action. In that case, maybe the life-energy sprung by environmental and climate tragedy is to be found precisely in the liberation from one pattern of self-understanding here, into a vitally different one – a new sense of the human self in evaluative action with which climate tragedy challenges us.

IV.

Tragedy, at its most basic, puts our world of value in jeopardy. It represents an anticipated triumph of what we take to be thoroughly and grievously bad over what we hold to be good, and it does so through the subversion from within, as it were, of qualities like courage or kingly authority or (in the environmental case) universalist commitment to the general welfare, which had seemed to us good and desirable. It makes sense, therefore, to start trying to get a grip on the issues which climate tragedy raises for our deep conception of human agency, by thinking about those which it raises for our stance as valuers.

Anticipating tragedy means seeing this prospective assault on our cherished values within the fully tragic framing outlined above – with disaster precipitated, that is, by destructive weaknesses recognised as inseparable from key strengths. This requires, in the first place, that what is coming cannot be understood simply as *unmitigated* disaster – sheer loss, mere catastrophe, felt only as pain and grief – because to experience it as such would be only to reaffirm, by the *via negativa* as it were, the values according to which it presents itself as disaster. Thus, to think that climate change will be irredeemably catastrophic because it will mean the halting and reversal of 'progress' is to anticipate it exclusively through continued, regretful but unchallenged attachment to the range of Enlightenment values, already noted, which inform that ideal. There is a very clear sense in which such an essentially defensive reaction doesn't do prospective tragedy anything like justice. Insofar as we are anticipating disaster as the upshot of weakness inherent in key strengths, that is, we must have at least begun to stand back from, to adopt a more ironic, detached and critical view of, the assumptions according to which what is coming would have to be seen as disaster unmitigated, the grievous defeat (by merely adverse circumstances) of a wholly commendable human enterprise.

But very importantly, that doesn't mean that we must instead think of climate chaos as potentially *mitigated* disaster – with prospective gains to be offset against the losses.

That kind of accounting, as I noted above, is also radically un-tragic, and now we can see more clearly why: it is, again, a way of trying to preserve essentially untouched by prospective tragedy certain relevant values which we hold prior to undergoing it. We may indeed come to see technological-progressivism as self-defeating, and so get beyond mere regret for the values driving it, but there is a danger that, if we then expect to recover things like greater physical robustness, the spirit of community solidarity and so on (all, obviously, good things in themselves), we do no more than turn back to existing values hitherto overshadowed by those in the 'progressive' package (until that was recognised as having breakdown built into it). Thinking in such terms does indeed mean that we leave room for *learning* something from tragedy, as merely regretting it does not; but to have done only this would be to have remained at a level which again we must recognise to be inadequate to the experience. Tragedy taken seriously must be expected to do much more than shift the balance of emphasis among our existing values, or free us from commitments to which we were mistakenly attached so that others can come unchallenged to the fore.

That is why, despite its force and clarity, Rupert Read's paper elsewhere in this Special Issue (Read 2017) points us in a crucially wrong direction. Read wants to argue that an escalating series of climate disasters will yet carry with them as an unexpected boon an opportunity for the development of community. He hopes that the attendant break-down of social relations founded on liberal–individualist values will be the necessarily traumatic spur to the emergence of alternatives founded in solidarity and co-operation. What this ignores is precisely that the climate disasters will cumulatively constitute climate *tragedy* – the revealed-to-be-inevitable self-undermining of the avowedly good, the genuinely admirable and strong. And tragedy, unlike mere disaster, is only itself if it strikes at our value-assumptions so deeply as to shake the *whole structure*.

This point is absolutely central to my argument. Tragedy shakes all our values, and not merely those which recognisably bring disastrous outcomes upon us, because it shakes our reliance on value – that is, our trust that we can make generally good choices by investing in an evaluative world-view. It tests to destruction our security in being able to make dependable moral sense of the world. Tragedy, as an art form, is such a vital part of the human heritage of self-knowledge precisely because moral sense-making tends so readily to become routinised, habitual (we 'have our principles', we 'know what's right'), and our moral reflexes to lose their living responsiveness. Tragedy shows us how values as explicit commitments in moral sense-making (rules, principles, codified virtues) so frequently aren't strong, subtle or complex enough for the charges of life-energy, the stresses of deep need and self-realising impulse, which have to pass through them. Honourable ambition, proper authority, passionate love ... all these can so easily lead us astray when we take them for granted as commitments – and if these can, what may not? Tragedy shows us how our values become a self-comforting carapace, some-thing in which to hide ourselves *from* ourselves, unless they are constantly being revitalised by a process of creative destruction. By the same token, it reveals on each tragic occasion not just the inadequacy of certain values as against others (which might then form the basis of compensation or mitigation), but the existential precariousness of our whole practice of evaluative living. That is why it leaves no values standing unquestioned, even when the destruction wrought out through a given tragic dilemma has been countered by superficially apparent positives.[6]

Tragedy looming for ourselves, in other words – tragedy acknowledged as such and honestly anticipated – can be foreseen neither as mitigated nor unmitigated disaster, because we recognise that the experience of it is going to unsettle the very basis of that dichotomy. Oncoming climate and environmental disaster is only being taken seriously as tragedy when it is being foreseen as something which will *transform* our relevant values, across the board – both those according to which the loss entailed will be disastrous *and* those by which we might have been consoled or compensated for it – and will do so in ways which beforehand we simply can't know or condition for.

Anticipated real-life tragedy thus insists on itself as a peculiarly acute case of what has recently been described by the American philosopher Laurie Paul as 'transformative experience'. The defining feature of such experience is that it provides you with knowledge which you cannot acquire except by personally undergoing the experience in question, and which, so acquired, could be sufficient to 'change your personal phenomenology in deep and far-reaching ways ... perhaps by replacing your core preferences with very different ones' (Paul 2013, 8). Her original example, in the paper from which this comes, is the classically life-changing experience of giving birth to a child. The main interest of this for Paul herself, as a theorist of rational choice, is that if an experience is likely to have this effect, it cannot be evaluated beforehand for the purposes of weighing up whether or not to undergo it (nor, presumably, afterwards for the purposes of retrospective justification) because it may be expected to change the *structure* of values (prudential or moral) essential to one's prospective or retrospective evaluation – either to delete some and substitute others, or to change how one's different values are interpretively felt to stand to one another, so that in neither direction are we ever comparing by a common standard or from a single perspective. Characteristic further examples of such potentially transformative experience offered by Paul include gaining a new sensory ability (as with a cochlear implant for someone born deaf), undergoing major surgery, participating in a revolution and embracing a religious conversion.

Of course, none of these (still less child-bearing) need be contemplated as a prospective tragedy. But to anticipate some genuinely tragic event which one knows one has to go through represents an acute case of the epistemological and existential jeopardy in which all these experiences place us, because here we know, just in virtue of the tragic framing within which what is coming presents itself to us, that our values *are* about to be wrenched and subverted across the board. And thus, the prospect of climate tragedy threatens us with a profound form of loss, quite over and above the material loss and damage which it will entail – a loss of *control* at the deep level where our sense of ourselves as persons is generated.

We can bring out what is involved here by contrast with a definition of ideal-type control offered by Daniel Dennett in one of his perversely illuminating discussions of free will: 'A controls B if and only if the relation between A and B is such that A can *drive* B into whichever of B's normal range of states A *wants* B to be in ... for something to be a *controller* its states must include desires ... about the states of something else' (Dennett 1984, 52 – emphases in original). What is not said here, but is necessarily implied, is that A's desires must be *independent* of B's changes in state. The notion that A is in control of B, in other words, is the complex notion both that B varies only (on the relevant occasion) in response to A's desires, and also that A doesn't co-vary as a desiring agent across such variations in B. I control something if it does my will, but this requirement has to hold my will constant across whatever the thing which I am controlling relevantly does.

This being so, and facing inevitable tragedy for ourselves being to face radically transformative experience, it must therefore also be to face the prospect of an absolute or 'metaphysical' loss of control. It is not just that a painful process will contingently escape our ability to govern it, but that it will be one which dissolves the possibility of control as a matter of the logic of both *tragedy* and *control*. It will be, precisely, a process across which the values and desires by which the will shapes itself must be *expected* not to hold constant. Rather, what we must look forward to is the transformation into something as yet unknown of motives to which, as we look forward, we are still very powerfully attached. Prospective loss of control is thus prospective loss of values which ground our present identity. This is in a very real sense to foresee the prospect of losing our sense of ourselves.

But now, we have already seen reason to suppose that the implications of this recognition run far wider than tragedy, which only presents such loss of control at its most acute and threatening. For by just the same token, the various challenging but comparatively ordinary experiences which Paul discusses as potentially transformative must be seen as involving the same possible dissolution of control for the agent undergoing them. Just to the extent that I cannot make a rationally-weighed decision beforehand about whether to commit myself to such an experience, nor know in advance how I will evaluate it afterwards if I should do so, I have ceased to be in control of what is going to happen. And this prospect, once we are brought to acknowledge it, can be seen to confront us across a wide range of decisions generally unavoidable in any ordinary life – in relationships (do I follow through on this deep attraction?), in work (do I make this rather scary career move?) or in connection with one's health (do I take this reputedly mind-altering medication?), to name but several. In action, we are always *embarked in change* rather than in Dennett's ideal agential control of what we are doing.

V.

As I indicated above, this paper is intended only as an exploratory foray. The topic deserves at least a book, which I at least hope to write. But for the purposes of provisional summary, I will now review briefly where I think the exploration has so far got us and suggest some directions in which it might continue.

The tragedy of anthropogenic climate change, honestly recognised as a radically transformative experience through which humanity has now shortly to pass, must surely compel us to admit, in the first place, the general truth which it so drastically exemplifies: that humans are not in control of the most serious, life-significant events in which they are implicated. Coming to accept that this is the case is one vitally important way in which we will have to accustom ourselves to letting go.

Where might this recognition of non-control leave us as creatures who formulate and act upon values? The guiding thought here is that if we are to respond creatively to the way in which tragedy will put all our values to the question, we must learn to do something which might be described as letting go *of our values*, without giving up on them. That would mean, I suggest, learning to treat our evaluative commitments and principles as at best ongoing heuristics, subject to revision and reinterpretation in the light of experience, while at the same time accustoming ourselves to condition for and trust in the moral robustness of the unsearchable whole self which such principles always express (unsearchable, ungraspable in thought, because thinking about it necessarily objectifies what must be subjective to be what it is).

This is too large an issue to do more than gesture towards here. A phrase like 'letting go of our values' might be expected to set alarm bells ringing: the opposite of letting go is *holding on,* and isn't holding on to one's values (through difficulties, in face of temptation...) the prime characteristic of moral strength? But one can hold onto values, as onto beliefs and relationships, as one holds onto Nurse – 'for fear of finding something worse'. There is a deeper moral resilience in trusting to what one's perhaps *changing* explicit values are expressing. One might live by a certain value, such as loyalty to a professed commitment or solemn promise, by striving always to control one's actions so that they were directed to goals which reflected the value. But mightn't one instead (and perhaps more realistically, given the above considerations about 'control') simply embark oneself in action, to whatever provisional goal made best sense, entrusting oneself to the spirit of the value? The difference would be that between always deliberately setting out to do this kind of thing rather than that, and always trying to bring one's predispositions creatively to bear on where one's action (in its quality of always tending to slip away from one's intentions) was actually taking one.

Here, we might note a worry about the whole idea of 'transformative experience': doesn't it in important kinds of case offer us a cheater's charter? After all, if my whole personal phenomenology and core preferences are liable to be altered by (say) plunging into this very tempting prospective affair, maybe my by-then-broken promise of faithfulness to my wife won't (then) look like such a big deal. But the point is that if I go ahead while tacitly banking on that self-gratifying outcome, I am actually refusing the real transformativity of the experience, while to embrace it will also be to accept that I might emerge having for the first time fully realised how precious to me my now-irretrievable faithfulness really was. Genuine creativity, in moral life as in art – as, indeed, anywhere – involves running radical risk. I honour values which have mattered to me no more by clutching them tightly to me than by slyly abandoning them: rather, I do so by taking their promptings with me into unpredictable life-change, where that is a decision of the whole being, in full awareness that this could renew me – or break me.

Letting go of one's values in this sense is not abandoning them. Abandonment is still (paradoxically) about control – I try to control my experience self-protectively by resiling from demands on myself which I have given up aspiring to meet. But creative letting go is more like a standing-aside of the would-be controlling ego so that the value can find its own living way. What one is letting go of is, at bottom, a certain relation of the self to value – that, in fact, which was noted at the end of Section III as defining our currently-favoured view of rational agency. It is exemplified *both* by anxious attachment to *and* by self-defensive abandonment of one's values, since these are both relations of which 'self' and 'value' form distinct terms. In letting go, one is recovering the self as ongoingly *constituted in* the values which we find our actions expressing.

To repeat, there is no creativity without risk. A serious risk here is the evidently large scope for bad faith which goes with such a conception of value in action. Letting go of principled control so that the whole, dark self which one's values creatively express can realise itself open-endedly sounds bold and brave, but it could also very easily become one's preferred way of disguising from oneself special pleading, a habit of backsliding or even moral nihilism. Certainly, philosophical work needs to be done to explore the implications for moral integrity and active responsibility of this kind of evaluative letting-go. (For some initial orientation, one might look to the recent revival of interest in a broadly intuitionist moral particularism – see for instance Dancy 2004.)

Some of the issues here may be sharpened by an example, and for this, it will be best to return to the climate situation, since broad policy considerations for that future represent another main head under which this work needs to be advanced. These considerations are going to be very difficult, since they involve anticipating now, and conditioning for, how we might (as valuers to be transformed by the experience of climate tragedy) hope to make case-by-case practical sense of the broken world with which that tragedy will leave us (or some of us) to deal.

I take the idea of the 'broken world' from Tim Mulgan's fascinating and inventive book *Ethics for a Broken World*: he defines it as 'a place where resources are insufficient to meet everyone's basic needs, where a chaotic climate makes life precarious and where each generation is worse off than the last' (2011, ix). Setting aside the interge-nerational issues for the moment, consider that such a world will contain by definition what Mulgan calls 'survival bottlenecks' – situations in which there are more people making a claim on available resources than those resources will support in meeting their basic survival needs. Indeed, the whole world will be a gigantic bottleneck of this kind – with a still-growing global population increasingly straitened by reductions in the availability of habitable land, food production capacity, usable water and easily deliver-able energy, all complicated by the ramifying infrastructural derangement which increasing climate chaos will also entail.

In any such situation, humanity will be faced with the novel but appalling demand for institutional and regulatory procedures to determine not just 'who gets what' (the classic distributional problem in politics) but *who survives*. How are resource allocation deci-sions to be made, given that a direct upshot of such decisions will be that some people (on a global scale, perhaps many millions of people) will die and others won't? Unless they are going to be made simply by *force majeure*, with the accompanying breakdown of anything resembling civilisation, we must hope that these decisions will be made on some kind of principle which will allow law and governance to continue operating, and the obvious candidate for such a principle is that of *justice*. But what would justice entail in such a case?

Looking at this question from where we are now, it would seem to involve finding some way to take seriously the idea (which Mulgan canvasses) of a survival *lottery*. And surely ideal-type justice for a survival bottleneck would mean (after perhaps excluding certain categories such as the very aged or the terminally ill who aren't going to make it anyway) something broadly equivalent to issuing everyone a lottery ticket, with only as many winning tickets as there are going to be packages of 'basic survival' resources available. Thereby, everyone would have an equal chance, and the fairness of the procedure might go some way to encouraging acceptance (if only among those charged, dismally, with enforcement), since *pure luck* would determine who wins through – rather than the historical–geographical and climatic good luck (improved through centuries of exploitation and canny management) by which people from certain areas within the broken world will remain comparatively well-provided with resources while others have been impoverished or indeed rendered destitute.

So much for the ideal. In actuality, of course, people finding themselves in anything approaching such straits will strive to protect their own families and communities, by institutional and legal means as far as possible and then in the last resort by force. And one possible, even tempting, response to this recognition is a kind of brutal realism: 'If justice requires me to put my kids into a survival lottery along with a lot of strangers, well, to hell with justice'. But for all the naturalness of that reaction, we will certainly need to hang onto some social organising principle with at least some of the characteristics of justice – some guiding rules for the allocation of responsibilities and benefits which have enough of equity, as well as of practicability, to be generally acceptable and thus workable – if all order, even in much more localised communities than we have recently been used to, is not to break down.

That being so, a response more in line with the considerations which we have been exploring – an attempt to let go of this crucial value without giving up on it – might be to say: given the radically transformative nature of the tragic process which will deliver us into the broken world, we simply can't know, *pre*-tragically, what the value of justice will mean for us post-tragically, nor the pattern of relations with our other values (those of family and community loyalty in particular) in which it will then sit. While we can hardly help viewing such a world prospectively with horror – that, after all, is why the prospect of it is tragic – we perhaps need not view it, in its moral dimensions, with either cynicism or nihilism. We could instead trust to our moral creativity, making what arrangements for the future we practically can while remaining as generous and as open-hearted as we are able.

And then, of course, comes the real work: somehow, the possible forms of such preparation for the future will need sketching.

VI.

By way of concluding (or at any rate, of stopping for the moment) I return to Nietzsche.

If the foregoing is at all persuasive, we can now perhaps recognise Yeats' 'tragic joy' or the Nietzschean Dionysiac as our indefeasible delight, at this great crisis of the human adventure, in re-evaluative energy itself, energy released by radical challenge – our delight in that opening up of our self-understanding to creative destruction and renewal which tragedy, properly acknowledged, must bring. In this creative energy, the indestructible might of *life*, though trampled on by overweening human billions worldwide, now reasserts itself. Any hope, which we can draw from the tragic prospect of what we must now endure, will then spring up as a renewed sense of that fundamental creativity: a sense that against whatever odds – even odds so great as massive climate change – life, in us as more widely, will go on re-making itself.

That sense affords us no guarantee. There is no certainty that life on Earth will not be ended by human actions. But we must let go of certainty, and of the desire for it. To do so is already to re-make life.

Notes

1. Ch2, v3; from Chen (1989).
2. And not, I can now add, the Trump presidency – though this will certainly bring climate tragedy on us more swiftly and decisively, and also exemplifies in its own way the tragic crisis of Enlightenment values which I discuss below.
3. I have discussed this problem in detail in Foster (2008).
4. By *we* I mean, for the present: those capable of such thinking.
5. "Hector is dead and there's a light in Troy;
   We that look on but laugh in tragic joy" ('The Gyres' in Yeats 1967, 337).
6. At the close of all great tragic drama, nothing remotely to be described as an unqualified positive is ever asserted. (The reader is invited to test this claim against his or her own reading.)

Disclosure statement

No potential conflict of interest was reported by the author.

References

Andrews, N. 2017. "Transformation, Adaptation and Universalism." *Global Discourse* 7 (1). doi:10.1080/23269995.2017.1300403.

Beddington, J. 2009. "World Faces 'Perfect Storm' of Problems by 2030, Chief Scientist to Warn." *The Guardian* 18 (3). https://www.theguardian.com/science/2009/mar/18/perfect-storm-john-beddington-energy-food-climate.

Chen, E. 1989. *The Tao Te Ching: A New Translation with Commentary*. St Paul, Minnesota: Paragon House.

Dancy, J. 2004. *Ethics without Principles*. Oxford: Clarendon Press.

Dennett, D. 1984. *Elbow Room: The Varieties of Free Will Worth Wanting*. Oxford: Clarendon Press.

Dyer, G. 2008. *Climate Wars*. Oxford: Oneworld.

Foster, J. 2008. *The Sustainability Mirage*. London: Earthscan.

Foster, J. 2015. *After Sustainability: Denial, Hope, Retrieval*. Abingdon: Routledge.

Hulme, M. 2009. *Why We Disagree about Climate Change*. Cambridge: Cambridge University Press.

Lynas, M. 2007. *Six Degrees: Our Future on a Hotter Planet*. London: Fourth Estate.

Mulgan, T. 2011. *Ethics for a Broken World*. Durham: Acumen.

Nietzsche, F. [1872] 1999. *The Birth of Tragedy*, ed. R. Geuss and R. Speirs. Cambridge: Cambridge University Press.

Oreskes, N. 2004. "The Scientific Consensus on Climate Change." *Science* 306 (5702): 1686–1686. doi:10.1126/science.1103618.

Paul, L. 2013. "What You Can't Expect When You're Expecting." *Res Philosophica* 92 (2): 1–23.

Read, R. 2017. "On Preparing for the Great Gift of Community that Climate Disasters Can Give Us." *Global Discourse* 7 (1). doi:10.1080/23269995.2017.1300440.

Rockstrom, J., W. Steffen, K. Noone, Å. Persson, F. S. I. I. I. Chapin, E. Lambin, T. M. Lenton, et al. 2009. "Planetary Boundaries: Exploring the Safe Operating Space for Humanity." *Ecology and Society* 14 (2): 32. doi:10.5751/ES-03180-140232.

Schopenhauer, A. [1819] 1958. *The World as Will and Representation, Volume I*. trans. E. F. J. Payne, New York: Dover.

Schultz, P.W. et al. 2005. "Values and Their Relationship to Environmental Concern and Conservation Behaviour." *Journal of Cross-Cultural Psychology* 36 (4): 457–475. doi:10.1177/0022022105275962.

Schwartz, S. 1994. "Are There Universal Aspects in the Structure and Contents of Human Values?." *Journal of Social Issues* 50 (4): 19–45. doi:10.1111/josi.1994.50.issue-4.

Smith, P., and N. Howe. 2015. *Climate Change as Social Drama*. Cambridge: Cambridge University Press.

Yeats, W. B. 1967. *Collected Poems*. London: Macmillan.

The future: compassion, complacency or contempt?

Rupert Read

This is a reply to:

Foster, John. 2017. "On letting go." *Global Discourse*. 7 (1): 171–187. http://dx.doi.org/10.1080/
23269995.2017.1300442.

John Foster's voice is one the world badly needs to hear. He ruptures the complacent assumptions of the legion advocates of narratives of 'progress', 'growth' and 'sustainable development'. His resolute willingness to face climate-reality head-on is, against the backdrop of such complacency, heartening. I have to state that point explicitly because such resolution is still *vanishingly* rare.

By my lights, *the vast majority of us are in climate-denial*. That is not just 'climate-sceptics'; not by a long chalk. Hardly *any* of us are willing, or perhaps able, to look in the eye what we are doing to ourselves, to our home, to our children and theirs.

And now I have to be brutally honest: this equates to *de facto* contempt for our descendants. If we bequeath to them a climate-ruined planet, what do you think they will feel for us? This thought already ought to wake us up.

What we have already to accept without reservation – and this is the starting point of 'Facing up to climate-reality', the new project of the think tank which I chair, Green House (co-founded by Brian Heatley, also a contributor to this special issue) – is that extremely substantial – unheard-of, appalling, partly irreversible – damage is going to be done to 'Gaia' and to humanity by human-triggered climate-change. As my piece in this issue bluntly puts it: we are committed for the remainder of the lifetimes of many of us to a rising level of climate-disasters. This is the *sine qua non* now of recognising climate-reality: that we are *committed* to a net-worsening situation for decades to come, and that the chances even of preventing runaway climate change may be low. This is bad enough and ought to be enough to 'satisfy' Foster.

But it would be an act of reckless uncaring to claim to know that the chances of stopping runaway climate change are as-good-as-zero. And to give the impression that we know the future in any such way risks encouraging an *apathetic* complacency.

Foster alleges that there is no *possibility* that we might yet transform ourselves to stop catastrophic climate change: but this is in profound tension with his claim (Foster 2017a, 4) that 'massively complex feedbacks and systemic sensitivities render human impacts on the biosphere into the medium-term future effectively indeterminable'. You can't have it both ways. As it happens, I think that the latter claim of his may well even be somewhat overstated.

But what is certainly true is, we do not know the future nearly as well as (extremely wide-spread) technoscientific hubris takes it that we do. This is the reason for our great need at this time for the Precautionary Principle (see, e.g. Taleb et al. 2014).

It is also a valid reason for not accepting the level of despair enjoined by Foster about the possibility of a transformation that would be enough.

Loss of control: yes, that is now our fate, to a large extent. We need to accept loss of a fantasised control over the planetary system, and over our own destiny. But that means we also do not get to be as confident as Foster is about how bad our future will be. We do not know, as he claims we do, that our chances of escaping climate-nemesis are negligible.

Letting go of certainty: yes. What that means is that we badly need to embrace a precautionary ethic. For such an ethic is a way of living in a world that we will never fully understand, let alone control. A way of living that 'builds down' our impacts until we might eventually no longer threaten our own future.

In sum: Foster's *knowingness about the inevitable failure of all existing projects overreaches.* We cannot know the future. Precaution warns us to guard against threats that may be far worse than we know; BUT it also warns us not to be too 'certain' in any doom-mongering.

Marx famously remarked that human beings only set themselves such problems as they can solve. We don't quite know this, either. The 'wicked' problem that is global overheat is going to be fiendishly difficult to solve; it may in practice be insoluble. And it certainly has tragic dimensions, some of them already irredeemable. But to claim to know categorically that it is insoluble is to make the same mistake as any Pollyannaish advocates of endless human progress: it is to claim to know that there is nothing new under the (now harsher) Sun. As Arendt stresses, there is *always* the possibility of something new coming into the world. Foster ought not to be too 'knowing', lest he fall back into the camp of those who he has brilliantly critiqued. No one really ever knows much at all of what is going to happen in the human future. This is a constitutive point. (It is the reason too why all precognition/time-travel narratives, the latest of which to hit our big screens is *Arrival*, are, literally nonsense.)

Who for instance could have anticipated, before it happened, that the biggest blockbuster in history would be a Gaia-centric eco-warrior epic featuring American marines and corporations as the would-be ecocidal *enemy*, a film so potentially incendiary that the Chinese government basically banned it from being viewed by their entire (restive) rural population? The thrilling consciousness-raising power of *Avatar* is one (not-so-)small indicator of what is possible for us. Imagine if, when its sequels appear, we were, together, ready to take advantage of that: to seek to use *Avatar* to help facilitate a *transformation* of consciousness…

Climate-disasters may yet facilitate a transformation of our consciousness. And, with the will, it would even now not be too difficult to change to a climate-sane path. The main things we'd have to do, at the level of on-the-ground policy-change, include the following: change from a path of ecosystem destruction to one of massive ecosystem-restoration (including large-scale rewilding); eliminate most intensive industrial animal husbandry; change our agricultural methods to more labour-intensive permacultural/agro-ecological methods; switch wherever feasible from building with cement and bricks to building with high-quality (and well-insulated) wood, in long-term programmes of *de facto* sequestration of carbon; radically relocalise our food systems and indeed our economic systems in general; as well as of course rapidly dropping fossil fuels in favour of (genuine) renewables (chiefly: wind, water and sun), and engaging in huge 'Green

New Deal'-style programmes of demand-reduction and energy-efficiency. Challenging indeed; but *all* of this could be done *within a few years*, if we willed it. The prospect undoubtedly seems remote; as does any revolution, before it happens.

Foster talks (2017a, 10) about the utter outdatedness at the present time of any and all 'unchallenged attachment to ... Enlightenment values'. Quite right. But what about a radically challenging transformation of Enlightenment values? That's what I am in favour of – following Wittgenstein (and Foucault, and Illich and Gorz). Taking these values far closer to communitarian, ecologistic, and truly conservative values. We ought to be conservative, in the (true) sense of seeking to conserve what we have, of respecting our elders and forebears, and of not too-hastily abandoning venerable and knowledge-rich traditions. This means abandoning neoliberalism, and indeed many features of the political philosophy of liberalism. Accepting anything like this requires a revolution in the cosy assumptions of virtue-signalling chattering classes: the valorization of the high-tech, the gigantic and the global needs to give way for something which will actually fit with (for example) what living communities struggling to deal with and 'grow' through climate-disasters need.

I find it slightly disappointing that Foster is not more excited about the values of community-solidarity, or about the prospects of localisation: including 'disaster-relocalisation', which we could envisage as a healthy alternative to 'Shock-Doctrine'-style responses to the coming slew of climate-caused disasters.[1] This *isn't* just a repackaging of the progressive package; it is a *transformation* of whatever is still living in that package, and a working in of stuff outside it (especially, of stuff that came *before* it; including, vitally, learning from the world's remaining indigenous peoples).

Still, I am glad to see Foster speaking in terms of the prospects of climate-change-triggered 'transformative experience' enveloping much of humanity. That is exactly what my climate disasters paper is about. I think that Foster equivocates on whether or not people/communities in (climate-) disasters can undergo just such experiences.

Finally, in his 'Caring for the future? – a response to Rupert Read', Foster (2017b) seeks to undermine my argument that caring for one's children mandates caring for the distant future because caring for one's children IS caring simultaneously for their children. He argues that the degree to which one cares about one's grandchildren is less than about one's children, and that this deterioration iterates.

I think that this is mistaken.

I would first anecdotally remark that many grandparents like their grandchildren *more* than their children. The intense relationship with one's children eases into a more even benignity, with regard to grandchildren. It is not coincidental that the classic image in Buddhism of mindful regard for one's thoughts is that of a benign *grandmother* watching her grandkids playing, not of a mother. But if those grandkids were threatened, Grandma would likely get tigerish. Well: they *are* so threatened.

Secondly, Foster's argument may derive a ring of plausibility from the elementary truth that, at average levels of replacement (i.e. if the average parent has two kids), one has twice as many grandkids as kids, four times as many great-grandkids, and so on. Thus, it is unsurprising if one's affection is less intense for one's grandkids considered as individuals, for it is more diffused. But my suggestion is that it remains at the same level if '*summed*' across each generation – on pain of otherwise one actually not caring even for one's kids.

Thirdly, I have argued elsewhere that my argument does not result in the utterly absurd conclusion that, for the sake of our very distant descendants, we have to act now to try to stop the Sun becoming a red giant, or to stop the Universe's heat death. Rather, my argument is that our care for our kids iterates into just as strong a care for their descendants *only so long as we can reasonably foresee and act on what needs to be done to protect them*. But, in the present case, it is pretty easy to see what that means. It means *doing our all* to head off the threat of runaway climate change in its full Damoclean awfulness, as indicated earlier. Failing to head off that threat is like discounting the future, or worse: it *is* equivalent to believing that future generations, after the next few, basically do not matter.

I am under no illusions that my argument concerning how caring for one's kids translates into caring for the whole human (and thus the whole biospheric) future will be enough alone to head off climate-catastrophe! Indeed, I think it on balance – tragically – highly unlikely that we *will* head it off. But we might. And, the more this argument gets known, the more that people come to think and feel long-term – compassionately – the more that slight chance *increases*.

And, in the darkness of this time, that is an encouraging thought.

Note

1. See, e.g. Norbert Hodge and Read (2016). See also http://www.theecologist.org/News/news_analysis/2988362/after_brexit_and_trump_dont_demonise_localise.html

Disclosure statement

No potential conflict of interest was reported by the author.

References

Foster, J. 2017a. "On Letting Go." *Global Discourse* 7 (1). doi:10.1080/23269995.2017.1300442.
Foster, J. 2017b. "Caring for the Future?" *Global Discourse* 7 (1). doi:10.1080/23269995.2017.1300441.
Norberg-Hodge, H., and R. Read. 2016. Post-Growth Localisation. http://www.greenhousethinktank.org/uploads/4/8/3/2/48324387/post-growth-localisation_pamphlet.pdf
Taleb, N., R. Read, R. Douady, J. Norman, and Y. Bar-Yam. 2014. "The Precautionary Principle." http://www.fooledbyrandomness.com/pp2.pdf

Index

For Product Safety Concerns and Information please contact our EU
representative GPSR@taylorandfrancis.com Taylor & Francis Verlag GmbH,
Kaufingerstraße 24, 80331 München, Germany

Printed and bound by CPI Group (UK) Ltd, Croydon, CR0 4YY
01/05/2025
01858459-0007